I0050290

Crafting Engineering Strategy

How Thoughtful Decisions Solve Complex Problems

Will Larson

O'REILLY®

Crafting Engineering Strategy

by Will Larson

Copyright © 2026 Will Larson. All rights reserved.

Published by O'Reilly Media, Inc., 141 Stony Circle, Suite 195, Santa Rosa, CA 95401.

O'Reilly books may be purchased for educational, business, or sales promotional use. Online editions are also available for most titles (*http://oreilly.com*). For more information, contact our corporate/institutional sales department: 800-998-9938 or *corporate@oreilly.com*.

Acquisition Editor: David Michelson
Development Editor: Sarah Grey
Production Editor: Kristen Brown
Copyeditor: Piper Content Partners
Proofreader: Krsta Technology Solutions
Indexer: Ellen Troutman-Zaig
Cover Designer: Susan Thompson
Cover Illustrator: Susan Thompson
Interior Designer: Monica Kamsvaag
Interior Illustrator: Kate Dullea

October 2025: First Edition

Revision History for the First Edition

2025-10-14: First Release

See *http://oreilly.com/catalog/errata.csp?isbn=9798341645523* for release details.

The O'Reilly logo is a registered trademark of O'Reilly Media, Inc. *Crafting Engineering Strategy*, the cover image, and related trade dress are trademarks of O'Reilly Media, Inc.

The views expressed in this work are those of the author and do not represent the publisher's views. While the publisher and the author have used good faith efforts to ensure that the information and instructions contained in this work are accurate, the publisher and the author disclaim all responsibility for errors or omissions, including without limitation responsibility for damages resulting from the use of or reliance on this work. Use of the information and instructions contained in this work is at your own risk. If any code samples or other technology this work contains or describes is subject to open source licenses or the intellectual property rights of others, it is your responsibility to ensure that your use thereof complies with such licenses and/or rights.

979-8-341-64552-3

[LSI]

Contents

Preface

In 2015, the Mini Sky City skyscraper, with 57 floors, was built in Changsha, China, in 19 days. Driving my son to school over the past few years, I've watched a nine-story building in San Francisco get built over three years. There's some argument that Mini Sky City's record isn't legitimate because it relied heavily on modular, prebuilt architecture, but I can assure you that the three-years-and-counting building in San Francisco is similarly being built from modular components. Why did one of these projects build three floors per day, and the other three floors per year?

How Big Things Get Done by Bent Flyvbjerg and Dan Gardner (Crown Currency, 2023) explores how strategy impacts the successful creation of complex buildings. The authors' foundational observation is that you go fast by making most of your mistakes where it's cheapest—for example, in simulation—and fewer where it's difficult to fix—for example, after you've built most of a physical building. In my experience, their observation applies equally well to software engineering strategy.

However, the problem in software engineering goes further. You'll never meet an architect who hasn't seen a building plan, but the majority of software engineers and even software executives will tell you that they've never seen a clear, written engineering strategy. There's a widespread belief that engineering strategy doesn't exist—but if you ask the right questions, you'll find that almost every engineer has a strong instinctive understanding of their current company's engineering strategy. Even if that strategy isn't particularly good, they'll know what it is.

I want this book to reshape the conversation around software engineering strategy in two ways. First, I hope to establish a sufficiently clear, shared definition of engineering strategy so that we agree on what we're talking about. With that definition, we can discuss how to improve our strategies, rather than debating whether they exist. My second goal is to make it easier for all of us to write down our companies' engineering strategies. If this book is particularly successful, a few years from now the ideas in this book will be obsolete through their own ubiquity. They'll be so obvious that they're not worth discussing—and that would be a triumph.

Strategy is often viewed as the domain of Staff-plus engineers and executives. I hope those folks think a lot about strategy, but I believe that *everyone* in an engineering organization can apply strategy. If you work within or even adjacent to an engineering organization, then this book wants to help you understand and improve on your company's engineering strategy. Certainly, different roles require different approaches, but *you* can contribute to improvement.

Finally, I believe a bit of rigor in our thinking can change our lives, our colleagues' lives, and the lives of the people who use the software that we create. Engineering organizations today routinely waste dozens or hundreds of years of their teams' lives by refusing to engage with the reality of their problems. Far from an abstract and aspirational endeavor, strategy invests our scarce time wisely—and that's the bare minimum we owe ourselves, our colleagues, and our users.

What This Book Is Not

This book is intended to be widely accessible, particularly for anyone working in or adjacent to software engineering. However, it certainly won't be everything to everyone, and I want to acknowledge some of its limitations.

First, the examples in this book are rooted in my personal experiences. I've done many things in my career, like starting a small iOS gaming startup in 2008, growing Calm's engineering organization, and contributing to Stripe's and Uber's periods of rapid growth. However, my experience has its gaps: I worked at Yahoo! when it was quite large, with a massive codebase, but I was there in a junior role, so I have an incomplete view of working at a company of that size. I've also never worked in government. Indeed, the list of things I *haven't* done is endless.

Second, this book is an opinionated introduction to engineering strategy, and it's intended to serve as your first introduction to that hopelessly broad topic. If you're looking for a more general book on strategy, particularly if you don't work in a software engineering–adjacent field, I'd probably suggest you instead start with Richard Rumelt's *Good Strategy, Bad Strategy* (Crown Currency, 2011).

Finally, this book touches on software architecture a number of times, as it's a common topic within engineering strategies. However, it is not a book *about* software architecture. Where one strategy focuses on software architecture, the next might focus just as heavily on managerial mechanisms, like approving headcount backfills. For a book on architecture, I might suggest *Fundamentals of Software Architecture: A Modern Engineering Approach* by Mark Richards and Neal Ford, now in its second edition (O'Reilly, 2025).

Navigating This Book

The default way to read this book is to start at the beginning and read through to the end. If you do that, you'll work through the book's five parts in order:

- Part I, "Introducing Engineering Strategy", introduces this book's overall thesis.
- Part II, "Steps for Building Engineering Strategies", breaks down the steps to craft, implement, and operate an engineering strategy into step-by-step instructions.
- Part III, "Refinement Tools", goes into further detail about refining strategy, which I believe is the most valuable and most neglected element of engineering strategy.
- Part IV, "Case Studies", provides 10 concrete engineering strategies, all of which are based on concrete work I've done in my career (although some are lightly anonymized).
- Part V, "Going Forward", wraps up the book with advice for evaluating strategies and improving your own strategy work.

If you want a more focused dive into the topic, I'd encourage you to start by reading the case studies, and then selectively read the chapters to understand any parts of the case studies that you find interesting or surprising. Reading this way will leave you without some of the relevant definitions, but it should still be a coherent read, and there's always the index to find anything you want to look up.

Using Code Examples

Supplemental material (code examples, exercises, etc.) is available for download at *https://craftingengstrategy.com*.

If you have a technical question or a problem using the code examples, please send email to *support@oreilly.com*.

This book is here to help you get your job done. In general, if example code is offered with this book, you may use it in your programs and documentation. You do not need to contact us for permission unless you're reproducing a significant portion of the code. For example, writing a program that uses several chunks of code from this book does not require permission. Selling or distributing examples from O'Reilly books does require permission. Answering a question by citing this book and quoting example code does not require permission. Incorporating a significant amount of example code from this book into your product's documentation does require permission.

We appreciate, but generally do not require, attribution. An attribution usually includes the title, author, publisher, and ISBN. For example: "*Crafting Engineering Strategy* by Will Larson (O'Reilly). Copyright 2026 Will Larson, 979-8-341-64552-3."

If you feel your use of code examples falls outside fair use or the permission given above, feel free to contact us at *permissions@oreilly.com*.

O'Reilly Online Learning

O'REILLY® For more than 40 years, *O'Reilly Media* has provided technology and business training, knowledge, and insight to help companies succeed.

Our unique network of experts and innovators share their knowledge and expertise through books, articles, and our online learning platform. O'Reilly's online learning platform gives you on-demand access to live training courses, in-depth learning paths, interactive coding environments, and a vast collection of text and video from O'Reilly and 200+ other publishers. For more information, visit *https://oreilly.com*.

How to Contact Us

Please address comments and questions concerning this book to the publisher:

O'Reilly Media, Inc.
141 Stony Circle, Suite 195
Santa Rosa, CA 95401
800-889-8969 (in the United States or Canada)
707-827-7019 (international or local)
707-829-0104 (fax)
support@oreilly.com
https://oreilly.com/about/contact.html

We have a web page for this book, where we list errata and any additional information. You can access this page at *https://oreil.ly/craftingEngStrategy*.

For news and information about our books and courses, visit *https://oreilly.com*.

Find us on LinkedIn: *https://linkedin.com/company/oreilly-media*.

Watch us on YouTube: *https://youtube.com/oreillymedia*.

Acknowledgments

Each book is the culmination of the prior writing I have done, the people I have had the chance to collaborate with, and the work itself that has educated me despite my best efforts. Thank you to each person who has helped me with this book itself, and with the work it stands on. I owe a particular deep debt to Sarah, Adi, Bobby, and David for their help in refining this book.

Above all else, I owe endless thanks to my wife, Laurel, and my son, Emerson. Thank you both for being part of this book's journey, and the much larger journey where this book is only a very small chapter.

PART | I

Introducing Engineering Strategy

Strategy is a very broad topic, and the first part of this book surveys that breadth while landing the foundation to dive into the details in the four following parts. It will establish the core definitions that we'll take through this book, and connect this book's ideas to the tradition they originated in.

It will also address the three most frequent concerns I hear from would-be strategy practitioners. First, is engineering strategy actually useful? (Yes.) Who gets to do it? (You do.) How much strategy is actually useful? (It depends on the altitude you're writing at.)

Introduction

I've worked alongside many talented people who spent years waiting for a chance to finally "do strategy." My hope is that this book convinces you—and maybe them—that waiting is optional. Strategy isn't reserved for executives. It's the practice of making thoughtful decisions, and it's accessible to everyone—including you.

Even if you'd prefer to avoid strategy, it's still happening all around you. My first big dose of strategy came when I was managing the team responsible for Uber's service migration (Document 16-1) while we desperately tried to survive an accelerating avalanche of inbound support requests. Since then, I've seen strategy everywhere I worked, from Stripe's acquisition of Index (Document 22-4) to Calm's focus on being a product engineering company (Document 21-1). There are even some strategy problems that I've encountered again and again at every company I've joined, such as deciding how to decompose monolithic codebases (Document 20-1).

This book is focused on *engineering strategy*—in other words, making thoughtful decisions about engineering. *Engineering* is defined both as the discipline of writing software, and also as the concerns of the Engineering department or organization within your company. If this seems like a hopelessly broad topic, then we agree on the scope of my definition. However, I would never agree that it's hopeless.

My decision making has significantly improved over the course of my career. I believe very strongly that my improvement had very little to do with my intrinsic ability and a lot to do with my learning to engage in structured thinking. I also believe the lessons that I learned slowly are eminently teachable in the next few hundred pages.

Grounded in My Direct Experience

Strategy is a broad topic, and many strategy books become awkwardly abstract. To avoid falling into that trap, I've anchored this book in my personal experiences doing strategy and the strategy work of colleagues that I had the opportunity to witness directly.

As much as possible, I've used examples that I worked on in real companies, which I mention by name. That's true for more than half the strategies included in this book, which describe strategies I collaborated on during my time at Stripe, Uber, and Calm. For the other half of the strategies, I have abstracted away from naming specific companies because they cover sensitive topics, such as how to work with private equity ownership (Document 18-1), or expose internal information better kept private, as in how to manage access to customer data (Document 19-1). In both sorts of examples, I've worked hard to remain honest, even when I've had to omit some details, out of respect for the companies and individuals involved.

You'll also notice that I try to be positive about all of these strategies. If I seem *too* positive at times, it's because all strategies age. Even the best eventually turn sour. It's most interesting to understand strategies in the context they were originally conceived. Of course, evaluation matters too, which I'll cover in Chapter 23.

Adapting Rumelt for Engineering

In addition to my own experience, the second-largest influence on this book is Richard Rumelt's *Good Strategy, Bad Strategy*. It's a quick read, and it was a life-changing discovery for me. Rumelt describes three pillars of effective strategy, which I'll paraphrase here:

Diagnosis
: A theory describing the nature of the challenge. This involves identifying the root cause(s) at play: for example, "high work-in-progress is preventing us from finishing any tasks, so we are increasingly behind each sprint" might be a good diagnosis.

Guiding policy
: A series of general policies which will be applied to grapple with the challenge. Guiding policies are typically implicit or explicit tradeoffs. For example, a guiding policy might be "only hire for the most urgent team; do not spread hires across all teams." If a guiding policy doesn't imply a

tradeoff, you should be suspicious of it. "Working harder to get it done" isn't really a guiding policy, for instance; the relevant guiding policy there might be "work folks hard and expect high attrition."

Coherent actions

A set of specific actions to address the challenge, directed by guiding policy. This is the most important part, and I think the most exciting, because it clarifies that a strategy is only meaningful if it leads to aligned action.

The first time I read this definition was eye-opening: it answered so many strategy questions I'd had for such a long time. However, although I was grateful to Rumelt for giving me my first framework for thinking about strategy, I continued noticing how little deliberate strategy existed in the engineering organizations I'd joined.

Eventually, I recognized that if applying Rumelt's work to engineering was trivial, we'd see a lot more disciplined engineering strategy in practice. We'd also, one hopes, see fewer obviously flawed engineering strategies. This book is the culmination of a decade spent understanding how to adapt Rumelt's approach to something that not only *could* work, but concretely *has* worked in the organizations that I've joined.

Iterative, Intellectual, and Mechanical

In addition to being anchored in my personal experience and building on Rumelt's approach, this book takes an iterative approach and embraces both the intellectual and the mechanical aspects of strategy.

Even my proudest strategy work eventually becomes obsolete. For some time, I was embarrassed by this realization. Eventually, I came to recognize that entropy is natural in strategy work; good strategy *embraces* change rather than fighting it. This solidified for me into the concept of strategy refinement (Chapter 8), where ideas are deliberately validated and improved rather than being treated as immutable.

If you've ever participated in executive hiring, you've probably interviewed someone who described strategic thinking as a personal strength. Those candidates often draw a distinction between directing how work should be done and being in the weeds of doing the work itself. It happens enough that you start to appreciate that many people view strategy as a fundamentally intellectual endeavor about how things *ought* to work, rather than a mechanical endeavor that studies how things actually *do* work in practice.

While strategy does indeed have intellectual elements, effective strategy is at least as dependent on the mechanical nuances of reality as it is on intellectual frameworks. Even the best policies will fail without attention to whether the team is actually adopting the policy's guidance. Similarly, very effective operational mechanisms to roll out a strategy won't help your company if the policy being rolled out is a bad one (see Chapter 10).

As obvious as these ideas seem, many organizations expect their strategies to manifest perfectly into existence from the very beginning. This book discusses how to bridge the gap between that pressing expectation of perfection and the reality that effective strategy development is grounded in iterative work that is both intellectual and mechanical.

This Book's Ambition

As I've worked on this book, one of my lingering concerns is that the ideas in it are perhaps too obvious to write down. But each time I've been tempted to set the project aside, I see a new example, or am reminded of an old experience, where some of the smartest people I've ever known have struggled unsuccessfully with a strategy problem that others would describe as quite simple.

The belief that strategy is complex often gets people in trouble. It's appealing to believe that strategies fail due to intricate errors in decision making or the unanticipated moves of an adversary. Maybe that is common when it comes to grand strategy. However, my experience is that engineering strategies fail for very mundane reasons—the most common of which is that executives assume their strategy will roll *itself* out. The second most common reason is forgetting to spend time validating the details. Both are avoidable with a bit of structure.

This book's framework is not an attempt to discredit all other approaches. Rather, it's a synthesis of the various approaches I've encountered, along with a few dimensions that I've not seen addressed in much detail elsewhere. Even if you don't agree with my framework, I hope it helps you refine your own framework. Either way, our industry will be much better for it.

2

Is Engineering Strategy Useful?

While I frequently hear engineers bemoan a missing strategy, their complaints rarely articulate why the missing strategy matters. Instead, it serves as more of a truism: the economy used to be better, children used to respect their parents, and engineering organizations used to have an engineering strategy.

This chapter starts by exploring something I believe quite strongly: there's *always* an engineering strategy, even if there's nothing written down. From there, we'll discuss why strategy, especially written strategy, is such a valuable opportunity for organizations that take it seriously.

We'll dig into:

- Why there's always a strategy, even when people say there isn't
- How strategies have changed companies I've encountered
- How inappropriate strategies create significant organizational pain without much compensating benefit
- How written strategy drives organizational learning
- The costs of not writing strategy down
- How strategy supports personal learning and development, even when you're not empowered to "do strategy" yourself

By this chapter's end, I hope you will agree with me that strategy is an undertaking worth investing your time—and your organization's.

There's Always a Strategy

Every company I've worked in has had at least one engineer who felt the company didn't have an engineering strategy. Once I became an executive and could document and distribute an engineering strategy myself, complaints about missing strategy didn't go away; they just shifted to focus on a missing product or company strategy.

This even happened at companies that definitively *had* engineering strategies, like the payment provider Stripe. When I joined in 2016, it had a clear engineering strategy with numerous guiding policies, including:

- Maintain backwards API compatibility, at almost any cost. (For example, force an upgrade from TLS 1.2 to TLS 1.3 to retain PCI compliance, but don't force upgrades from the `/v1/charges` endpoint (*https://oreil.ly/P19yM*) to the `/v1/payment_intents` endpoint (*https://oreil.ly/lk7pv*).)
- Work in Ruby within a monorepo, unless it's the PCI environment, data processing, or data science work.
- Engineers are fully responsible for the usability of their work, even when product or engineering managers are involved.

I found it to be generally clear what the company's engineering strategy was on any given topic—even if finding it sometimes required asking around. Over time, certain decisions became sufficiently contentious that it became hard to definitively answer what the strategy was. For example, the question of whether to adopt Ruby or Java became contentious enough that I distributed a strategy document (*https://lethain.com/magnitudes-of-exploration*) attempting to mediate the disagreement. It wasn't a particularly successful effort, for reasons that are obvious in hindsight—particularly the lack of any enforcement mechanism.

William Gibson has said, "The future is already here—it's just not very evenly distributed." In the same sense, there is *always* a strategy embedded into an organization's decisions—even if that strategy is only visible to a small group and is quickly forgotten.

I've simply never found an organization with no engineering strategy at all. If you ever find yourself thinking that your organization doesn't have one, I'd encourage you to seek out where the strategy might live in practice, even if it isn't codified in documentation. Whatever you find practitioners doing is their strategy. Repeated decisions are always made according to some rule or set of rules, even if the only rule is a powerful disregard for prior decisions.

Strategy Changes Companies

In Chapter 21, I discuss the meditation app Calm's engineering strategy to address pervasive friction within its engineering team. The core of that strategy was about clarifying how Calm makes major technology decisions, along with documenting the motivating goal steering those decisions: to maximize the time and energy Calm spent on creating its product rather than on investing in platform changes.

That strategy eliminated the cause of ongoing friction by increasing the burden of proof required to adopt new technologies, canceling a planned service decomposition, and narrowing our innovation efforts to those that directly improved our product. It was successful in resetting the team's focus. It also caused several engineers to leave the company, because experimenting with new technologies was more important to them than making progress on Calm's product. A clear, documented strategy made it clear to everyone involved what sort of game we were playing and what the rules for that game were, so that for the first time they could make an informed decision about whether they wanted to play that game with the wider team.

Creating alignment is one of the ways that strategy makes an impact, but it's certainly not the only way. Some of the other ways that strategies support organizations are:

Concentrating company investment into a smaller space
: For example, deciding not to decompose a monolith (see Chapter 20) allows you to invest the majority of your tooling efforts into one language, one test suite, and one deployment mechanism.

Making many interesting properties only available through universal adoption
: Moving to an "N-1 policy" on backfilled roles, discussed in Document 18-2, is a significant opportunity for managing costs, but it only works if it's consistently adopted. As another example, many strategies for disaster recovery and multiregion availability are only viable if *all* infrastructure has a common configuration mechanism.

Focusing execution on what truly matters
: Stripe's Sorbet strategy (Document 22-3) allowed a team of 10 engineers to push the company's Ruby monolith toward static typing incrementally, without distracting the larger organization. This was a difficult project that

could have consumed the entire organization for many months, but this focus allowed a small team to accomplish the majority of the early work.

Creating a knowledge repository of how your organization thinks
Onboarding new hires, particularly senior new hires, is much more effective with a documented strategy.

For example, the strategy for accessing user data (Document 19-1) requires that all access to user data must be supported by a clear, user-understandable rationale. While this might be obvious to new hires from larger companies, folks with only small-company experience are likely to be completely unaware that such a rule is necessary. If it isn't documented, compliance with the policy will quickly decline.

There are some things that a strategy, even a cleverly written one, cannot do. It cannot guarantee business growth, hire a particular individual, or guarantee that lobbying will change an existing legal framework like General Data Protection Regulation (GDPR). However, it's always been my experience that developing a strategy creates progress, even if that progress consists of understanding the inherent disagreement.

Inappropriate Strategy Is Especially Impactful

While good strategy can accomplish many things, it sometimes feels like inappropriate strategy is far more impactful—in all the wrong ways. Digg V4 (*https://lethain.com/digg-v4*) remains the worst-considered strategy I've personally participated in. It involved completely rewriting the Digg V3.5 codebase from a PHP monolith to a PHP frontend and backend composed of a dozen Python services. It also moved the database from sharded MySQL to an early version of Cassandra. Perhaps worst, it replaced the nuanced algorithms developed over a decade with a hack implemented a few days before launch.

Digg would likely have struggled to become profitable anyway, since it relied on search engine optimization for traffic, and in that era Google's search algorithm changed frequently. However, the engineering strategy ensured that it died quickly, closing off any opportunity to rebuild before we ran out of money.

Importantly, it's not just Digg. Almost every engineering organization you drill into will have its share of unused platform projects that captured decades of engineering years, to the detriment of an important opportunity. A shocking number of senior leaders join new companies and initiate a grand migration (*https://lethain.com/grand-migration*) that attempts to entirely rewrite the architecture, switch programming languages, or otherwise shift their new organization to resemble a prior organization where they understood things better.

Inappropriate Versus Bad

When I first wrote this section, I labeled this sort of strategy as "bad." The problem with that term is that the same strategy might well have been very effective in a different set of circumstances. For example, if Digg had been a three-person company with no revenue, rewriting from scratch could have been the right decision!

I've thus tried to favor the term *inappropriate* rather than *bad* to avoid getting caught up in whether a given approach *might* work in other circumstances. Every approach undoubtedly works in *some* organization.

Written Strategy Drives Organizational Learning

When I joined Carta, I noticed that we had an inconsistent approach to a number of important problems. Teams had distinct "standard kits" that defined which technologies could be used in new projects. We were inconsistent about adopting existing internal platforms and about funding new ones. There was widespread agreement that we were in the process of decomposing our monolith, but no agreement on how we were doing it.

Carta was a *permissive strategy environment*: there was explicit guidance, but individual teams were allowed to interpret that guidance according to their own beliefs. Over time, the variation in interpretation across teams resulted in many strongly differing perspectives on the ideal path forward.

As such, one of my first projects was writing down an explicit engineering strategy along with our newly formed Navigators team (*https://lethain.com/navigators*), itself a part of Carta's new engineering strategy. This program explicitly named individuals as technical leaders who would represent key parts of the engineering organization in a small leadership group of about 10 engineers. The group made it possible to iterate on strategy without taking on the impossible task of negotiating with 400 engineers directly.

The process of writing this strategy made it possible to describe the problems we saw explicitly and discuss how we wanted to navigate them. We could iterate on the strategy in the small group, then share the artifact widely for feedback from teams we might have missed. We did just that, and talked about it frequently in engineering all-hands meetings. Then we came back to it each year—or when things stopped making much sense—and revised it.

As an example, our initial strategy didn't talk about artificial intelligence (AI) at all. A few months later, we extended it to mention a very conservative approach to using large language models (LLMs). We recently revised the AI portion again, as we dive deeply into agentic workflows (*https://oreil.ly/oqtWQ*).

A lot of people have disagreed with parts of the strategy, which is great: *making it possible to disagree more precisely* is one of the key benefits of having a written strategy. From those disagreements, we've been able to evolve our strategy—sometimes in response to new information, like the current rapid evolution of AI practices, and other times to improve our initial approach, like changing how we selected members for the Navigators team over time.

New hires can disagree, too, and when strategy is written down, they can do it from an informed place rather than coming across as being too attached to their prior company's practices. In particular, they can understand the thinking that motivated past decisions, even when that context is no longer obvious. When Carta paused the decomposition of our monolith, there was significant friction in service provisioning—but since that's far less true today, the decision might seem a bit arbitrary. Only a written document can consistently communicate that context across a growing, shifting organization.

With oral history, what you believe about the past and the present highly depends on who you talk with. With written history, it's far more possible to agree at scale, which is a prerequisite for *growing* at scale—rather than isolating growth within small pockets of senior leadership.

Implicit Strategy Comes at a Cost

I've just finished talking about written strategy, and Chapter 11 of this book is devoted entirely to that topic. My emphasis on that topic isn't just because of the positives written strategy creates, but also because of the damage *unwritten* strategy does. When your strategy isn't written down:

It's vulnerable to misinterpretation

In organizations that rely foremost on verbal communication, information flow depends on an individual being in a given room for a decision, then accurately repeating that information to others who need it. However, those individuals often fail to repeat the information, or they repeat it incorrectly to some degree. Both create significant problems.

Two-Headed Organizations

Some years ago, I shifted toward a model where most engineering organizations I worked with had two leaders: a manager and a senior engineer. This was partially to ensure that engineering context would be included in decision making at the senior level, but it was also intended to reduce communication errors. Having two leaders where one might be sufficient sounds like an expensive investment, which it is, but I've always found it worth the price.

Errors in one-to-one communication are so prevalent, and the cost of communication errors is so high, that I now structure organizations and communication mechanisms to ensure that I always convey important updates (like those related to strategy) to *at least two people in each area of the organization*.

It creates inconsistency across teams

At one company I worked in, promotions to Staff-plus roles happened at a much higher rate in the infrastructure engineering organization than in the product engineering team. This created a constant drain on product engineering to work on infrastructure-shaped problems, even if those problems weren't particularly valuable to the business.

New leaders had no idea that this informal policy of preferring infrastructure work for Staff-plus promotions existed, and they would routinely run into trouble in calibration discussions (*https://lethain.com/perf-management-system*). They *also* weren't aware they needed to go argue for a better policy. Worse, no one was sure if this was a real policy or not, so whether the preference for infrastructure work was represented in any given promotion was ultimately random. Sometimes good promotions would be blocked; sometimes borderline cases would be approved.

It creates inconsistency over time

Implementing a new policy tends to be a mix of persistent and one-time actions. For example, let's say you want to standardize all HTTP operations to use the same library across your codebase to avoid dealing with the nuances of error handling across numerous HTTP clients. You add a linter check to reject known alternatives and do a one-time pass across your codebase to standardize on that library.

However, two years later, there are another three random HTTP libraries in your codebase, creeping into the cracks surrounding your linting. If the standardization policy is written down and a few people read it, then there are a number of ways this could be prevented. If it's not written down, it's much less likely someone will remember the policy, let alone the rationale, well enough to argue about it.

It poses a hazard to new leaders

When a new Staff-plus engineer or executive joins a company, it's common for the current team to blame them for failing to understand the existing context behind past decisions. That's fair: a big part of senior leadership is uncovering and understanding context. It's also unfair: explicit documentation of the thinking that led to the prior decision would make this much easier for them.

Every particularly bad new-leader onboarding that I've seen has involved a new leader coming into an unfilled role that the new leader's manager didn't know how to do. These leaders' success depended entirely on their learning ability (and interest).

The practice of documenting strategy has a lot in common with succession planning (*https://lethain.com/succession-planning*), in that the full benefits accrue to the *organization* rather than to the individual doing the planning. It's possible to maintain the status quo when the original authors are present, but appreciating the value of documentation requires stepping outside yourself for a moment to consider what will matter most to the organization when you're no longer a member.

Information Herd Immunity

A frequent objection to writing strategy down is that "no one reads anything." There's some truth to this: it's extremely hard to get everyone in an organization to know something. However, I've never found that goal to be particularly important.

I view information dispersal in an organization as being a lot like herd immunity (*https://oreil.ly/R2DLb*): you don't need *everyone* to know something; you just need *enough* people to know it that any confusion doesn't propagate too far.

It may be impossible for *all* engineers to know the details of your strategy, but you certainly can make sure every Staff-plus engineer and engineering manager knows them.

Writing Strategy Supports Personal Learning

While I believe that the biggest beneficiary of written strategy is the organization, I also believe that creating strategy is an underrated avenue for individual self-development.

The ways that I've seen strategy support personal development are:

Building self-awareness
: I've worked with several engineers who viewed themselves as extremely senior, but frequently demanded that projects be implemented using new programming languages or technologies because they personally wanted to learn about that technology. Their internal strategy was clear—they wanted to work on something fun—but following the steps to build an engineering strategy (discussed in Chapter 5) would have created a strategy that even they agreed didn't make sense.

Supporting situational awareness in new environments
: Wardley mapping (covered in Chapter 15) talks a lot about situational awareness as a prerequisite to good strategy. This is about ensuring you understand the realities of your circumstances, which is the most destructive failure of new senior engineering leaders. If you explicitly state the diagnosis to which the strategy should be applied, it's easier to see why reusing a prior strategy in a new team or company might not work.

Serving as your personal archive
: Just as documented strategy is institutional memory, it also serves as personal memory, helping you to understand the impact of your prior approaches. Each of us is an archivist of our prior work, pulling out the most valuable pieces to address the problem at hand. Over a long career, memory fades—and motivated reasoning creeps in—but explicit documentation persists.

Indeed, part of the reason I started working on this book *now* rather than later is that I realized I was starting to forget the details of the strategy work I did earlier in my career. If I wanted to preserve the wisdom of that era and ensure I didn't have to relearn the same lessons in the future, I had to write it now.

Summary

This chapter has covered why strategy can be a valuable learning mechanism for both your engineering organization and for you. I've shown how strategies have helped organizations deal with service migrations, monolith decomposition, and right-sizing backfilling. I've also discussed how inappropriate strategy contributed to Digg's demise.

However, if I had to pick two things to emphasize as this chapter ends, it would be two themes that I find are frequently ignored:

- There's always a strategy, even if it isn't written down.
- The single biggest action you can take to further strategy in your organization is to *write strategy down* so that the organization can debate it, agree upon it, and explicitly evolve its approach.

Discussions around topics like strategy often get caught up in high-prestige activities like making controversial decisions, but the most effective strategists I've seen make more progress by actually performing the basics: writing things down, exploring widely to see how other companies solve the same problem, and incorporating feedback into their draft from folks who disagree with them. Strategy *is* useful—and doing strategy can be simple, too.

3

Who Gets to Do Strategy?

If you talk to enough aspiring leaders, you'll become familiar with the prevalent idea that they need to be promoted before they can work on strategy. It's widely accepted as true, but I've found this idea fundamentally incorrect: you can work on strategy from anywhere in an organization. It just requires different tactics to do so.

This chapter explains my belief that *anyone* within an organization can make meaningful progress on strategy, particularly if you are honest about the tools accessible to you and thoughtful about how to use them.

The themes I'll dig into are:

- How to do strategy as an engineer, particularly an engineer who hasn't been given explicit authority to do strategy
- Doing strategy as an engineering executive who is responsible for your organization's decision making
- How you can develop engineering strategy even in difficult situations, such as when there's no existing strategy, when acknowledging certain problems is politically sensitive, or when misaligned incentives make consensus challenging
- If this book's argument is that everyone should do strategy, is there anyone who, nonetheless, really should *not* do strategy?

By the end, you'll hopefully agree that engineering strategy is accessible to everyone, even though you're always operating within constraints.

Doing Strategy as an Engineer

It's easy to get so distracted by an executive's top-down approach to strategy that you convince yourself that there aren't other approachable mechanisms to doing strategy. There are!

Staff Engineer introduces an approach I call "take five, then synthesize" (*https://oreil.ly/aMso-*), which does strategy in two stages. The first stage involves documenting how five related current and historical decisions have been made in your organization. This is an extended exploration phase. In the second phase, you're synthesizing those five documents into a diagnosis and a policy. You are naming the implicit strategy, so it's impossible for someone to reasonably argue that you're not empowered to do strategy: you're just describing what's already happening.

At that point, either the organization feels comfortable with what you've written—which is their current strategy—or it doesn't, in which case you've forced a conversation about how to revise the approach. Creating awareness is often enough to drive strategic change, and doing so doesn't require any explicit authorization from an executive.

When awareness is insufficient, the other pattern I've found highly effective in low-authority scenarios is an approach I wrote about in *An Elegant Puzzle* and call "model, document, and share" (*https://lethain.com/model-document-share*):

1. Model the approach you want others to adopt. Make it easy for them to observe how you've changed the way you're doing things.
2. Document the approach, the thinking behind it, and how to adopt it.
3. Share the document around. If people see you succeeding with the approach, then they're likely to copy it from you.

You might be skeptical, because this is an influence-based approach. However, as we'll discuss in the next section, even executive-driven strategies are highly dependent on influence.

Strategy Archaeology

Vernor Vinge's *A Deepness in the Sky* (Tor Books, 1999) introduced the term *software archaeologists*, meaning folks who create functionality by cobbling together millennia of scraps of existing software.

Although it's a somewhat different usage, I sometimes think of the "take five, then synthesize" approach as performing strategy archaeology. Simply by recording what has happened in the past, we make it easier to understand the present—and influence the future.

Doing Strategy as an Executive

The biggest misconception about executive roles, frequently held by nonexecutives and new executives who are about to make a series of regrettable mistakes, is that executives operate without constraints. That is false: executives operate under an extremely high number of constraints—budgets to meet, CEO visions to fulfill, peers to satisfy, and a team to motivate. They can disappoint any of these temporarily, but in the long term they have to satisfy all of them.

Nonetheless, it is true that executives have more latitude to mandate and cajole participation in the strategies that they sponsor. *The Engineering Executive's Primer*'s chapter on strategy (*https://lethain.com/eng-strategies*) is a brief summary of this entire book, but it doesn't say much about how executive strategy differs from nonexecutive strategy.

How the executive's approach to strategy differs from the engineer's can be boiled down to:

- Mandates only matter if there are consequences. Executives have the advantage that they can mandate adherence to their strategy, which gives them more options for making effective policy. An engineer can't prevent the promotion of someone who refuses to follow their policy, but an executive can. If an executive can't or won't enforce consequences for not complying with a mandate, it isn't a meaningful mandate.
- Even if an executive doesn't have sufficient support or is unwilling to use mandates, they have significant visibility and access to their organization to advocate for their preferred strategy.
- Neither access nor mandates improve an executive's ability to diagnose problems. However, both often create the *appearance* of progress. This is why executive strategies can fail so spectacularly and endure so long despite failure.

As a result, my experience is that executives have an easier time doing strategy, but a much harder time learning how to do strategy *well*. They also have fewer guardrails to help them avoid serious mistakes, and the consequences of an executive's poor strategy tend to reach much further than an engineer's. Waiting to do strategy until you are an executive is a recipe for disaster, even if it looks easier from a distance.

Doing Strategy in Other Roles

Even if you're neither an engineer nor an engineering executive, you can still do engineering strategy. It'll just require an even more influence-driven approach.

The engineering organization is generally right to believe that they know the most about engineering, but that's not always true. Sometimes a product manager used to be an engineer and has significant relevant experience. Other times, such as with the early adoption of LLMs (Document 17-1), engineers don't know much either and benefit from outside perspectives.

Doing Strategy in Challenging Environments

Good strategies accurately diagnose the circumstances and introduce policies that address those circumstances. You are likely to spend time in organizations where internal limitations make both of those challenging, so it's worth acknowledging that and discussing how to navigate those challenges.

LOW-TRUST ENVIRONMENT

Diagnosing problems is a skill. Sometimes you may be too inexperienced to write an effective strategy for your current problem. In that case, the solution isn't easy, but it is straightforward: do more strategy work to build your expertise. In other cases, you may see the problems fairly clearly, but you know that your organization's culture would frown on acknowledging them. The latter is a diagnosis problem rooted in low trust, and it does make things more difficult.

Sometimes you have to whisper the controversial parts of a strategy: translate difficult messages into softer, less direct versions that are acceptable to state. If your goal is to hold people accountable, this can feel dishonest or like an ethical compromise, but the goal of strategy is to make better decisions, which is an entirely different concern than holding folks accountable for the past. Chapter 7 recognizes this problem and discusses it in more detail.

Karpman Drama Triangle

Sometimes, when the diagnosis seems particularly obvious to you and yet people don't agree with you, it's because you are wrong. When I've been obviously wrong about things I understand well, it's usually because I've fallen into viewing a situation through the lens of the Karpman Drama Triangle (*https://oreil.ly/4Z3QL*), where all parties are mapped onto the roles of persecutor, rescuer, and victim.

POOR-JUDGMENT ENVIRONMENT

Even when you do an excellent job diagnosing challenges, it can be difficult to drive agreement within the organization about how to address them. Sometimes this is due to genuinely complex tradeoffs. For example, in Stripe's acquisition of Index (discussed in Document 22-4), there was debate about how to deal with Index's Java-based technology stack. It culminated in a compromise that didn't make anyone particularly happy: deferring the decision until after launching the initial release.

That compromise is a good example of a difficult tradeoff: although parties disagreed with the approach, everyone understood the conflicting priorities that had to be addressed.

In other cases, though, there are policy choices that simply don't make much sense, generally driven by poor judgment. Sometimes that's poor technical judgment; other times, people choose to prioritize their own interests at the expense of the company's needs. Calm's strategy to focus on being a product engineering organization (discussed in Document 21-1) dealt with some aspects of that, acknowledging in its diagnosis that "most of our disagreements stem around adopting new technologies or rewriting existing components into new technology stacks." In that situation, your strategy is an attempt to educate your colleagues about the tradeoffs they are making.

Sometimes people will disagree with your strategy. In that case, remember that most interesting problems require iterative solutions. Writing your strategy down and sharing it will start a process that can change the organization's mind. Don't get discouraged, even if that change is initially slow.

Dealing with Missing Strategies

The strategy laid out in Document 18-1 for dealing with new private equity ownership introduces a common problem: lack of clarity about what other parts of your own company want. In that case, a layoff seemed likely, but it was unclear how large that layoff would be. Many leaders encounter that sort of ambiguity and decide that they cannot move forward with a strategy of their own until that decision is made. While it's inconvenient not to know the details, getting blocked by ambiguity is *always* the wrong decision.

Instead, do what the private equity strategy does: *accept* that ambiguity as a fact and work around it. Rather than giving up, that strategy adopted a series of new policies to reduce cost growth by changing the organization's seniority mix (Document 18-2). The strategy also recognized that once there was clarity on reduction targets, additional actions would be needed.

Whenever you're working on challenging problems, you can always find justifications for not making progress. Leadership is about finding a way to move forward despite those issues. A missing strategy will always be part of your diagnosis, but it should never be a reason that you *can't* do strategy.

Who Shouldn't Do Strategy?

In my experience, there's almost never a reason why *you* cannot do strategy, but there are two particular scenarios where doing strategy probably doesn't make sense. The first is not a "who" problem, but a "when" problem (the focus of the next chapter): sometimes there is so much strategy already happening that doing more would be a distraction. If another part of your organization is already working on the same problem, do your best to work with them directly rather than generating competing work.

The other time to avoid strategy is when you're trying to satisfy an emotional need to make a direct, immediate impact. Sharing a thoughtful strategy always drives progress, but it's often the slow, incremental progress of changing your organization's beliefs. Even definitive, top-down strategies from executives are often ignored in pockets of an organization, and bottom-up strategies spread slowly, as they are modeled, documented, and shared. Embarking on strategy work requires a tolerance for winning in the long run, even when there's little progress this week or this quarter.

Summary

As you finish reading this chapter, my hope is that you also believe that *you* can work on strategy in your organization, whether you're an engineer, an executive, or in another role. I also hope that you appreciate that the tools you use will vary greatly depending on who you are within your organization and the culture in which you work. Whether you need to model or can mandate, there's a mechanism that will work for you.

4

When Should You Write Strategy—and How Much?

Even if you believe that strategy is generally useful, it is difficult to decide that today is the day to start writing engineering strategy. When you do start writing strategy, it's easy to write such an overwhelming amount of strategy that your organization ignores it rather than investing time into understanding it.

Fortunately, these are universal problems, and there are a handful of useful mental models to help you avoid both extremes. This chapter covers:

- When to write strategy
- How much strategy your organization can tolerate
- Using *strategy altitude*—how permissive a given strategy is and where it's implemented—to manage the overhead that strategies create
- Mechanisms to debug whether you're doing too much or too little strategy work

When you're done reading it, you should have a clear perspective on when to start writing strategy, determining how many strategies to write, and using strategy altitude to reduce overhead when you do decide to write a high volume of strategies.

When to Write Strategy

Shortly after becoming Calm's CTO, I opened a document, titled it "Engineering Strategy," and then stared into that blank abyss before putting it away for a year. When I came back to it, I documented three guiding principles:

- Choose boring technology (*https://oreil.ly/P3TY9*)
- Resolve conflict with curiosity
- Prefer vendors for commoditized functionality

These simple statements greatly reduced our conflict in decision making, and allowed us to focus more energy on improving our product. When I started, I felt like we needed a clearer strategy, but I just didn't know what to write—so I wrote nothing.

Often, writing nothing is the best available choice. Indeed, a common slur against leaders is that they "want to be strategic," implying that they're too focused on abstract ideas rather than on the concrete needs of today. Behind that allegation is an important truth: strategy work isn't always the most valuable way you can spend your time. Sometimes working on strategy is just a way of "snacking" (*https://oreil.ly/2SBEY*) to avoid doing something more important.

Before you start working on strategy, you have to decide whether now is the correct time. That depends on your organization's current strategic state, the trend of that strategic state over time, and whether you have enough context to be effective.

CURRENT STRATEGIC STATE

The first of those three criteria is the idea of strategic state. Using the example of service architecture strategy (Document 20-1), your engineering organization is going to be in one of three strategy states:

Globally consistent

There is a clearly agreed-upon strategy, even if it's not written down. When you ask different members of the team how to approach a given problem, you get similar answers. For example, everyone agrees to write new product functionality in the existing monolithic codebase.

Consistent within teams

There is a clear strategy within pockets of the organization, but there's some inconsistency across pockets. For example, product engineering believes all new functionality should be in a new service within a shared monorepo, but platform engineering believes all new functionality should be implemented in a monolith.

Highly varied
There's little agreement across individuals within engineering on how to approach problems. For example, some engineers want to do work in new services in a monorepo, others in new services in polyrepos, and some believe in implementing new functionality in an existing monolithic service.

If your organization is globally consistent, then it's unlikely that doing more strategy work will be useful, unless your organization is consistently deciding upon undesirable approaches. If you're in one of the latter two states, then it's likely a useful time to write some strategy.

TRENDS IN STRATEGIC STATE

Even if the organization's current state is good, if it's trending toward a worse state, now is a valuable time to start doing strategy work. Conversely, if the current state is decent and trending toward something better, it's likely not a valuable opportunity.

There are a handful of recurring causes that can lead to abrupt, sometimes unexpected, shifts in state—making it a good opportunity to consider writing strategy. These include:

How much you are—or aren't—hiring
Uber doubled its engineering headcount every six months for four years and opened many distributed engineering offices, which led to highly varied approaches. It also meant that most engineers were recent hires, driving up inconsistency even more.

Whether your newly hired external leaders tend to be playbook-driven or respond to the organization's current context
Although it's a known antipattern in executive onboarding (*https://lethain.com/first-ninety-days-cto-vpe*), many leaders are so desperate to make an early impact that they forget to diagnose their new environments before making sweeping changes. This creates a strategy rift between teams that align with the new direction and teams maintaining the existing software and infrastructure.

How frequently you have significant organizational changes
: Changes such as reorganizations or layoffs can break the mechanisms that propagate organizational culture, which are the sort of subtle glue work (*https://noidea.dog/glue*) that often gets ignored in spreadsheet-driven exercises.

How effectively you document and communicate historical decisions
: Communication during onboarding is key: some companies drill new hires on how decisions are made, and others expect teams to do the training locally. Both approaches can work well. Both can work poorly.

YOUR CONTEXT LEVEL

Finally, even if the current state is poor and getting worse, you have to assess whether *you* understand the organization well enough to start doing useful strategy work. Many new leaders jump in, make assumptions without testing them, and attempt a massive migration (*https://lethain.com/grand-migration*) or some other grand, sweeping gesture. That might *feel* like an audacious example of driving strategy, but it's mostly just anxiety and ego wrapped in a Gantt chart.

Do you understand the history around the areas you want to change? Do you understand the individuals who made the decisions, and the context that made them good decisions at the time? If so, then you're ready to step into strategy. If not, it's worth slowing down to build the relationships and context necessary to make your subsequent work useful.

If things could be better or are trending down, and you know enough about the company to get started, then it's time to start working on strategy.

How Much Strategy to Write

The next question you'll run into is: *how much* strategy should you undertake? Should you write something about programming language choice? Or service decomposition? Or how you prioritize bugs? Or should it be about data warehouses? What about doing all four at once?

The potential strategies you could work on are genuinely infinite, so it's hard to decide where to start. By far the most valuable decision you can make is to limit the work you have in progress (*https://lethain.com/limiting-wip*) at any given time, even if it means starting smaller than you want. Generally, what I've found effective is to start with small pieces of strategy, iterate until you get them working, and only then move on to something larger. Limit yourself to developing one or two strategies at a time. This gives you bandwidth to ensure that your strategies actually work.

To remain effective while limiting concurrent strategy development, it's important to have a clear, but lightly held, point of view about where you want to get over time. This clarity makes it possible to align small chunks toward the same destination such that they build into something larger, while also remaining flexible enough to adjust as each step teaches you more about the path you're on.

Grounding that in a concrete example: at Uber, we were having reliability and productivity issues related to the monolithic Python codebase. My team didn't have the ability to forbid commits there, but we did have the ability to make service provisioning really, really easy. So we created a strategy around making service provisioning and operation as painless as possible. The strategy aimed to solve a later problem of decomposing and departing from the monolith, but we didn't address that directly. We focused on the first step, believing that it was a necessary prerequisite for the subsequent steps. After we proved out the first step, it then became possible to work strategy on the subsequent steps.

If we had started with the broader strategy, we might have gotten stuck having an intellectual debate about what should happen in the future, and success would have required many different teams to buy into our future vision without having any concrete step for them to take right then and there. By narrowing our focus, we were able to iterate on the prerequisites and delay building consensus until there was a concrete step we needed folks to take. At that point, there was no intellectual debate about whether it was possible, because most people were already operating as we intended.

One of the challenges with reducing the volume of your concurrent strategies is that it appears unambitious. In the Uber example, we *needed* to solve development in the monolithic codebase, but instead we were talking about service provisioning. From a distance, it must have seemed like we'd lost the plot. This is a recurring challenge: effective strategy development can appear overly conservative. To solve that apparent lack of ambition, you have to pair your focused approach with broader, proactive storytelling to your stakeholders. This allows the team's execution to remain focused while also explaining to stakeholders how the incremental initiative will expand into something remarkable over time.

Sometimes this isn't just a stakeholder problem: it can feel slow to you as well. In those moments, I try to remember that friction isn't velocity (*https://lethain.com/friction-vs-velocity*): driving down the highway with windows down feels faster, but is actually slower, and the same holds true in software engineering. For example,

Digg's engineering strategy when I joined had an extremely clear and consistent architecture (a PHP frontend, Python services, Cassandra for all storage), but the company still collapsed around us. A few strategies that work are more valuable than a bunch of strategies, even good ones, in a burning building.

Strategy Altitude

Sometimes you *do* want to lay out a broad, comprehensive strategy, and you want to do it quickly. That violates the general rule of developing one strategy at a time, but there's one helpful idea that can often make this possible: *strategy altitude.*

It's easiest to explain this idea by starting with a few examples of operating at different altitudes (Figure 4-1):

A permissive strategy at the engineering organization altitude
: A developer experience team wants to increase code quality. They create a mechanism that allows teams to define linting rules for their own builds. The developer experience team creates opinionated defaults for teams to adopt, but each team is empowered to override those defaults locally.

A prescriptive strategy at the engineering organization altitude
: A CTO wants to increase code quality. They mandate that every pull request must include a test and that continuous integration/continuous delivery (CI/CD) should block merging pull requests that reduce code coverage.

A permissive strategy at the team altitude
: A product engineering team wants to decrease security vulnerabilities in its software. They tell engineers that it's important to consider a number of security issues when implementing software, and include resources for engineers to educate themselves.

A prescriptive strategy at the team altitude
: A product engineering team wants to reduce user-impacting bugs. They decide that their planning sprints will schedule bug fixes first, and only schedule features after draining the bug backlog.

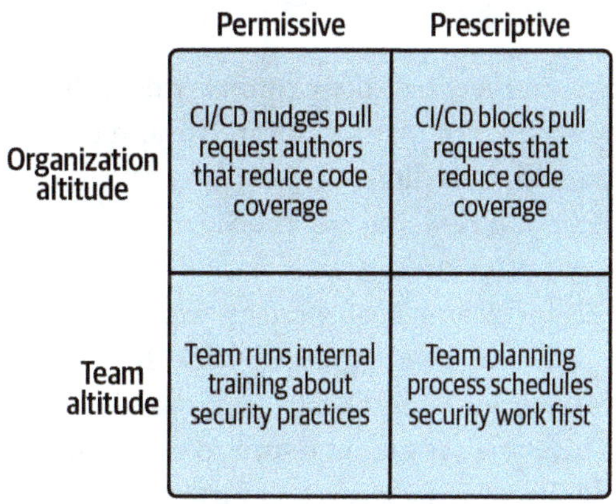

Permissive
Prescriptive
Organization altitude
CI/CD nudges pull request authors that reduce code coverage
CI/CD blocks pull requests that reduce code coverage
Team altitude
Team runs internal training about security practices
Team planning process schedules security work first

Figure 4-1. Example strategies at different strategy altitudes

Permissive strategies are less expensive than prescriptive strategies because they require little to no enforcement. Lower-altitude strategies (such as team strategies) are less expensive than higher-altitude strategies (like org or company strategies) because they can rely on local mechanisms for rollout and maintenance. Mechanisms for wider communication are often oversaturated and lossy: for instance, communicating in engineering-wide chat channels is, at best, ineffective.

Pulling these ideas together, the formula to increase strategy volume is to either reduce altitude, increase permissiveness, or both.

Going into a concrete example, when I joined Carta, I worked across engineering to roll out quite a bit of strategy work in the first six months. Some of this was documenting existing strategy so that adopting it didn't require much overhead. Other parts were shifts in approach, so we focused on developing permissive strategies. Every strategy included an escalation path to support local customization, generally asking each team's Navigator (*https://lethain.com/navigators*) (a Staff-plus engineer responsible for that area) to override the strategy as appropriate. There was only one place where I was highly prescriptive, which was around provisioning new services—there, the escape hatch was more restrictive, requiring escalation to the CTO.

Because we focused on permissive strategies, we were able to cover a broad range of topics at high altitude. If I'd been more proscriptive, the approach would have certainly failed, even though I might have looked like a more courageous leader. Annoyingly, *looking* effective and *being* effective tend to be only lightly correlated.

Are You Doing Too Much?

Although many engineers feel that their company doesn't have a clear engineering strategy, it's my experience that significantly more leaders fail by attempting too *much* strategy work than too little.

To debug whether you're doing too much, the most valuable question you can ask is whether your prior strategy work has affected subsequent decisions.

If you've shared out a bunch of strategy work, but it doesn't seem to be changing how your software is written, scale back. Instead, focus on getting just a single strategy working well and deeply understanding what's gone wrong in your prior efforts. Then, and only then, return to that work and fix it. Finally, and *only* after completing the prior steps, expand further.

You may be doing good work, but simply overwhelming the organization with too much. Adopting new approaches is hard, and changing everything at once is overwhelming. Adjust your strategy altitude to make your strategies easier to adopt, and you slow down on adding more until the existing ones have been fully adopted.

Summary

After reading this chapter, you know when it's effective to write strategy, and how to pace yourself to write a reasonable volume of strategies. You can use strategy altitude to make strategies easier to adopt, and can debug whether you're overwhelming your organization with too much strategy work.

If you take nothing else away from this chapter, try to *always be working on exactly one strategy*. Doing more feels like progress, but usually fails. Doing less is always a missed opportunity.

PART | II

Steps for Building Engineering Strategies

Because strategy is often treated as an abstract topic, advice on how to do strategy is often a collection of general advice. The second part of this book goes in the opposite direction, breaking strategy into five concrete steps to follow to create effective engineering strategies. These steps are reproducible, practical, and things you can begin today.

This part ends with practical advice on writing readable strategies and tactics for overcoming the many obstacles that often impact strategy work: chaotic environments, lack of executive sponsorship, and unrealistic timelines.

Steps to Build an Engineering Strategy

Often you'll see a disorganized collection of ideas labeled as a "strategy." Even when they're dense with ideas, such documents can be hard to parse. This is a major reason why most engineers will claim their company doesn't have a clear strategy—even though, as you saw in Chapter 1, *all* companies follow some strategy, even if it's undocumented.

This chapter lays out a repeatable, structured approach to drafting strategy and introduces each step of that approach. I'll detail each step further in its respective chapter. Here, I'll cover how these five steps fit together to facilitate creating strategy, especially by preventing practitioners from skipping steps that feel awkward or challenging. I'll also look at how to decide for yourself whether to follow these exact steps for your own strategy work or adjust them.

Here is a high-level summary of each step:

Step 1: Exploring
: Exploring the wider industry's ideas and practices around the strategy you're working on. Exploration is understanding what recent research might change your approach, and how the state of the art has changed since you last tackled a similar problem.

Step 2: Diagnosing
: Diagnosing the details of your problem. It's hard to slow down to understand your problem clearly before attempting to solve it, but it's even more difficult to solve anything well without a clear diagnosis.

Step 3: Refining
: Refinement is taking a raw, unproven set of ideas and testing them against reality. Three techniques are introduced to support this validation process: strategy testing, systems modeling, and Wardley mapping.

Step 4: Setting policy
: Policy makes the tradeoffs and decisions to solve your diagnosis. These can range from specifying how software is architected, to how pull requests are reviewed, to how headcount is allocated within an organization.

Step 5: Operations
: Operations are the concrete mechanisms that translate policy into an active force within your organization. These can be nudges that remind you about code changes without associated tests, or weekly meetings where you study progress on a migration.

From this chapter's starting point, you can decide where you want to read further.

How the Steps Become Strategy

You can't create effective strategy through the rote incantation of a formula; following these steps doesn't guarantee that you'll create a great strategy. However, what I've consistently found is that strategies fail more often due to avoidable errors than to fundamentally unsound thinking. Busy people skip steps—especially steps they dislike or have failed at before.

These steps are the way to avoid those errors. By practicing them routinely, you'll build powerful habits and intuition around which approach is most appropriate for the current strategy you're working on. They also help turn strategy into a community practice that you, your colleagues, and the wider engineering ecosystem can participate in together.

Each step is an input that flows into the next step: Your exploration is the foundation of a solid diagnosis. Your diagnosis helps you search the infinite space of policy for what you currently need. Operational mechanisms help you turn policy into an active force supporting your strategy, rather than an abstract treatise.

If you're skeptical of the steps, you should certainly maintain your skepticism, but do give them a few tries before discarding them entirely. You may also appreciate the discussion in Chapter 12 on bridging between theory and practice when doing strategy.

STEP 1: EXPLORING

Exploration is the deliberate practice of searching through a strategy's problem and solution spaces before allowing yourself to commit to a given approach. It's understanding how other companies and teams have approached similar questions, and whether their approaches might also work well for you. It's also learning why what brought you success at your former employer isn't necessarily the best solution for your current organization.

The Uber service migration strategy (Document 16-1) used exploration to understand the service ecosystem by reading industry literature:

> *As a starting point, we find it valuable to read "Large-Scale Cluster Management at Google with Borg" (https://oreil.ly/95B_Q), which informed some elements of the approach to Kubernetes, and "Mesos: A Platform for Fine-Grained Resource Sharing in the Data Center" (https://oreil.ly/6HQID), which describes the Mesos/Aurora approach.*

It also used a Wardley map to explore the cloud compute ecosystem, as shown in Figure 5-1.

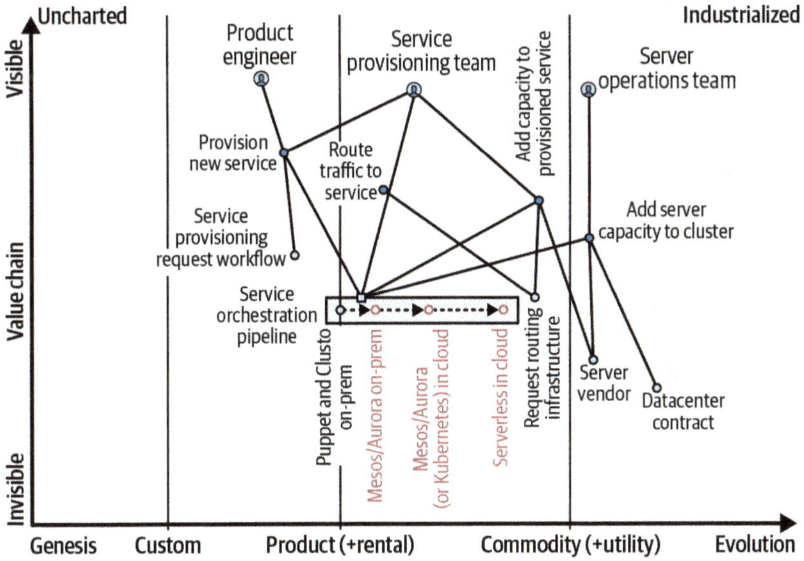

Figure 5-1. Evolution of service orchestration in 2014

For more details on exploration, see Chapter 6; Chapter 15 is a deep dive into Wardley mapping.

STEP 2: DIAGNOSING

Diagnosis is your attempt to correctly recognize the context that the strategy needs to solve before deciding on the policies to address that context. Building a diagnosis starts from what you learned in Step 1 and your understanding of your current circumstances. This step forces you to delay thinking about solutions until you fully understand your problem's nuances.

A diagnosis can be largely data-driven, such as the strategy for navigating a private equity ownership transition, discussed in Chapter 18:

> *Our Engineering headcount costs have grown by 15% YoY this year, and 18% YoY the prior year. Headcount grew 7% and 9% respectively, with the difference between headcount and headcount costs explained by salary band adjustments (4%), a focus on hiring senior roles (3%), and increased hiring in higher cost geographic regions (1%).*

It can also be less data-driven, instead aiming to summarize a problem, such as the Index acquisition strategy's summary of the known and unknown elements of the technical integration prior to the acquisition closing:

> *We will need to rapidly integrate the acquired startup to meet this timeline. We only know a small number of details about what this will entail. We* do *know that point-of-sale devices directly operate on payment details (e.g., the point-of-sale device knows the credit card details of the card it reads).*
>
> *Our compliance obligations restrict such activity to our "tokenization environment," a highly secured and isolated environment with direct access to payment details. This environment converts payment details into a unique token that other environments can utilize to operate against payment details without the compliance overhead of having direct access to the underlying payment details.*

The approach, and challenges, of developing a diagnosis are detailed in Chapter 7.

STEP 3: REFINING

Strategy refinement is a toolkit of methods to identify which parts of your diagnosis are most important, and verify that your approach to solving the diagnosis actually works. Chapter 8 discusses three methods in particular, each of which also has its own chapter: strategy testing (Chapter 13), systems modeling (Chapter 14), and Wardley mapping (Chapter 15).

Why Doesn't Refinement Come Earlier (or Later)?

A frequent point of disagreement with the steps I've laid out here is that refinement should occur *before* diagnosis. Another is that mapping and modeling are two distinct steps, and that mapping should occur before diagnosis, while modeling should occur after policy. A third is that refinement ought to be the final step of strategy, turning the steps into a looping cycle. These are all reasonable objections, so let me unpack my rationale for this structure.

By *far* the biggest risk for most strategies is not that you model too early or map too late, but that you skip both steps entirely. My foremost concern is minimizing the required investment into mapping and modeling so that more folks do these steps at all. Refining *after* exploring and diagnosing allows you to concentrate your efforts on a smaller number of load-bearing areas.

That said, it's common to refine at many places in your strategy creation. You're just as likely to have three small refinement steps as one bigger one.

STEP 4: SETTING POLICY

Setting *policy* is interpreting your diagnosis into a concrete plan that works. This requires careful study of what's worked within your company and any new ideas you've discovered while exploring the current problem.

Policies can do many things. The user-data control strategy discussed in Document 19-1 provides directional guidance:

> *Good security discussions don't frame decisions as a compromise between security and usability. We will pursue multi-dimensional tradeoffs to simultaneously improve security and efficiency. Whenever we frame a discussion on trading off between security and utility, it's a sign that we are having the wrong discussion, and that we should rethink our approach.*
>
> *We will prioritize mechanisms that can both automatically authorize and automatically document the rationale for access to customer data. The most obvious example of this is automatically granting access to*

> *a customer support agent for users who have an open support ticket assigned to that agent. (And removing that access when that ticket is reassigned or resolved.)*

Stripe's strategy for acquiring Index (Document 22-4) postponed making a decision until later:

> *Defer making a decision regarding the introduction of Java to a later date: the introduction of Java is incompatible with our existing engineering strategy, but at this point we've also been unable to align stakeholders on how to address this decision. Further, we see attempting to address this issue as a distraction from our timely goal of launching a joint product within six months.*
>
> *We will take up this discussion after launching the initial release.*

Chapter 9 goes further into evaluating policies, overcoming ambiguous circumstances that make it difficult to decide on an approach, and developing novel policies.

STEP 5: OPERATIONS

Even the best policies have to be interpreted. There will be new circumstances their authors never imagined, and the policies may be in effect long after their authors have left the organization. *Operational mechanisms* are the concrete implementation of your policies.

The simplest mechanism is an explicit escalation path, as shown in Calm's product engineering strategy (Document 21-1):

> *Exceptions are granted by the CTO, and must be in writing. The above policies are deliberately restrictive. Sometimes they may be wrong, and we will make exceptions to them. However, each exception should be deliberate and grounded in concrete problems we are aligned both on solving and how we solve them. If we all scatter toward our preferred solution, then we'll create negative leverage for Calm rather than serving as the engine that advances our product.*

From that starting point, the mechanisms can get far more complex. Chapter 10 works through evaluating mechanisms, composing an operational plan, and the most common sorts of operational mechanisms that I've seen across strategies.

Is the Structure Sacrosanct?

When you're struggling to write a strategy document, one of the first tools people recommend is a *strategy template*. Templates are great: they reduce the ambiguity in an already broad project into something more tractable. If you're wondering if you should use a template to craft strategy: sure, go ahead!

However, I find that well-meaning, thoughtful templates often turn into lumbering, callous documents that serve no one well. The secret to making a good template is that someone has to *own* it, and that person has to *care about the template's user* first and foremost, rather than the various constituencies that want to insert requirements into the strategy creation process. The security, compliance, and costs of your plans matter a great deal, but many organizations start to layer more and more requirements into these sorts of documents until writing them becomes prohibitively painful.

The best advice I can give is to discard every element of strategy that gets in your way *as long as you can explain what that element was intended to accomplish*. For example, if you're drafting a strategy and you don't find any operational mechanisms that fit, fine, discard that section. Ultimately, the structure is not sacrosanct: it's the *thinking* behind the sections that really matters. This topic is explored in more detail in Chapter 11.

Summary

Now you know the foundational steps to conducting strategy. From here, you can dive into the details with strategy case studies (see Part IV of this book), or you can maintain a high altitude, starting with the next chapter, about how exploration creates the foundation for an effective strategy.

Whichever you start with, I encourage you to eventually work through both to get the full perspective.

6

Exploring

A surprising number of strategies are doomed from inception because their authors get attached to one particular approach without considering alternatives that would work better for their current circumstances. This happens, for instance, when engineers want to pick tools solely because they are trending, and when executives insist on adopting the tech stack from their prior organization where they felt comfortable.

Exploration is the antidote to early anchoring. It forces you to consider the problem widely *before* evaluating any of the possible paths forward. Exploration is about verifying your prior experience remains relevant, rather than assuming the industry's been stagnant since you last worked on a given problem. Exploration is continuing to believe that things can get better when you're not watching.

This chapter covers:

- The goals of the exploration phase of strategy creation
- When to explore (always first!) and when it makes sense to stop exploring
- How to explore a topic, including common mechanisms like mining for internal precedent, reading industry papers and books, and leveraging your external network
- Why you must avoid making judgments while exploring

By the end of this chapter, you'll be able to conduct an exploration for your current strategy or the next one you work on.

What Is Exploration?

One of the frequent antipatterns I've encountered among senior leadership is the Grand Migration (*https://lethain.com/grand-migration*), where a new leader declares that a massive migration to a new technology stack—typically the stack used by their former employer—will solve every pressing problem. What distinguishes the Grand Migration is not the initially bad selection, but the single-minded ferocity with which the senior leader pushes for their approach, even when it becomes abundantly clear to others that it doesn't solve the problem at hand.

These senior leaders are very intelligent, but have allowed themselves to be trapped by their initial thinking from prior experiences. Accepting those early thoughts as the foundation of their strategy, they build the entire strategy on top of those ideas, and eventually so much weight rests on those early assumptions that it becomes impossible for the leader to acknowledge the errors.

Exploration is the deliberate practice of searching through a strategy's problem and solution spaces before allowing yourself to commit to an approach. It's understanding how others have approached the same problem, recently and in the past, both in trendy companies you admire and in practical companies that actually resemble yours.

Exploration is usually more external than internal, but the proportion will depend on the size of your company. If you're in a massive engineering organization of 100,000, there are likely existing internal solutions to your problem that you've never heard of. Conversely, if you're in an organization of 50 engineers, it's likely that much of your exploration will be external.

When to Explore

Exploration is the first step of good strategy work. You will always regret skipping it, because you'll inadvertently box yourself into whatever approach you focus on first. Especially when it comes to problems that you've solved previously, exploration is the only thing preventing you from overindexing on your prior experiences.

Try to continue exploring until you know how three similar teams within your company (if it's a large company) and three similar companies have recently solved the same problem. Make sure you can explain the thinking behind those decisions. At that point, you should be ready to stop exploring and move on to the diagnosis step of strategy creation (covered in the next chapter).

Exploration should always come with a minimum and maximum time frame: less than a few hours is very suspicious, and more than a week is questionable as well.

How to Explore

While the details of each exploration will differ a bit, the overarching approach tends to be pretty similar across strategies. After I open up the draft strategy document I'm working on, my general approach to exploration has five steps:

1. Gather every resource you can think of related to that problem. For example, in the Uber service migration strategy, I started by collecting recent papers on Mesos, Kubernetes, and Aurora to understand the state of the industry on orchestration.
2. Do some web searching and foundational-model prompting, and check with a few current and prior colleagues about what topics and resources you might be missing. For example, for the Calm engineering strategy, I focused on talking with industry peers about tools they had used to focus a team with diffuse goals.
3. Summarize the list of resources you've gathered, separating those you want to explore from those you won't spend time on but which are worth mentioning. For example, the LLM adoption strategy's exploration section documents the variety of resources the team explored before completing it.
4. Work through the list one by one, continuing to collect notes in the strategy document. When you're done, synthesize those into a concise, readable summary of what you've learned. For example, the monolith decomposition strategy synthesizes the exploration of a broad topic into four paragraphs, with links to references.
5. Once you generally understand how a handful of similar internal and external teams have recently approached this problem, stop.

Of all the steps in strategy creation, exploration is the most inherently open-ended, and you may find that a different approach works better for you. If so, go ahead and try that instead—as long as it's not skipping exploration! If you're not sure what to do, though, try following the preceding steps closely.

Note

You can also use techniques like Wardley mapping (*https://oreil.ly/LbaqL*), covered in Chapter 8, to support your exploration phase. Wardley mapping is a tool designed within a different strategy tradition, and categorizing it as solely either an exploration tool or a refinement tool ignores some of its potential uses.

There's no perfect way to do strategy: take what works for you and use it.

MINE YOUR ORGANIZATION FOR INTERNAL PRECEDENT

One of the most powerful forms of strategy is simply documenting how similar decisions have been made internally: it's often enough to steer how your organization makes similar decisions in the future. This approach, documented in *Staff Engineer*'s "Write five, then synthesize" (*https://oreil.ly/aMso-*), is also the most valuable step of exploration for those working in established companies.

If you are a tenured engineer, then it's somewhat safe to assume that you are aware of your organization's typical internal approaches. Even so, it's worth poking around to see if there are any related experiments happening internally. This is doubly true if you've joined the organization recently or if your work is distant from the codebase itself.

Sometimes the internal approach isn't ideal, but it's still superior because it's already been implemented and there's someone else maintaining it. In the long run, your strategy can ride along as someone else addresses the issues that aren't a perfect fit.

USING YOUR NETWORK

There are some topics you can't learn much about without talking directly to practitioners—especially security, compliance, operating at truly large scales, and competitive processes like optimizing advertising spend. Further, people often publicly describe solving a problem very differently from how they actually approach the problem.

This is why having a broad personal network is exceptionally powerful, and makes it possible to quickly understand the breadth of possible solutions. It also provides you with access to the practical downsides to various approaches, which people often omit when speaking publicly.

In a recent strategy session, a proposal came up that seemed off to me. I was able to text industry peers and get answers to those texts before the meeting ended—answers that invalidated the room's assumptions about what was and was not possible. A disagreement that might have taken weeks to resolve was resolved in a few minutes, and we were able to figure out next steps then and there.

Of course, it's *also* important to evaluate information from your network with skepticism rather than accepting it without question. I've certainly had my network be wrong, and the people in your network never know how your current circumstances differ from theirs.

If you're looking for more detailed coverage on building your network, this topic also comes up in *Staff Engineer*'s chapter "Build a network of peers" (*https://oreil.ly/VwIeD*), and *The Engineering Executive's Primer*'s chapter "Building your executive network" (*https://lethain.com/building-exec-network*). It feels silly to cover the same topic a third time, but networking is a foundational technique for effective decision making.

READ WIDELY; READ NARROWLY

Reading has always been an important part of my strategy work. There are two distinct motions within this approach: read widely on an ongoing basis to broaden your thinking, and read narrowly on the specific topic you're working on.

Starting with reading widely, I make an effort each year to read 10 to 20 industry-relevant works. These are not necessarily new releases, but they're new *to me*. Importantly, I try to read on topics that I don't know much about or arguments that I initially disagree with. Some of my recent reads include Chris Miller's *Chip War* (Scribner, 2022); Curry, Hsu, and Bergman's *Building Green Software* (O'Reilly, 2024); Kent Beck's *Tidy First?* (O'Reilly, 2023); and Flyvbjerg and Gardner's *How Big Things Get Done* (Crown Currency, 2023). From each of these books, I learned something or stored away some ideas that might apply to new problems.

On the other end of things is reading narrowly. When I recently started working on a strategy related to AI agents, the first thing I did was read through Chip Huyen's exceptionally helpful survey *AI Engineering* (O'Reilly, 2024). Similarly, when the team at Uber started thinking about Uber's service migration (Document 16-1), they read a number of industry papers, including "Large-scale Cluster Management at Google with Borg" (*https://oreil.ly/95B_Q*) and "Mesos: A Platform for Fine-Grained Resource Sharing in the Data Center" (*https://oreil.ly/6HQID*).

None of these readings had *all* the answers to the problems I was working on, but they did an excellent job at helping me understand the range of options and identify other references to consult in my exploration.

I highly encourage getting comfortable with skimming books. Even tightly edited books will have a lot of content that isn't particularly relevant to your current goals, and you should skip that content liberally. Second, what you read doesn't have to be books. It can also be blog posts, essays, interview transcripts, or even nontext sources like conferences and talks. I got a lot out of Dan Na's excellent talk "Pushing Through Friction" (*https://oreil.ly/65U9x*).

EACH JOB IS AN EDUCATION

Experience—spending time working on the details of meaningful problems—is the most effective, and the slowest, mechanism for exploring. You probably shouldn't pick every job to prioritize learning (*https://lethain.com/forty-year-career*), when there are so many other things to optimize for, like financial stability, but doing so occasionally allows you to explore complex problems over time—recognizing that some of your prior knowledge will have gone stale along the way—which is uniquely valuable.

SAVE JUDGMENT FOR LATER

The point of exploration is to go broad with the goal of understanding approaches you might not have considered and invalidating things you initially think are true. Both of those things are only possible if you save judgment for later. If you're passing judgment about whether approaches are "good" or "bad," then your exploration is probably going astray.

As a soft rule, if no one involved in a strategy has changed their mind about something they believed when you started the exploration step, then you're not done exploring. This is *especially* true when it comes to strategy work by senior leaders. Their beliefs are often well-justified by years of experience, but even they begin each exploration unclear whether their prior experiences have gone stale over time.

Summary

At this point, I hope you feel comfortable exploring as the first step of your strategy work, and that you understand the likely consequences of skipping this step. It's not an overstatement to say that every one of the worst strategic failures I've encountered would have been prevented if its primary author had taken a few days to explore the space before anchoring on a particular approach. A few days of feeling slow are always worth avoiding years of misguided efforts.

7

Diagnosis

Once you've written your strategy's exploration, the next step is working on its diagnosis. Diagnosis is about understanding the constraints and challenges your strategy needs to address. In particular, it's about slowing yourself down from jumping to solutions before fully understanding the nuances and constraints of the problem.

You may find yourself wanting to skip the diagnosis phase—let's get to the solution already! So it's worth acknowledging that every strategy that I've seen fail did so due to a lazy or inaccurate diagnosis. It's very challenging to fail once you have a proper diagnosis, and it's almost impossible to succeed without one.

This chapter will cover:

- Why diagnosis forms the foundation of an effective strategy and effective policies depend upon it
- Why skipping the diagnosis phase consistently ruins strategies
- How to diagnose your strategy's circumstances, step by step
- How to incorporate data into your diagnosis effectively
- Where to focus on adding data
- How to deal with controversial elements of your diagnosis, such as pointing out that your own executive is one of the challenges
- Why it's more effective to view difficulties as part of the problem to be solved than as obstacles blocking forward progress
- Why humility and self-awareness are crucial to making an effective diagnosis

Into the details we go!

Diagnosis Is Strategy's Foundation

One of the challenges in evaluating strategy is that, after the fact, many effective strategies are so obvious that they're boring. Similarly, most ineffective strategies are so clearly flawed that their authors look lazy. That's because, as you operate a strategy, the reality around it becomes clear. When you're writing your strategy, you don't know if you can convince your colleagues to adopt a new approach to specifying APIs; a year later, though, you know very definitively whether it's possible.

Diagnosis is your attempt to correctly recognize the problem that the strategy needs to solve before deciding on the policies to address that problem. Done well, the subsequent steps of writing strategy often feel like an afterthought, which is why I think of diagnosis as strategy's foundation.

Where exploration was an evaluation-free activity, diagnosis is all about evaluation. How do teams feel today? Why did that project fail? Why did the last strategy go poorly? What distractions must you overcome to make this new strategy successful?

That said, not all evaluation is equal. If you state your judgment directly, it's easy to dispute. An effective diagnosis is hard to argue against because it's a web of interconnected observations, facts, and data. Even those who dislike your conclusions will find the weight of evidence hard to shift.

> **Note**
>
> Strategy testing, explored in Chapter 8, takes advantage of the reality that it's easier to diagnose by doing than by speculating. It proposes using a recursive diagnosis process until you have real-world evidence that the strategy is working.

How to Develop Your Diagnosis

Your strategy is almost certain to fail unless you start from an effective diagnosis, but how to build that diagnosis is often left unspecified. That's because, for most people, diagnosis is a dark art: unspecified, undiscussed, and uncontrollable. I've been guilty of this as well; *The Engineering Executive's Primer*'s chapter on strategy (*https://lethain.com/eng-strategies*) is notably silent on how to perform diagnosis.

So, yes, there is some truth to the idea that diagnosis is an emergent, organic process rather than a structured, mechanical one. However, over time I've come to adopt a fairly structured approach:

Step 1: Braindump

Starting from a blank sheet of paper, write down your best understanding of the circumstances that inform your current strategy. Then set that piece of paper aside for the moment.

Step 2: Summarize exploration

On a new piece of paper, review the contents of your exploration. Pull in every piece of diagnosis from similar situations, internal or external, that resonates with you. For each diagnosis, tag whether it fits your current circumstances perfectly or needs to be adjusted. Then, once again, set the piece of paper aside.

Step 3: Mine for distinct perspectives

Devote yet another blank page to talking to different stakeholders and colleagues who you know are likely to disagree with your early thinking. Your goal is not to agree with this feedback; it's to understand their views. *The Crux* by Richard Rumelt (PublicAffairs, 2022) anchors diagnosis in this approach, emphasizing the importance of "testing, adjusting, and changing the frame, or point of view."

Step 4: Synthesize views into one internally consistent perspective

Sometimes the different perspectives you've gathered don't mesh well. People might explicitly differ in what they believe the underlying problem is, as is typical of the common tension between platform and product engineering teams. The goal is to represent each of these perspectives competently in the diagnosis, even the ones you disagree with, so that later on you can evaluate your proposed approach against each of them.

When synthesizing feedback goes poorly, it tends to fail in one of two ways. The first is that the author's opinion shines through so strongly that it renders the diagnosis suspect. Your goal isn't to agree with every perspective, nor should your diagnosis crown one viewpoint as correct: readers should see detailed perspectives without clearly sensing the author's biases.

The second common issue is when a group tries to own the synthesis jointly, but creates fractured perspectives rather than a unified one. I generally find that holding one author accountable for representing all views works best to address both of these issues.

Step 5: Test drafts across perspectives

Once you've written your initial diagnosis, sit down with the people you expect to disagree most fervently. Iterate with them until they agree that you've accurately captured their perspectives.

Even if they disagree with some viewpoints, they should be able to agree that others hold those views. If they argue that the data you've included doesn't capture their full reality, you have to pick between collecting more data to address their concern, or documenting their disagreement that the data presented is comprehensive. Collecting more data to address concerns is the preferred option, but you have to be careful not to allow requests for data to prevent forward progress indefinitely: fulfill one or two requests per stakeholder, but hold the line at delaying further.

Don't worry about getting the details perfectly right in your initial diagnosis. You're trying to get the right crumbs to feed into the next phase, strategy refinement. Allowing yourself to be directionally correct rather than perfectly correct makes it possible to cover a lot of territory quickly. Getting caught up in perfecting the details is an easy way to anchor yourself in one perspective prematurely.

At this point, I hope you're starting to predict how I'll conclude any recipe for strategy creation: if these steps feel overly mechanical to you, adjust them to something that feels more natural and authentic. There's no perfect way to understand complex problems. That said, if you feel uncertain or are skeptical of your own track record, I encourage you to start with the preceding approach.

Incorporating Data into Your Diagnosis

The diagnosis behind Stripe's creation of Sorbet (discussed in Document 22-3) includes data to help readers understand the author's reasoning, such as staffing numbers for relevant teams and the extent of test coverage in the Ruby codebase.

If everyone has the same data and the same assumptions about how that data is likely to change going forward, then evaluating the strategy becomes vastly simpler. Data is also your mechanism for supporting or critiquing the various views that you've gathered when drafting your diagnosis; to an impartial reader, data will speak louder than passion. If you're confident that a perspective is true, then include a data narrative that supports it. If you believe another perspective is overstated, then include any data that the reader will require to come to the same conclusion.

Do your best to include data analysis, with a link out to the full data, rather than requiring readers to interpret the data themselves while reading. As your strategy document travels further, there will be inevitable requests for different cuts of data to help readers understand your thinking, and you can prevent this somewhat by linking to your original sources.

In strategy work, it's common to find that much of the data you want doesn't currently exist. After all, if you already had the data to make the decision easy, you probably would have already made a decision rather than needing to run a structured thinking process. (The next chapter, on refining strategy, covers tools for building confidence in low-data environments.)

Whisper the Controversial Parts

I once worked for a company that rolled out a "bar-raiser" program, styled after Amazon's, that aimed to improve the quality of new hires by requiring an interviewer from outside the team to approve every hire. I spent some time arguing against adding this additional step: I didn't understand the problem we were solving for, and management seemed surprisingly uninterested in learning if the new process actually improved hiring outcomes.

What I didn't realize until much later was that most of the senior leadership distrusted one of their peers and felt that the CTO wasn't holding that leader accountable. They had rolled out the bar-raiser program solely to create a mechanism to control that manager's hiring decisions. (I also learned that these leaders didn't care much about implementing this policy, resulting in hiring managers frequently ignoring the bar-raisers' rejections, but that's a discussion for Chapter 10.)

This is a good example of a strategy that makes sense when you have the full diagnosis but makes little sense without it. It's also a case where stating part of the diagnosis out loud is nearly impossible: even senior leaders are not generally allowed to write a document that says, "The Director of Product Engineering is a bad hiring manager."

When you're writing a strategy, you'll often find yourself trying to choose between two awkward options: say something awkward or uncomfortable about your company or someone working within it, or omit a critical piece of your diagnosis that's necessary to understanding your wider thinking. Whenever you encounter this sort of dilemma, my advice is to find a way to include the full diagnosis, but to reframe the difficult part into a palatable statement that avoids casting blame too narrowly.

I think it's helpful to discuss a few concrete examples of this. The strategy for navigating private equity, discussed in Chapter 18, has a diagnosis that includes:

> *Based on general practice, it seems likely that our new Private Equity ownership will expect us to reduce R&D headcount costs through a reduction. However, without concrete details, we cannot yet make structured decisions. Our strategy will depend significantly on the scale of any proposed reductions.*

The authors of this strategy are probably upset about the likely possibility that their new private equity ownership will eliminate colleagues. They may also be upset that, with no clear plan for what they need to do, they are stuck preparing for a wide range of potential outcomes. However they feel, though, their diagnosis sticks to precise, factual statements.

For a second example, we can look to the Uber service migration strategy (Document 16-1):

> *Within infrastructure engineering, there is a team of four engineers responsible for service provisioning today. While our organization is growing at a similar rate as product engineering, none of that additional headcount is being allocated directly to the team working on service provisioning. We do not anticipate this changing.*

The team didn't *agree* that their headcount should not be growing, but it was the reality they were operating in. They acknowledged that reality with a factual statement, without any additional commentary.

In both of these examples, the authors found professional, nonjudgmental ways to acknowledge the circumstances that had created the problems they were solving. The authors would have preferred that the leaders behind those decisions take explicit accountability for them, but attempting to make that happen within their strategy writeup would have undermined the strategy work.

Excluding critical parts of your diagnosis makes your strategies particularly hard to evaluate, copy, or recreate. To make the strategy effective, find a way to say things politely. Strategies are always more about realities than ideals.

Reframe Blockers as Part of Your Diagnosis

When I work with early-career leaders, they often argue that a certain problem they've identified makes strategy work impossible. For example, they might argue that they can't do strategy work at their current company because the members of the executive team change their minds too often.

That core insight is almost certainly true, but it's much more powerful to reframe it as a diagnosis: "If we don't find a way to show concrete progress quickly and use that to excite the executive team, our strategy is likely to fail." This transforms the thing preventing your strategy into a condition your strategy needs to address.

Whenever you run into a reason why your strategy, or strategy overall, seems difficult or unlikely to work, you've found an important piece to include in your diagnosis. There are never reasons why strategy simply cannot succeed—only diagnoses you've failed to recognize.

For example, in the strategy for resourcing Engineering-driven projects discussed in Document 21-2, we knew that Calm's informal approach to prioritization wasn't going to change. Even if we convinced our peers in product management to change how *they* planned, the executive team's informal planning wasn't going to change. Rather than *preventing* us from implementing a strategy, those dynamics clarified what sort of approach could actually *succeed*.

The Role of Self-Awareness

Every problem of today is partially rooted in the decisions of yesterday. If you've been with your organization for any duration at all, this means that *you* are, directly or indirectly, responsible for a portion of the problems that your diagnosis ought to recognize.

Recognizing the impact of your prior actions in your diagnosis is a powerful way to demonstrate self-awareness. It also suggests that your next strategy's success will be rooted in your self-awareness about your prior choices. Don't be afraid to recognize the failures in your past work. While changing your mind *without* new data is a sign of chaotic leadership, changing your mind *with* new data is a sign of thoughtful leadership.

Summary

Because diagnosis is the foundation of effective strategy, I've always found it the most intimidating phase of strategy work. While I think that's a somewhat unavoidable reality, my hope is that this chapter has somewhat prepared you for that challenge.

The four most important things to remember are:

- Form your diagnosis before deciding how to solve it.
- Try especially hard to capture perspectives you initially disagree with.
- Supplement intuition with data where you can.
- Accept that sometimes the data you need will be missing.

The last piece, in particular, is why many good strategies never get shared. It's also the topic of the next chapter.

Refining

In the book *Great by Choice* (Random House Business, 2011), Jim Collins and Morten T. Hansen develop a concept they call "Fire Bullets, Then Cannonballs" (*https://oreil.ly/hUYUF*). Their premise is that you should test new ideas cheaply before fully committing to them. Your organization can only afford to fire a small number of cannonballs, but it can bankroll far more bullets. Why not use bullets to derisk your cannonballs' trajectories?

This chapter introduces the practice of strategy refinement and presents a series of concrete techniques that I have personally used to refine strategies before they reach the cannonball stage. We'll work through:

- Why strategy refinement is the highest-impact step of strategy creation
- How mixed incentives often lead people to skip the refinement stage, even though doing so leads to worse organizational outcomes
- How to build your personal strategy-refinement toolkit for refining strategy with techniques like strategy testing, systems modeling, and Wardley mapping
- How to avoid antipatterns that skip refinement or that manufacture consent to create the illusion of refinement without providing its benefits

Each of these refinement techniques is also covered in greater detail in its own chapter of this book.

What Is Strategy Refinement?

Most strategies succeed because they properly address narrow problems within a broader strategy. While fully implementing a strategy to validate it is possible, this approach is typically inefficient and slow. Worse, it's easy to get so distracted by miscellaneous details that you lose sight of the levers that will make your strategy impactful.

Strategy refinement is a toolkit of methods to identify those narrow problems that matter most, and validate that your solutions to those problems will be effective. The right tool within the toolkit will vary depending on the strategy you're working on. It might be using Wardley mapping to understand how the ecosystem's evolution will impact your approach. Or it might be systems modeling to determine which part of a migration is the most valuable lever. In other cases, it's slowing down committing to your strategy until you've done a narrow test drive to derisk the pieces you don't quite have conviction in yet.

Whatever tools you've relied on to refine strategy thus far in your work, there are always new refinement tools to pick up. This book presents a workable introduction to several tools that I find reliably useful, while providing a broader foundation for deploying other techniques that you develop toward strategy refinement.

DOES REFINEMENT MATTER?

At Stripe, the head of engineering rolled out Agile techniques in one meeting. This change was aimed at our difficulties with planning in periods longer than a month, which was becoming an increasing challenge as we started working with enterprise businesses who wanted us to commit to specific functionality as part of signing their contracts. On the other hand, the approach worked poorly, because it assumed that the issue was engineering managers being generally unfamiliar with Agile techniques. The challenge of adoption wasn't awareness, but rather the difficulty of prioritizing tasks from numerous stakeholders in an environment where saying no was frowned upon.

In this Agile rollout, the lack of a shared planning paradigm was a real, apt problem. However, the solution solved the easiest part of the problem, without addressing the messier parts, and consequently failed to make meaningful progress. This happens a surprising amount, and can be largely avoided with a small dose of refinement.

On the opposite end, we created Uber's service adoption strategy (Chapter 16) exclusively through refinement, because the infrastructure engineering team didn't have any authority to mandate wider changes. Instead, we relied on two different kinds of refinement to focus our iterative efforts. First, we used systems modeling to understand what parts of adoption we needed to focus on. Second, we used strategy testing to learn by migrating individual product engineering teams over to the new platform.

In the Agile adoption example, failure to refine turned a moderately challenging problem into a strategy failure. In the service migration example, focus on refinement translated an extremely difficult problem into a success. Refinement is, in my experience, the kernel of effective strategy.

IF IT MATTERS, WHY IS IT SKIPPED?

When a small team creates a strategy—called a *low-altitude strategy*—they almost always spend a great deal of time refining it. This isn't because most teams believe in refinement. Rather it's because most teams lack the authority to force others to align with their strategy. This lack of authority means they must incrementally prove out their approach until other teams or executives believe it's worth aligning with.

High-altitude strategy is typically the domain of executives, who generally have the ability to mandate adoption. They routinely skip the refinement stage, even when it's inexpensive and is almost guaranteed to make them more successful. Why is that? When executives start a new role (*https://lethain.com/first-ninety-days-cto-vpe*), they know making an early impression matters. They also, unfortunately, know that sounding ambitious often resonates more loudly than doing good work. So, while they do hope to eventually be effective, early on they kick off a few aspirational initiatives like a massive overhaul of the codebase (*https://lethain.com/grand-migration*), believing it'll establish their reputation as an effective leader at the company.

This isn't uniquely an executive failure; it also happens frequently in permissive strategy organizations that require an ambitious, high-leverage project to get promoted into senior engineering roles (*https://oreil.ly/esVRq*). For example, you might see a novel approach to networking or authorization implemented, whose adoption fails after solving some easier proof points, and trace its heritage back to the company's promotion criteria. In many cases, the promotion will come before the rollout stalls out, disincentivizing the would-be-promoted engineer from worrying too deeply about whether this was net-positive for the organization. The executive responsible for the promotion rubric will eventually recognize the flaw, but it's not the easiest tradeoff for them to pick between an organization that innovates too much while empowering individuals or an organization with little waste but restricted room for creativity.

Another reason refinement can get skipped is that sometimes you're forced to urgently create and commit to a strategy, usually because your boss tells you to. This doesn't actually prevent refinement—just say you're committed and refine anyway—but often this interaction turns off the strategist's mind, tricking them into thinking they can't change their approach because they've already committed to it. This is never true; all decisions are up for review with proper evidence, but it takes a certain courage to refine when those around you are asking for weekly updates on completing the project.

There's one other important reason that strategy refinement gets skipped: many people haven't built out a toolkit to perform strategy refinement, and they haven't worked with someone who has a toolkit.

Building Your Toolkit

I'm eternally grateful to my father, a professor of economics, who brought me to a systems modeling workshop in Boston one summer when I was in high school. This opened my eyes to the wide world of techniques for reasoning about problems, and systems modeling became the first tool in my toolkit for strategy refinement.

Part III of this book, on refinement, will go into three refinement techniques in significant detail: strategy testing, systems modeling, and Wardley mapping, as well as surveying a handful of other techniques more common to strategy consultants. I adopted systems modeling early, whereas Wardley mapping I only learned while working on this book. Few individuals are proficient users of many refinement tools, but it's extraordinarily powerful to unlock your first tool, and worthwhile to slowly expand your experience with other tools over time. All tools are flawed, and each is best at illuminating certain types of problems.

If all of these are unfamiliar, then skim over all of them and pick one that seems most applicable to a current problem you're working on. You'll build expertise by trying a tool against many different problems, and talking through the results with engaged peers.

As you practice, remember that the important thing to share is what you learn from these techniques, and try to avoid getting too caught up in sharing the techniques themselves. I've seen these techniques meaningfully change strategies, but I've never seen those changes successfully justified through the inherent insight of the refinement techniques themselves.

STRATEGY TESTING

Sometimes you'll need a strategy to solve an ambiguous problem, or a problem where a diagnosis is difficult because the issues blocking progress are poorly understood. At Carta, one strategy problem we worked on was improving code quality, which is a good example of both of those. It's difficult to agree on what code quality is, and it's equally difficult to agree on appropriate, concrete steps to improve it.

To navigate that ambiguity, we spent relatively little time thinking about the right initial solution, and a great deal of our time deploying the strategy-testing technique discussed in Chapter 13:

1. Identify the narrowest, deepest available slice of your strategy. Iterate on applying that slice until you see some evidence it's working.
2. As you iterate, identify metrics that help you verify the approach is working.
3. Operate from the belief that people are well-meaning, and strategy failures are due to excess friction and poor ergonomics.
4. Keep refining until you have conviction that your strategy's details work in practice, or that the strategy needs to be approached from a new direction.

In this case, we achieved some small wins, funded a handful of specific bets that we believed would improve the problem long-term, and ended the initiative early without making a large organizational commitment. You could argue that's a failure, but my experience is quite different: having a problem doesn't mean you have an elegant solution, and strategy testing helps you validate if the solution's efficiency and ergonomics are viable.

If you're dealing with a deeply ambiguous problem and there's no agreement on the nature of the reality you're operating in, strategy testing is a great technique to start with.

SYSTEMS MODELING

When you're unsure where leverage points might be in a complex system, systems modeling (Chapter 14) is an effective technique to cheaply determine which levers might be effective (Figure 8-1). For example, the systems model for onboarding drivers in a ride-share app (Document 16-2) shows that in a mature market, reengaging drivers who've left the platform matters more than bringing on new drivers.

Similarly, in the Uber service migration example (Document 16-1), systems modeling helped us focus on eliminating upfront steps during service onboarding, shifting to reasonable defaults and away from forcing teams to learn the new service platform before it had shown any usefulness to them.

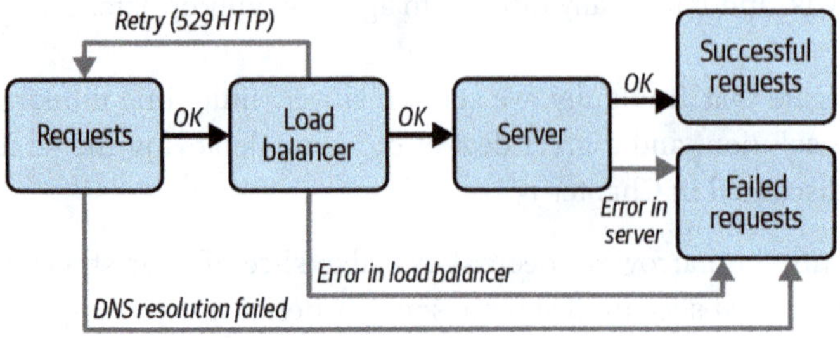

Figure 8-1. Systems model of errors in a load balancer

While you can certainly reach these insights without modeling, modeling tends to make the insights immediately visible. In cases where your model doesn't immediately illuminate what matters most, studying how your model's projections conflict with real-world data will guide you to understand where your assumptions are contorting your understanding of the problem.

If you generally understand a problem, but need to determine where to focus efforts to make the largest impact, then systems modeling is a valuable technique to deploy.

WARDLEY MAPPING

Many engineering strategies implicitly make the assumption that the ecosystem we're operating within is static. However, that's certainly false. Many experienced engineers and engineering leaders have great judgment, and great intuition, but nonetheless deploy a flawed strategy because they've anchored on their memory of how things work rather than noticing how things have changed over time.

If, rather than being hit over the head by them, you want to incorporate these changes into your strategy, Wardley mapping is a great tool to add to your kit.

Wardley maps allow you to plot users and their needs, and then study how the solutions to those needs will shift over time. For example, today there is a proliferation of narrow platforms built on recent advances in LLMs, but studying a Wardley map of the LLM ecosystem (Figure 8-2) suggests that it's likely that this ecosystem will consolidate to fewer, broader platforms rather than remaining so widely scattered across distinct vendors.

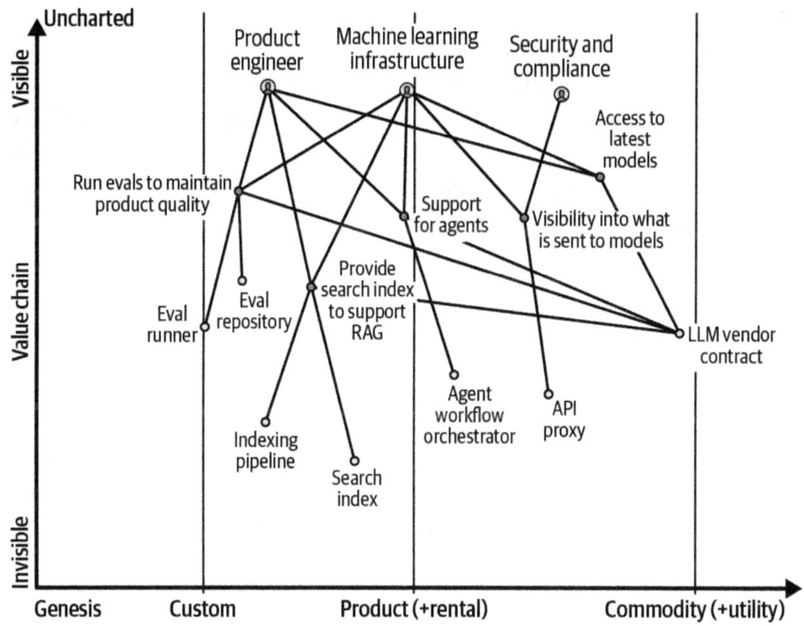

Figure 8-2. Wardley map of large language model ecosystem

If your strategy involves adopting a highly dynamic technology, such as observability in the 2010s, or if your strategy is intended to span five-plus years, then Wardley mapping will help surface how industry evolution will impact your approach.

Antipatterns in Refinement

We've already discussed why refinement is often skipped, which is the most frequent and most damning refinement antipattern. At Calm, we decomposed our monolithic codebase because that was what we saw similar companies doing around us; we had no reason to believe this was improving developer productivity, but we continued to pursue this strategy for a year before recognizing that we were suffering from skipping refinement.

The second most common antipattern is creating the impression of strategy refinement through manufactured consent. A new senior leader joined Uber and mandated a complete technical rearchitecture, justifying this in part through the evidence that a number of internal leaders had successfully adopted the same techniques on their teams. When I spoke with those internal leaders, they themselves were skeptical that the proposal made sense, despite the fact that their surface-level agreement was being used to convince the wider organization that they believed in the new approach.

Finally, refinement often occurs, but counterevidence is then discarded because the refining team is optimizing for a side goal of some sort. My first team at Yahoo! adopted Erlang for a key component of Yahoo! Build Your Own Search Service (*https://lethain.com/datahub*), which proved to be an excellent solution to our problem of wanting to use Erlang, but a questionable solution to the core problem at hand. Only three of the engineers on our 15-person team were willing to touch the Erlang codebase, but that counterevidence was ignored because it conflicted with the side goal.

Summary

This chapter has introduced the concept of strategy refinement, surveyed three common refinement techniques—strategy testing, systems modeling, and Wardley mapping—and provided a framework for building your personal toolkit for refinement.

9

Setting Policy

Chapter 1 started by defining strategy as "making decisions." Then we dug into exploration, diagnosis, and refinement. Those are three chapters where you could argue that we didn't decide anything at all. Clarifying the problem to be solved is a prerequisite for effective decision making, but eventually decisions do have to be made. Here, in this chapter on policy and the following chapter on operations, we finally start making some decisions.

In this chapter, we'll dig into:

- How we define policy, and how *setting* policy differs from *operating* policy (as discussed in the next chapter)
- The structured steps for setting policy
- How many policies should you set? Is it preferable to have one policy or many, or does it not matter much either way?
- Recurring kinds of policies that appear frequently in strategies
- Why it's valuable to be intentional about your strategy's altitude, and how engineers and executives generally maintain different altitudes in their strategies
- Criteria for evaluating whether your policies are likely to be impactful
- How to develop novel policies, and why it's rare
- Why having multiple bundles of alternative policies generally indicates a gap in your diagnosis
- How policies that ignore constraints sound inspirational, but accomplish little
- Making progress on your strategy even when your cross-functional stakeholders have an unclear strategy

By the end, you'll be ready to evaluate why an existing strategy's policies aren't making an impact, and to start iterating on policies for a strategy of your own.

What Is Policy?

Policy is interpreting your diagnosis into a concrete plan. That plan will be a collection of decisions, tradeoffs, and approaches that could include coding practices, hiring mandates, architectural decisions, and guidance about how choices are made within your organization.

An effective policy solves the entirety of the strategy's diagnosis, although the diagnosis itself should specify which aspects can be ignored. For example, Document 18-1's strategy for working with private equity ownership acknowledges in its diagnosis that the authors don't have clear guidance on what kind of reduction to expect:

> *Based on general practice, it seems likely that our new Private Equity ownership will expect us to reduce R&D headcount costs through a reduction. However, without concrete details, we cannot yet make structured decisions. Our strategy will depend significantly on the scale of any proposed reductions.*

Faced with that uncertainty, the policy simply acknowledges the ambiguity and commits to reconsidering when more information becomes available:

> *We believe our new ownership will provide a specific target for Research and Development (R&D) operating expenses during the upcoming financial year planning. We will revise these policies again once we have explicit targets, and will delay planning around reductions until we have those numbers to avoid running two overlapping processes.*

There are two frequent points of confusion when creating policies that are worth addressing directly. The first thing to understand is that policy is a *subset* of strategy, rather than the *entirety* of strategy, because policy is only meaningful in the context of the strategy's diagnosis. For example, the "N-1 backfill policy" makes sense in the context of new private equity ownership. The policy wouldn't work well in a rapidly expanding organization. It's true that any strategy without a policy is useless, but you'll find that policies without context aren't worth much either. This is unfortunate, because so often strategies are communicated without those critical sections.

Second, policy describes how tradeoffs should be made, but it doesn't verify *how* the tradeoffs are actually made in practice. Chapter 10, on operations, covers how to inspect an organization's behavior to ensure policies are followed.

When you're reworking a strategy to be more readable (see Chapter 11), it often makes sense to merge the policy and operation sections together. However, when drafting strategy, it's valuable to keep them separate. Yes, you *might* use a weekly meeting to review whether the policy is being followed, but whether it's an effective policy is independent of having such a meeting, and the operational mechanisms you use will vary depending on the number of policies you intend to implement.

With this definition in mind, now we can move on to the more interesting discussion of how to set policy.

How to Set Policy

Every part of writing a strategy feels hard when you're doing it, but I personally find that writing policy either feels uncomfortably easy or painfully challenging. It's never a happy medium. Fortunately, the exploration and diagnosis usually come together to make writing your policy simple—even if that simple conclusion is sometimes difficult to swallow.

The six steps I follow to write a strategy's policy are:

Step 1: Review diagnosis
: Review your diagnosis to ensure it captures the most important themes. It doesn't need to be perfect, but it shouldn't have any glaring omissions.

Step 2: Select policies that address the diagnosis
: Explicitly match each policy to one or more diagnoses that it addresses. Continue adding policies until every diagnosis is covered. This is a broad instruction, but it's simpler than it sounds, because you'll typically select from policies you identified during your exploration phase. However, there certainly is space to tweak those policies, and to reapply familiar policies to new circumstances.

Step 3: Consolidate policies
: Consolidate overlapping or adjoining policies. For example, two policies about specific teams might be generalized into a policy about all teams in the engineering organization.

Step 4: Backtest
: Backtest the new policy against recent decisions you've made. This is particularly effective if you maintain a decision log (*https://oreil.ly/YTdl3*) in your organization.

Step 5: Mine for conflict
: Mine for conflict once again, much as you did in developing your diagnosis. Emphasize feedback from teams and individuals with different perspectives than your own, but don't wholly eliminate those you agree with. Just as it's easy to crowd out opposing views during diagnosis if you don't solicit their input, it's possible to accidentally crowd out your own perspective if you anchor too much on others' perspectives.

Step 6: Refine
: If you finish writing, and you just aren't sure your approach works, refine it! Deploy one of the refinement techniques you learned about in Chapter 8 to increase your conviction. Remember that, while people *talk* about strategy like it's all done in one pass, almost all real strategy takes many refinement passes.

The steps of writing policy are relatively pedestrian, largely because you've done so much of the work already in the exploration, diagnosis, and refinement steps. If you skipped those phases, you might still follow the preceding steps for writing policy, but its quality would be far lower.

How Many Policies?

Addressing the entirety of the diagnosis is often complex, which is why most strategies feature a set of policies rather than just one. For example, the strategy for decomposing a monolithic application (see Document 20-1) is not one policy deciding not to decompose, but a series of four policies:

1. Business units should always operate in their own code repository and monolith.
2. New integrations across business unit monoliths should be done using gRPC.
3. Except for new business unit monoliths, we don't allow new services.
4. Merge existing services into business unit monoliths where you can.

Four isn't universally the right number either—it's simply the number that was required to solve *that* strategy's diagnosis. With an excellent diagnosis, your policies will often feel inevitable, perhaps even boring. That's a great thing. What makes a policy good is that it's *effective*, not that it's novel or inspiring.

Kinds of Policies

While there are *so many* policies you can write, I've found they generally fall into one of four major categories: approvals, allocations, direction, and guidance. This section introduces those categories.

APPROVALS

Approvals define the process for making a recurring decision. This might require invoking an architecture advice process or involving an authority figure, like an executive.

In the Index post-acquisition integration strategy (Document 22-4), there were a number of complex decisions to be made, and the approval mechanism was:

> *Escalations come to paired leads: Given our limited shared context across teams, all escalations must come to both Stripe's Head of Traffic Engineering and Index's Head of Engineering.*

Consulting both the acquired and acquiring teams before any decision was finalized allowed them to start building mutual trust. On the other hand, the user data access strategy's approval mechanism (Document 19-1) was more focused on managing corporate risk:

> Exceptions must be granted in writing by the CISO. *While our overarching Engineering Strategy states that we follow an advisory architecture process as described in* Facilitating Software Architecture, *the customer data access policy is an exception and must be explicitly approved, with documentation, by the CISO. Start that process in the* `#ciso` *channel.*

These two different approval processes had different goals, so they made different tradeoffs between safety, productivity, and trust.

ALLOCATIONS

Allocations describe how resources are split across multiple potential investments. Allocations are the most concrete statement of organizational priority, and articulate the organization's beliefs about how productivity happens in teams. Some companies believe you go fast by swarming more people onto critical problems; others go fast by forcing teams to solve problems without additional headcount. Both methods can work, and both teach you something important about the company's beliefs.

The strategy for Uber's service migration, discussed in Document 16-1, has two concrete examples of allocation policies. The first describes the infrastructure engineering team's allocation between manually provisioning tasks and investing in creating a self-service provisioning platform:

> *Constrain manual provisioning allocation to maximize investment in self-service provisioning. The service provisioning team will maintain a fixed allocation of one full-time engineer on manual service-provisioning tasks. We will move the remaining engineers to work on automation to speed up future service provisioning. This will degrade manual provisioning in the short term, but the alternative is permanently degrading provisioning by the influx of new service requests from newly hired product engineers.*

The second allocation policy is implicitly noted in this strategy's diagnosis, where it describes the allocation policy in the Engineering organization's higher-altitude strategy:

> *Within infrastructure engineering, there is a team of four engineers responsible for service provisioning today. While our organization is growing at a similar rate as product engineering, none of that additional headcount is being allocated directly to the team working on service provisioning. We do not anticipate this changing.*

Allocation policies often create a surprising amount of clarity for the team, and I include them in almost every policy I write—either explicitly or, in a higher-altitude strategy, implicitly.

DIRECTION

Direction provides explicit instruction on how a decision *must* be made. This is the right tool when you know where you want to go and the exact route you want to take there. Direction is appropriate for problems you understand clearly, especially when you value consistency more than empowering individual judgment.

Direction works well when you need an unambiguous policy that doesn't leave room for interpretation. For example, Calm's policy for working in the monolith (Document 21-1) includes the following:

> *We write all code in the monolith. It has been ambiguous if new code (especially new application code) should be written in our JavaScript monolith, or if all new code* must *be written in a new service outside of the monolith. This is no longer ambiguous: all new code must be written in the monolith.*
>
> *In the rare case that there is a functional requirement that makes writing in the monolith implausible, then you should request an exception as described below.*

In that case, the team couldn't agree on what should go into the monolith. Individuals would often make incompatible decisions, so creating consistency required removing personal judgment from the equation.

Sometimes judgment is the issue, and sometimes consistency is difficult due to misaligned incentives. A good example of this comes in the private equity strategy (Document 18-1):

> *We will move to an "N-1" backfill policy, where departures are backfilled with a less senior level. We will also institute a strict maximum of one Principal Engineer per business unit.*

It's likely that hiring managers would simply ignore this backfill policy if it was stated more softly, although sometimes less forceful policies are useful.

GUIDANCE

Guidance provides a recommendation about how a decision *should* be made. Guidance is useful when there's enough nuance, ambiguity (*https://lethain.com/navigating-ambiguity*), or complexity that you *can* explain the desired destination, but you *can't* mandate the path to reaching it.

One example of guidance comes from the Index acquisition integration strategy (Document 22-4):

> *Minimize changes to tokenization environment: Because point-of-sale devices directly work with customer payment details, the API that directly supports the point-of-sale device must live within our secured environment where payment details are stored.*
>
> *However, any other functionality* must not *be added to our tokenization environment.*

This might read like direction, but it's clarifying the *desired outcome* of avoiding unnecessary complexity in the tokenization environment. However, because it can't articulate what complexity is necessary, it requires significant judgment to interpret—making it guidance rather than direction.

A second example of guidance comes from the strategy on decomposing a monolithic codebase (Document 20-1):

> *Merge existing services into business unit monoliths where you can. We believe that each choice to move existing services back into a monolith should be made "in the details" rather than from a top-down strategy perspective. Consequently, we generally encourage teams to wind down their existing services outside of their business unit's monolith, but defer to teams to make the right decision for their local context.*

This is another case of knowing the desired outcome, but encountering too much uncertainty to direct the team on how to get there. If you ask five engineers about whether it's possible to merge a given service back into a monolithic codebase, you'll probably get five different answers. That's fine. Guidance makes it possible to make incremental progress in areas where more concrete direction would cause confusion.

When you're working on a strategy's policy section, it's important to consider all of these categories. Which feel most natural to use will vary, depending on your team and role, but they're all usable. For instance:

- If you're a developer productivity team, you might have to lean heavily on guidance in your policies and provide increased support for that guidance within the details of your platform.

- If you're an executive, you might lean heavily on direction. Indeed, executives often lean *too* heavily on direction, even though guidance often works better for areas where you understand the direction but not the path.
- If you're a product engineering organization, you might have to narrow the scope of your direction to the engineers within that organization, to deal with the realities of complex cross-organization dynamics.

Finally, if you have a clear approach you want to take that doesn't fit cleanly into any of these categories, then don't let this framework dissuade you. Give it a try, and adapt if it doesn't initially work out.

Maintaining Strategy Altitude

Chapter 4 introduced the concept of *strategy altitude*, or being deliberate about where certain kinds of policies are created within your organization. Altitude is particularly relevant when considering if or how your new policies eliminate flexibility within your organization. Consider these two somewhat opposing strategies:

- Stripe's Sorbet strategy (Document 22-3) could only have worked in an organization that enforced the use of a single programming language across (essentially) all teams.
- Calm's strategy for resourcing Engineering-driven projects (Document 21-2) acknowledged that resourcing had to be managed by the team directly. Attempting to solve the problem at another level would simply result in someone talking to the team directly to rewrite their priorities to incorporate a new urgent project.

Stripe's organization-altitude policy took away individual teams' freedom to select their preferred technology stacks. In return, it unlocked their ability to centralize investment in a powerful way. Calm went the opposite way, empowering only teams to manage the contents of their roadmap; executives were more senior, but frequently overridden by other executives' out-of-band instructions.

Both altitudes make sense. Both have consequences.

Criteria for Effective Policies

In *The Engineering Executive's Primer*'s chapter on engineering strategy, I introduced three criteria for evaluating policies. First, they ought to be *applicable*, or useful for navigating complex real-world scenarios, particularly when making tradeoffs. Second, policies should be *enforced*, meaning teams are held accountable for following them. Third, policies should *create leverage* with a compounding or multiplicative impact.

The last of these three, creating leverage, made sense in the context of a book about engineering executives, but probably doesn't make as much sense here. Some policies certainly should create leverage (for instance, the policy to avoid deprecating APIs makes other customer retention mechanisms more effective) but others might not (like moving to an N-1 backfill policy). Outside the executive context, what's important isn't necessarily creating leverage, but that a policy solves for part of the diagnosis.

That leaves the other two—being applicable and enforced—both of which are necessary for a policy to actually address the diagnosis. Any policy you can't determine how to apply or aren't willing to enforce simply won't be useful.

Let's apply these criteria to a handful of potential policies. First let's think about policies we might write to improve the talent density of our engineering team:

We only hire world-class engineers.

This isn't applicable, because it's unclear what "world-class engineer" means. Because there's no mutually agreeable definition in this policy, it's also not consistently enforceable.

We only hire engineers who get at least one "strong yes" in scorecards.

This is applicable, because there's a clear definition. It's also enforceable, depending on the organization's willingness to reject otherwise good candidates who don't happen to get a strong yes.

Next, let's think about a policy regarding code reuse within a codebase:

We follow a strict Don't Repeat Yourself policy in our codebase.

There's room for debate within a team about whether two pieces of code are truly duplicative, but this is generally applicable. Because there's room for debate, enforcing it will be a very context-specific determination.

Code authors are responsible for determining if their contributions violate Don't Repeat Yourself, and rewriting them if they do.

This is much more applicable, because now there's only a single person's judgment to assess the potential repetition. In some ways, this policy is also more enforceable, because there's no longer any ambiguity around who decides whether a piece of code is repetitive.

The challenge is that enforceability now depends on one individual, and making this policy effective will require holding individuals accountable for the quality of their judgment. I think adopting a service-oriented architecture was absolutely the best available choice at Uber, but I immediately paused service rollouts at Calm and Carta after joining. One policy, but very different outcomes depending on circumstances. If an organization is unwilling to make that sort of distinction, and hold decision-makers accountable for those making decisions that reflect those distinctions, it won't get any value out of the policy.

If you ever find yourself wanting to include a policy that for some reason can't be applied or enforced, stop. Ask yourself what you're trying to accomplish and if there's a different policy that might be better suited to that goal.

Developing Novel Policies

My experience is that there are vanishingly few truly novel policies to write. Someone else has almost always done something similar to your intended approach already. Calm's engineering strategy (Document 21-1) is such a case: the details are particular to the company, but the general approach is common across the industry.

The most likely place to find truly novel policies is during the widespread-adoption phase of a new technology, such as mobile phones, cloud computing, or LLMs. Even then, as Document 17-1 explores, you can engage with the new technology as a generic technology:

Develop an LLM-backed process for reactivating departed and suspended drivers in mature markets. Through modeling our driver lifecycle, we determined that improving onboarding time will have little impact on the total number of active drivers. Instead, we are focusing on mechanisms to reactivate departed and suspended drivers, which is the only opportunity to meaningfully impact active drivers.

You could simply replace "LLM-backed" with "data-driven" and it would be equally readable. In this way, policy can generally sidestep areas of uncertainty by being a bit abstract. This avoids being overly specific about topics you simply don't know much about.

However, even if your policy isn't novel to the industry, it might still be novel to you or your organization. The steps that I've found useful to debug novel policies are the same steps as running a condensed version of the strategy process, with a focus on exploration and refinement:

1. Collect a number of *similar* policies and articulate how those policies differ from the policy you are creating.
2. Create a systems model (see Chapter 14) to articulate how the new policy will work, as well as how it will differ from the similar policies you're considering.
3. Run a strategy testing cycle for your proto-policy to discover any "unknown unknowns" about how it works in practice.

Whether you run into this scenario is largely a function of the extent of your, and your organization's, experience. Early in my career, I found myself doing novel (for me) strategy work very frequently; these days, it's much rarer for me than adapting well-known policies to new circumstances.

Are Competing Policy Proposals an Antipattern?

When creating policy, you'll often have to engage with the question of whether you should develop one preferred policy or a series of potential policies to pick from. Developing a set of options is a useful stage of setting policy, but rather than helping you refine your policy, I'd encourage you to think of it as a way to expose gaps in your diagnosis.

For example, when Stripe developed the Sorbet Ruby-typing tooling, there was debate between two policies:

> *Should we build a Ruby-typing tool to allow a centralized team to gradually migrate the company to a typed codebase?*
>
> or
>
> *Should we migrate the codebase to a preexisting strongly typed language, like Golang or Java?*

These were, initially, equally valid hypotheses. Only when we clarified our diagnosis around resourcing did it become clear that it would be better to incur the bulk of costs in a centralized team than to spread the costs across many teams. Specifically, we recognized that we wanted to prioritize short-term product-engineering velocity, even if it led to a longer migration overall.

If you do develop multiple policy options, I encourage you to move the alternatives into an appendix rather than including them in the core of your strategy document (see Chapter 11 on readable strategy documents). Focusing on the selected approach makes it easier for readers to understand how to follow your policies without the distraction of other possible approaches.

Recognizing Constraints

Another frequent policy failure is developing a policy that you cannot possibly fund. It's easy to get enamored with policies that would only work in an alternate universe where it was possible to enforce and resource them—but adopting them would be bad policy.

To consider a few examples:

- The strategy for controlling access to user data (Document 19-1) might have proposed requiring manual approval of every access to customer data by a second party. However, that would have gone nowhere, because it would have harmed customer experience by greatly slowing down internal workflows.
- Our approach to Uber's service migration (Document 16-1) might have required more staffing for the infrastructure engineering team—but we knew that wasn't going to happen, so it would have been a meaningless policy to propose.
- The strategy for navigating private equity ownership (Document 18-1) might have argued that the new owners should not hold engineering accountable to a new standard on spending. But they would have just invalidated that strategy in the next financial planning period, because your leadership is never bound to honor a policy you write that they disagree with.

An impractical policy isn't just a poor one: it also suggests your diagnosis is missing an important pillar. Rather than debating the policy options, the fastest path to resolution is to align on a diagnosis that would invalidate some of the potential paths forward.

In cases where aligning on the diagnosis isn't difficult (for example, because you simply don't understand the possibilities of a new technology, as encountered in the strategy for adopting LLMs), then you've likely found a valuable opportunity to use strategy refinement to build alignment.

Dealing with Missing Strategies

At a recent company offsite meeting, we were debating policies to deal with annual plans that kept getting derailed after less than a month. Someone remarked that this would be much easier if we could get the executive team to commit to a clearer written strategy about which business units the organization was prioritizing.

They were, of course, right. It would have been much easier. Unfortunately, this goes back to the problem I discussed in Chapter 7 about reframing blockers into diagnoses. If a strategy from the company or a peer function is missing, the empowering thing to do is to include the absence in your diagnosis and move forward.

Sometimes, even when you do this, it's easy to fall back into the belief that you cannot set a policy because a peer function might set a conflicting policy in the future. Whether you're an executive or an engineer, you'll never have all of the details you want to make the ideal policy. Meaningful leadership requires taking meaningful risks, which is never comfortable.

Summary

After working through this chapter, you know how to develop policy, how to assemble policies to solve your diagnosis, and how to avoid a number of the frequent challenges that policy writers encounter. At this point, there's only one phase of strategy left to dig into: operating the policies you've created.

Operations

Even the best policies fail if the teams they're intended to serve don't adopt them. Can you persistently change your company's behaviors with a one-time announcement? No, probably not.

I refer to the art of making policies work as *operations* or *strategy operations*. The good news is that effectively operating a policy is two-thirds avoiding common practices that simply don't work. The other one-third takes some repetition, but can be practiced in any engineering role: there's no need to wait until you're an executive to start building mastery.

This chapter will dig into those mechanisms, with particular focus on:

- How operations support policies with mechanisms that ensure they work well
- Evaluating operational mechanisms to select the most effective choice
- Composing an operational plan to support your specific set of policies
- Operations mechanisms, effective and otherwise, including approval forums, inspection mechanisms, and nudges
- How to adjust your approach to operations if you are in an engineering role
- The largest threat to effective strategy operations: cargo-culting

Let's unpack the details of making sure your *potentially* good policy has a positive impact. In addition to showing you how to roll out a strategy of your own, this chapter also provides a rescue toolkit you can use to put an existing, floundering strategy back on track. If you don't see an opportunity to write new strategy within your organization, then there's still probably room to flex your operational skill.

What Are Operational Mechanisms?

Operations are how a policy is implemented and reinforced. Effective operations ensure that your policies actually accomplish something. Examples of operations could include a recurring weekly meeting, an alert that notifies the team when a threshold is exceeded, or new requirements for promotions.

The strategy for working with new private equity ownership (Document 18-1) introduces a policy to backfill hires at a lower level, and cap the number of principal engineers:

> *We will move to an "N-1" backfill policy, where departures are backfilled with a less senior level. We will also institute a strict maximum of one Principal Engineer per business unit, with any exceptions approved in writing by the CTO—this applies for both promotions and external hires.*

That introduces an explicit operational mechanism—escalations go to the CTO. It also introduces an implicit, undefined mechanism: how do we ensure the backfills are actually down-leveled as the policy instructs? Here are three potential operational solutions to implementing this policy:

- The CTO approves the levels of backfilled roles in a group chat with engineering recruiting.
- Enforcing downleveling becomes the Recruiting team's responsibility.
- Take it on trust that hiring managers will do the right thing.

Operations is the art of picking the right option for your circumstances, running it, and tweaking it as you learn.

Operations in Government

For another interesting take on how critical operations are, *Recoding America* (*https://oreil.ly/gpOfM*) by Jennifer Pahlka (Metropolitan Books, 2023) is well worth the read. It explores how well-intended government legislation often isn't feasible to implement, which results in policies that require massive IT investments but provide little benefit to constituents.

How to Evaluate Mechanisms: A Rubric

In order to determine the most effective operational mechanisms for the problems you're working on, it's useful to have a standardized evaluation rubric. While the rubric presented here isn't perfectly universal, having any rubric will make it easier to evaluate your options consistently, and you can customize it for your needs.

The rubric I use to evaluate whether an operational mechanism will be effective consists of six factors:

Measurability
: Can you measure both leading and lagging indicators to inspect (*https://lethain.com/inspection*) the mechanism's impact? If you have to choose, measuring leading indicators allows much quicker evaluation so you can iterate on your mechanisms.

Adoption cost
: How much work will migrating (*https://lethain.com/migrations*) to this mechanism require? Can this work be done incrementally or does it require a major, coordinated shift?

User ease (or burden)
: After adopting this policy, how much easier (or harder) will it be for users to perform their work? If things will be harder, can those users tolerate the additional effort?

Provider ease (or burden)
: How much additional ongoing maintenance will this mechanism require from the centralized or platform team providing it? For example, if every new architecture proposal requires a thorough review by your Security team, can the Security team actually support those reviews?

Reliance on authority
: How much does this mechanism depend on a top-down authority's active support? If the sponsoring executive departs, will this mechanism remain effective? Is that an effective tradeoff in this case?

Cultural alignment
: Is this something that your organization wants to do, or something it will fight at each step? Is there a way you can adjust the framing to make it more acceptable to your organization's culture?

Generally, I find folks are good at evaluating mechanisms against these criteria, but somewhat worse at accepting the consequences of their evaluation. For example, someone might fall in love with a particular mechanism whose adoption cost is unbearably high and try to force the organization to accept it. Or someone might introduce a mechanism that creates significant user burden for a team already struggling with tight efficiency goals.

Self-awareness helps here, but so does consulting others who are willing to point out the errors in your reasoning—which is a core part of how I've found success in adopting operational mechanisms.

Composing an Operational Plan

Your *operational plan* is the sum of the mechanisms used to support your policies. While evaluating each individual mechanism in isolation is part of creating an operations plan, it's also valuable to consider how the mechanisms will work together:

- Review the policies you've developed. What sort of mechanisms seem most likely to support these policies? How might you pool these mechanisms together to avoid redundancy?
- Review the operational mechanisms used in your organization. Which have had the best effects, and which have left too bad an aftertaste to be reused?
- Which new mechanisms showed up in your exploration phase? If any of them seem particularly well suited to the policies you're considering and none of your organization's frequently used mechanisms are good fits, consider testing a new one.
- Evaluate each of the mechanisms you're considering using against the evaluation rubric.
- Consolidate the full set of mechanisms into one coherent operational plan. Be particularly mindful of any ease or burden the integrated plan creates for users and/or platform providers.
- Validate your plan with users and providers to make sure they don't impose an unreasonable burden or a workflow that simply won't work.
- If you run this process and still can't agree with stakeholders on your proposed plan, commit to running a strategy testing process that includes the plan. This will build confidence in the approach before people feel forced to commit to following it long-term.

Even if you don't use strategy testing for your plan, at least schedule a review in three months to reflect on how things have worked out. Your operational plan is the vehicle that delivers your policies to your organization. It's extremely tempting to skip refining the details here, but doing so is a relatively quick step that can completely change your strategy's outcomes.

Effective Mechanisms and Patterns

Most companies have a handful of frequently used operational mechanisms. Some are company-specific, such as Amazon's weekly business review (*https://oreil.ly/rDwce*); others repeat across companies, like requiring executive approval. This section categorizes the mechanisms I've found consistently effective.

APPROVAL AND ADVICE FORUMS

At a high level, new policies are obvious and simple; they apply cleanly to the problem they are intended to solve. However, when you apply those policies to detailed, complex circumstances, it isn't always clear how to stay loyal to the policy's intentions. Approval and advice forums are a common solution to that problem.

Calm's product engineering strategy (Chapter 21) shows what the simplest, most common approval forum looks like in practice:

> *Exceptions are granted by the CTO, and must be in writing. The above policies are deliberately restrictive. Sometimes they may be wrong, and we will make exceptions to them. However, each exception should be deliberate and grounded in concrete problems we are aligned both on solving and how we solve them. If we all scatter toward our preferred solution, then we'll create negative leverage for Calm rather than serving as the engine that advances our product.*
>
> *All exceptions must be written. If they are not written, then you should operate as if it has not been granted. Our goal is to avoid ambiguity around whether an exception has, or has not, been approved. If there's no written record that the CTO approved it, then it's not approved.*

This example also has several weaknesses that are common in approval forums. Most importantly, it doesn't explicitly specify how to get approvals (perhaps by asking in a `#cto-approvals` Slack channel) or to research prior requests and approvals.

Approvals don't necessarily need to come from senior leadership. Instead, the senior leadership can loan their authority on a topic to another group. The LLM adoption strategy in Document 17-1 provides a good example of this:

Start with Anthropic. We use Anthropic models, which are available through our existing cloud provider via AWS Bedrock. To avoid maintaining multiple implementations, where we view the underlying foundational model quality to be somewhat undifferentiated, we are not looking to adopt a broad set of LLMs at this point. This is anchored in our Wardley map of the LLM ecosystem.

Exceptions will be reviewed by the Machine Learning Review in `#ml-review`.

In a more community-minded organization, approval forums might not require senior leadership to be involved at all. Instead, the culture might create an environment where the forums' feedback is taken seriously on its own merits.

Every company does approval forums a bit differently. At Carta, the Navigators (*https://lethain.com/navigators*) program experimented with granting executive authority for technical decisions to named engineers in each area. I recommend Andrew Harmel-Law's discussion of this topic in *Facilitating Software Architecture* (O'Reilly, 2024). You can spend a lot of time arguing the details here. My experience is that having the right participants and a good executive sponsor matter a lot, and the other pieces matter a lot less.

INSPECTION

While even the best policies can fail, it's more common for a policy to *sort of* work and need some modest adjustments. An inspection mechanism (*https://lethain.com/inspection*) allows you to evaluate whether your policy is succeeding and if you need to make adjustments.

The user-data access strategy in Document 19-1 provides an example:

Measure progress on percentage of customer data access requests justified by a user-comprehensible, automated rationale. This will anchor our approach on simultaneously improving the security of user data and the usability of our colleagues' internal tools. If we only expand requirements for accessing customer data, we won't view this as progress because it's not automated (and consequently is likely to encourage workarounds as teams try to solve problems quickly). Similarly, if we only improve usability, charts won't represent this as progress, because we won't have increased the number of supported requests.

As part of this effort, we will create a private channel where the security and compliance team has visibility into all manual rationales for user-data access, and will notify the manager of anyone who repeatedly uses a manual justification for accessing user data.

This example is a good start, but fully realizing an inspection mechanism requires concretely specifying where and how the data will be tracked. A better version of this would include a dashboard link and a commitment to reviewing the data at specified intervals.

For a recent inspection mechanism, I created a recurring invite for the working group members who had agreed to review the data, with a link to the relevant data dashboard and a specific chat channel for discussion. This wasn't a synchronous meeting, but rather a commitment to independently review the data and discuss anything that felt surprising.

Your particular mechanisms could be threshold-triggered alerts, something you fold into an existing metrics review meeting, a script you commit to running and reviewing periodically, or something else. The most important thing is that it cannot silently fail: if your mechanisms fail without triggering inspection, then they won't accomplish anything.

NUDGES

It's common to hear complaints about how a team isn't following a new policy, as if it were a deliberate choice they'd made. I find that people usually *want* to do things the new way, but rarely take time to learn how. *Nudging* means providing individuals with context to inform them about a better way they might do something. Nudges are an exceptionally effective mechanism.

At Stripe, we had a policy of allowing teams to self-authorize new cloud hosting costs. This worked well almost all the time. However, sometimes teams would accidentally introduce large cost increases—almost always without realizing it. Even if we'd told them not to introduce unapproved spending spikes, they simply didn't perceive they'd done it.

We had a choice: prevent all teams from introducing new spend, or try a nudge. The nudge we added did a few things:

- Informed teams whenever their cloud spend accelerated month over month
- Directed them to charts that explained the acceleration
- Told them where to go to ask questions

Nudges pair well with inspections, so the Efficiency Engineering team reviewed any spikes monthly and reached out where necessary.

Maybe we could have forced all teams to review new spend, but this nudge approach didn't require an authoritative mandate. It also meant we only spent time advising teams that *actually* spent too much, instead of having discussions with every team that *might* spend too much.

As another example: At Carta, some managers had said they didn't know when or why their team members merged untested pull requests. The working group added a nudge to inform managers anytime this occurred. This made it easy to detect and also respected their attention by only sending a notification if there was a new, untested pull request.

With poor ergonomics, nudges can be an overwhelming assault on your colleagues' attention, but done well, I continue to believe they are the most effective operational mechanism. Stay in the latter camp by limiting the total number of nudges, ensuring that each nudge has an explicit action that the recipient can take, and including clear instructions on how to take that action.

People can't enforce policies if they don't know they exist or how to follow them. In my experience, nudges are the most effective way to solve both of those problems, because nudges bring information to people at exactly the moment that information would be useful. At most companies, well-done nudges are relatively uncommon, and the far more common solution to lack of information is documentation and training.

DOCUMENTATION AND TRAINING

There are so many approaches to documentation and training. I've not found my own approaches particularly effective, so I hesitate to give much advice. Following standard practices for your company, even if the outcomes seem imperfect, is probably your best bet. Internal knowledge bases tend to rot quickly, and introducing yet another knowledge base is almost always an illusion of progress (even when you really don't like the current one).

Finally, remember that for documentation and training, the measure of success is not necessarily that everyone in the company knows how the new policy works. A more useful goal is "informational herd immunity": as long as someone on each team understands your policy, the team will generally be capable of following it.

AUTOMATION

Relying on humans to respond to new policies is slow, and the quality of response will vary. In many cases, automation is the most effective and scalable mechanism to support your policies' rollout.

Automation was key in the Uber service migration strategy (Document 16-1), moving us out of a slow manual process that was taking up a great deal of user and provider time:

> *Move to structured requests, and out of tickets. Missing or incorrect information in provisioning requests create significant delays in provisioning. Further, collecting this information is the first step of moving to a self-service process. As such, we can get paid twice by reducing errors in manual provisioning while also creating the interface for self-service workflows.*

In that case, better automation allowed us to eliminate a series of back-and-forth negotiations to collect data, instead providing the necessary information in a single step. Occasionally we still ran into users who couldn't fill in the form, but now we could focus on providing a good manual experience for those rare exceptions.

Automation can't have a positive impact as a core strategy mechanism without an effective user experience. If you view user experience as a secondary concern, automation is unlikely to make much impact.

DEFERRAL TO FUTURE WORK

Sometimes there's something you really want a policy to do, but you also know that you have no reasonable mechanism to do it. In that case, explicitly deferring action can be useful.

The strategy for integration of the Index acquisition at Stripe (Document 22-4) used this mechanism:

> *Defer making a decision regarding the introduction of Java to a later date: the introduction of Java is incompatible with our existing engineering strategy, but at this point we've also been unable to align stakeholders on how to address this decision. Further, we see attempting to address this issue as a distraction from our timely goal of launching a joint product within six months.*
>
> *We will take up this discussion after launching the initial release.*

So did the strategy for working with a private equity acquirer (Document 18-1):

> *We believe there are significant opportunities to reduce R&D maintenance investments, but we don't have conviction about which particular efforts we should prioritize. We will kick off a working group to identify the features with the highest support load.*

There's no shame in deferral. As much as you want to make progress on a certain area, it's better to explicitly acknowledge that you can't right now—and clarify when you will be able to—than to allow the organization to continue churning on an intractable problem.

MEETINGS

You can fit any and all of the preceding mechanisms into a meeting. Meetings are a universal mechanism, although frequently overused, because they can do an adequate job of operating almost any policy. Meetings are almost always the most expensive mechanism you can find to solve a problem, but they are easy to suggest, run, and iterate on.

The most common type is reporting meetings. The LLM adoption strategy (Document 17-1) suggests reporting progress in the Executive Weekly Meeting:

> *Develop an LLM-backed process for reactivating departed and suspended drivers in mature markets. Through modeling our driver lifecycle, we determined that improving onboarding time will have little impact on the total number of active drivers. Instead, we are focusing on mechanisms to reactivate departed and suspended drivers, which is the only opportunity to meaningfully impact active drivers.*
>
> *Report on progress monthly in* Exec Weekly Meeting, *coordinated in* `#exec-weekly`.

Another common meeting archetype is the weekly working meeting, discussed in Chapter 13.

If you can't find any other mechanism you believe in, then a meeting is a decent starting point. Just don't get too fond of them—and try to iterate your way to canceling every recurring meeting that you start.

Antipatterns and Ineffective Mechanisms

In addition to the effective operational methods discussed in this chapter, there are a number of frequently used mechanisms that I consider antipatterns. They can provide some value, but there's almost always a better alternative. These include:

Top-down pronouncements
: Sometimes leaders operationalize a policy by simply declaring that it must be followed. For example, some "return to office" policies dictate that the team must work from a central office, but driving a real change requires motivating those individuals to actually return.

Education-as-announcement rollouts
: Many companies roll out policies through one-time "education" by default, often as an all-company announcement for existing employees. They might follow up by updating training for onboarding new hires.

Education sounds great, but a couple of trainings will never change the whole organization's behavior. Changing that requires ongoing reminders, visible role models, inspections to understand why some teams are *not* adopting the behavior, and so on. Education can be a good component of operationalizing a policy, but it cannot stand on its own.

Mandatory recurring trainings
: These are a staple of compliance-driven policies, generally because of laws mandating a certain number of hours of relevant training each year.

There are two deep challenges with mandatory trainings. First, because attendance is *required*, trainers tend to make little effort to make their content good. Second, many trainees don't pay attention because they expect low-quality content. It's not uncommon to hear people who've been trained on a policy annually for years say that they've never heard of that policy.

It's possible to overcome these barriers, but in a situation where you're accountable for actually changing the outcomes (as opposed to simply shifting legal obligations away from the company), mandatory trainings tend to work poorly.

"Just change the culture"

Some leaders frame most problems as cultural problems, which is reasonable and often useful. Unfortunately, it's common for those who rely heavily on cultural framings to have simplistic views about how to change culture.

Changing an organization's culture is tricky. It requires a combination of many techniques to create visible leaders role-modeling the new behavior, as well as reinforcement mechanisms to weed out pockets of dissent. Anyone who frames culture change as a simple or instant change is living in an imaginary world.

If you're using one of these approaches, it isn't necessarily a bad choice. Just make sure you can explain why you're using it—and make sure you *believe* that explanation. If you don't, look for a more effective mechanism.

What If You're Not an Executive?

It's easy to get discouraged when you think about which operational mechanisms are unavailable to you as a nonexecutive, like running mandatory recurring meetings or starting a binding architecture review process.

However, there's always a related mechanism that can be implemented with less authority. The binding architecture process can be replaced with an architectural advice process. A mandatory review of pull requests can be replaced with a nudge.

Although authoritative mechanisms may be more common, my experience as an executive has been that they don't work particularly well. They do a great job of technically shifting accountability to the wider organization, but they often don't change anyone's behavior at all.

Instead of getting frustrated by what you can't do, focus on the mechanisms that are available to you today. Add nudges, focus on the real dynamics of how colleagues do work in your organization, and build a real dataset.

It's very hard to get an executive to support your initiative before you have mechanisms and data to support it, and very easy to get their support once you do. Once you've done what you can without authority to build confidence, if you really do need more authority, then you're in a good place to escalate to get an executive to support your policies.

Beware Cargo-Culting

Cargo-culting is recreating a process that previously solved a problem without understanding the circumstances that made that process effective. In some cases, that's enough: you can kick a ball without understanding physics. However, it's often disastrous: how my toddler thinks driving a car works is very different from how driving a car actually works.

The longer I work in the software industry, the more I am surprised by how few strategists seem to care if their approaches actually work. Instead, they seem focused on doing something that *might* work, offloading accountability to the organization or some team, and then moving off to the next problem.

Perhaps this is driven by the unfortunate reality that leaders are often evaluated by how they appear, rather than by what they accomplish. Either way, it's surprisingly difficult to know which patterns to borrow from strategy rollouts and implementations. The best advice, unfortunately, is to remain skeptically optimistic. Collect ideas widely, but force them to prove their merit.

Summary

Now that you've finished this chapter, you're significantly more qualified to write a complete, useful strategy than I was a decade into my career. The operations behind your strategy are at least as essential as any other step, but are often skipped; any strategy without them will fade quietly into your organization's history.

Writing Readable Engineering Strategies

You've learned by this point in the book that a complete engineering strategy has five components: explore, diagnose, refine, set policy, and operate. That's an effective sequence for *creating* a strategy, but it's challenging for those trying to quickly *read and apply* a strategy without necessarily wanting to understand the complete thinking behind each decision. The order in which you write your strategy isn't necessarily the order in which your audience should read it.

This chapter covers:

- Why the order for writing a strategy is hard to read
- How to organize a strategy document for reading
- How to refactor and merge components for improved readability
- Additional tips for writing effective strategy documents

After reading it, you should be able to take a written strategy and rework it into a version that's much easier for others to read.

Why Writing Structure Inhibits Reading

Most software engineers learn to structure documents as students. Academic essays present evidence to support a clear thesis and generally build an argument forward toward a conclusion. Some business consultancies train their new hires in business writing—for instance, McKinsey teaches Barbara Minto's *The Pyramid Principle: Logic in Writing and Thinking* (Prentice Hall, 2010)—but that's the exception.

While academic essays want to develop an argument, professional writing is a bit different. Professional writing typically has one of three distinct goals:

Refining thinking about a given approach
: "How do we select databases for our new products?" This is an area where the academic structure can be useful, because it focuses on the *thinking* behind the proposal rather than the proposal itself.

Seeking approval from stakeholders or executives
: "What database have we selected for our new analytics product?" The academic structure creates a great deal of confusion here, because it focuses on the thinking rather than the specific proposal—which stakeholders view as the primary topic to review.

Communicating a policy to your organization
: "Databases are allowed for new products." This type of writing is about helping engineers at your company understand the permitted options for a given problem, as well as explaining the rationale behind the decision for those who want to understand or challenge the current policy.

The ideal format for the first case is generally at odds with the other two, which is a frequent reason why strategy documents struggle to graduate from brainstorming to policy. Most strategy writers resist the idea that it's worth their time to restructure their initial documents, so let me expand on challenges I've encountered when I've personally tried to make progress without restructuring.

TOO LONG, DIDN'T READ

Thinking-oriented structures leave policy recommendations at the very bottom, but the vast majority of strategy readers are simply trying to understand the policy so that they can apply it to their specific problem. Many—perhaps most—of those readers give up before they reach the sections that answer their questions. They assume that the document doesn't provide clear direction because finding that direction takes too long.

This is very much akin to the core lesson of Steve Krug's classic book on web usability, *Don't Make Me Think* (Peachpit, 2013): users (and readers) don't understand, they muddle through. It's an act of hubris to assume that readers will invest significant time to deeply understand your document.

APPROVAL MEETING TO NOWHERE

There are roughly three types of approval meetings. The first is where you go in and no one has any feedback. Maybe someone gripes that "this meeting could've been an email," but your document is approved.

The second type of approval meetings has two sets of stakeholders with incompatible goals who need a senior decision-maker to mediate between them. This is a very useful meeting, because you generally can't make progress without that senior decision-maker breaking the tie.

The third sort of meeting is when you get derailed early with questions about the research, whether you'd considered another option, and whether this is even relevant. You might think this happens because your strategy is wrong, but in my experience, it's usually because you failed to structure the document to present the policy up front. Stakeholders might disagree with many elements of your thinking, yet still agree with your ultimate policy. It's only useful for them to dig into your rationale if they actually disagree with the policy itself. Avoid getting stuck debating the details when you agree on the overarching approach. Present the policy *first*, and only dig into those details when there's disagreement.

TRANSIENT ALIGNMENT

Sometimes you'll see two distinct strategy documents, with the first covering the full thinking and the second including only the policy and operations sections. This tends to work quite well initially, but over time, team members depart and new people are hired. At some point, a new member will challenge the thinking behind a strategy as obviously wrong (generally because it's a different set of policies than they used at the previous employer). If you omit the diagnosis and exploration sections entirely, they can't trace through the reasoning to understand the decision. Instead, they often leap to simplistic conclusions, like the ever-popular "I guess the previous engineers here were just dumb."

As annoying as each of these challenges is, the solution is simple: use the writing structure for writing, and invert that structure for reading.

Inverting the Document Structure for Reading

To reiterate a point from Chapter 5: it's always appropriate to change the structure you use to develop or present a strategy, as long as you are making a *deliberate, informed* decision.

While "explore, diagnose, refine, set policy, and operate" generally works well for writing policy, I've consistently found it a poor format for *presenting* strategy. I recommend a mostly inverted structure:

Policy
: What does the strategy require or allow?

Operation
: How is the strategy enforced and carried out? How are exceptions granted?

Refine
: What load-bearing details informed the strategy?

Diagnose
: What general trends and observations steered the thinking?

Explore
: What is the high-level, wide-ranging context that we brought into creating this strategy?

The key rule for structuring a written strategy is to prioritize what the readers are most likely to care about: if you know what they care about most, put that first. When seeking approval from executives, you'll probably focus on the *Policy* section. When rolling a policy out to your organization, you'll probably focus on the *Operation* section more. In both cases, those are the critical components and you want them right up front. Very few strategy readers want to understand the full thinking behind your strategy. The vast majority just want to understand how it will impact them or their function. These are your least motivated readers, so you need to provide the details they care about early in the document before they stop reading.

Someone who wants to really understand the thinking will invest time reading through the document, even if it isn't perfectly structured for them. Someone who just wants an answer will frequently give up and make up an answer, rather than reading all the way through to where the document does in fact answer their question.

Zooming out a bit, this is a classic "lack of user empathy" problem. The document's authors are so deep in the details that they can't put themselves in the readers' shoes. They don't see how overwhelming the document is to someone simply trying to pop in, get an answer, and then pop out. This lack of empathy also means that most strategy writers refuse to structure their documents to support the large population of answer seekers. Try it a few times, though, and I think you'll see it helps a great deal. For an even faster perspective, go read someone else's strategy document that you aren't familiar with. If its authors have followed the academic structure, you'll quickly appreciate how challenging it can be to identify the actual proposal.

Strategy Refactoring

Inverting the structure is the first step of optimizing a document for readability, a process I think of as *strategy refactoring*. But you don't have to stop there. Even the inverted strategy structure can be somewhat confusing. For example, the LLM adoption strategy (Document 17-1) makes two refactors to the inverted format. First, it merges *Refine* into *Diagnose*, which keeps the map and models closer to the specific topics it explores. Second, it discards the *Operation* section entirely and includes the relevant details alongside the policies to which they apply in the *Policy* section.

Strategy refactoring is about discarding structure where it interferes with usability. The strategy structure is very effective at separating concerns while reasoning through decision making, but most readers benefit more from engaging with the full implications of the strategy at once. Once you're done thinking, refactor away the thinking tools: don't let the best tools for one workflow mislead you into thinking they're the best ones for an entirely different workflow.

Additional Tips for Writing Effective Strategy Documents

In addition to the preceding advice, this section offers a handful of smaller tips that I've found helpful for creating readable strategy documents.

Before releasing a document widely, find someone entirely uninvolved with the strategy thus far and have them read it. Ask them to point out any areas that are difficult to understand. Anyone who's been thinking about the strategy is going to gloss over areas that might be inscrutable to those who are approaching it with fresh eyes.

Every strategy document should be rolled out with an explicit commenting period where you invite discussion, as well as office hours where you are available to explain how to apply the strategy correctly. These steps help with adoption, but even more importantly, they help you identify dissenters, so you can follow up to better understand their concerns.

Every company should maintain its own internal engineering strategy template. Your template should include consistent metadata, particularly when the document was created, the current approval status, and where to ask questions. Of these, a clear, durable place to ask questions is the most important, as it extends the life of the document. Consider incorporating some of the material from this chapter into your template.

After you release your strategy, disable in-document commenting. This isn't intended to prevent further discussion, but rather to move the discussion outside of the document. Nothing creates the impression of an unapproved, unfinished strategy document faster than a long string of open comments. Open comments also distract readers from the strategy document.

Summary

While it's helpful to impose rigid structures while creating a strategy, you now know how to escape those structures to create a readable document that is easier for others to both approve and apply. Beyond initially inverting the structure for easier reading, you also understand how to refactor away sections that may have been essential for creating the strategy but interfere with understanding how to apply it. Remember that applying the strategy is by far the most common task for strategy readers.

I hope you finish this chapter agreeing that it's worth your time to rework your thinking-optimized draft. Deliberately refusing to structure documents for readers' benefit causes a surprising number of good strategies to fail utterly.

12

Bridging Theory and Practice

Some people I've worked with have lost hope that engineering strategy actually exists within *any* engineering organization. I imagine them unimpressed as they read through the steps to build engineering strategy or the strategy for resourcing Engineering-driven projects. They probably see these ideas as theoretical at best. In less polite company, they might even describe them as fake constructs.

Let's talk about it! Because they're right. In fact, they're right in two different ways. First, this book explains how to create clean, refined, and definitive strategy documents, but most real strategy artifacts initially look rather messy. Second, applying these techniques can require a fair amount of creativity. It might sound easy, but it's quite difficult in practice.

This chapter will cover:

- Why strategy documents need to be clear and definitive, especially when strategy development has been messy
- How to iterate on strategy when there are demands for unrealistic timelines
- Using strategy as a nonexecutive
- Handling dynamic, quickly changing environments where the diagnosis can change frequently
- Working with indecisive stakeholders
- Surviving other people's bad strategy work

Let's dive into the many ways that praxis doesn't quite line up with theory.

Clear, Definitive Documents

The last chapter explored why documents that feel intuitive to write are often fairly difficult to read. That's because thinking tends to be a linear-ish journey from a problem to a solution. Most readers, on the other hand, usually just want to know the solution and then move on. That's because good strategies are read for direction (like when a team wants to understand how to solve a specific issue) far more frequently than to build agreement (the way you build stakeholder alignment during initial strategy development).

However, many organizations only produce writer-oriented strategy documents and have no reader-oriented documents at all. If you've predominantly worked in those sorts of organizations, the first reader-oriented documents you encounter may seem superficial because they present decisions before explaining how those decisions were reached. That's true, but it's not superficial; it's simply prioritizing what most readers care about: the decision itself.

There are also organizations with many reader-oriented documents that omit the rationale for the strategy. Those documents feel prescriptive and heavy-handed, because the infrequent readers who *do* want to understand the thinking can't find it. Further, anyone who wants to propose an alternative has to do so without the rationale behind the current policies. The absence of that context often transforms a collaborative problem-solving opportunity into a political conflict.

With that in mind, I'd encourage you to see the frequent absence of reader-oriented, fully justified documents as a major opportunity to drive strategy within your organization, rather than evidence that these documents don't work. My experience is that they do.

Doing Strategy Despite Unrealistic Timelines

The most frequent failure mode I see for strategy is when it's rushed. Authors often accept that they must stop thinking when the artificial deadline is reached. Stripe executive Claire Hughes Johnson, in her book *Scaling People: Tactics for Management and Company Building* (Stripe Press, 2023), argues that planning expands to fit any timeline, and consequently sets a short annual planning timeline of several weeks. Some teams accepted that as a fixed timeline and *stopped planning* when the timeline ended, whereas effective teams never stopped planning before or after the planning window.

When strategy work is given an artificial or unrealistic timeline, you should deliver the best draft you can. Afterward, rather than being "finished," you should view yourself as starting the refinement process. It's an open secret that many strategies never leave the refinement phase and are tweaked throughout their lifespans. Why should a strategy with an early deadline be any different?

Well, there is one important problem to acknowledge: the executive who imposes the unrealistic timeline often intends it to force people into action and quick thinking. Even if you know that an executive's artificial deadline denotes when refinement starts rather than when strategy development ends, your colleagues who are also working on strategy might believe that all decisions must be finalized by that deadline. Ideally, you can appeal directly to the executive to clarify their timeline.

Sometimes having the conversation with the responsible executive is quite difficult. In that case, you do have to work with individuals taking the strategy literally and as unalterable until either you can have the conversation or something goes wrong enough that the executive starts paying attention again. Usually, though, you can find someone who has a communication path, as long as you can articulate the issue clearly.

Using Strategy as a Nonexecutive

Some engineers will argue that the only valid strategy altitude is the highest one—the executive level—because any other strategy can be invalidated by a new, higher-altitude strategy. They claim that teams simply *cannot* do strategy, because executives might invalidate it. Some engineering executives argue the same thing, claiming that they can't work on an engineering strategy because the missing product strategy or business strategy might introduce new constraints.

I don't agree with this line of thinking at all. To do strategy at any altitude, you have to come to terms with the certainty that new information will show up and you'll need to revise your strategy to deal with it.

The strategy for controlling access to user data (Document 19-1) is a good counterexample against the premise that effective strategy requires executive support. In this particular case, the Security team had framed their lack of progress as the result of limited executive engagement, which had led to a disengaged team. However, as I dug into the ergonomics of the problem with the Security team, we came to realize that we could significantly reduce unnecessary access to user data without any top-down support at all by making the workflows easier to use.

When it comes to using strategy, effective diagnosis trumps authority. At least as many executives' strategies are ravaged by reality's pervasive details as are overridden by higher-altitude strategies. The only way to be certain your strategy will fail is to wait until you're certain that no new information might show up.

Doing Strategy in Chaotic Environments

Chapter 17 discusses how a company should plot a path through the rapidly evolving LLM ecosystem. Periods of rapid technological evolution are one reason your strategy might encounter a pocket of chaos, but there are many others. Pockets of rapid hiring or layoffs create chaos. Load-bearing senior leaders departing can change a company quickly. Slowing revenue in the company's core business can also initiate chaotic actions in pursuit of a new business.

Strategies don't require stable environments; they require awareness of the environment that they're operating in. In a stable period, you might expect a strategy to run for several years with relatively little deviation from the initial approach. In a dynamic period, the strategy authors might know that they can only protect capacity in two-week chunks before a new critical initiative pops up. It's possible to execute good strategy in either scenario, but it's impossible to execute good strategy if you don't diagnose the context effectively.

Unreliable Information

Often, the way forward is very obvious—if only a few key decisions could be made. You know who is supposed to make those decisions, but you simply cannot get them to decide. My most visceral experience of this was conducting a layoff where the CEO wouldn't define a target cost reduction or specify how much various functions (like Engineering, Marketing, and Sales) should contribute to those reductions. Those two decisions would have made Engineering's approach obvious; without that clarity, things felt impossible.

Although I was frustrated at the time, I've since come to appreciate that missing decisions are the norm rather than the exception. The strategy on navigating private equity ownership (Document 18-1) deals with this problem by acknowledging a missing decision and expressly blocking one part of the strategy's execution until that decision is made. Other parts of its plan, like changing how roles are backfilled, went ahead to address the broader cost problem.

Rather than blocking on missing information, your strategy should acknowledge what's missing and move forward where you can. Sometimes that means moving forward by taking risks; sometimes it means delaying for clarity—but it never means accepting that you're stuck without options other than pointing a finger.

Surviving Other People's Bad Strategy Work

Sometimes you will be told to follow something described as a strategy, but it's really just a policy without any strategic thinking behind it. This is an unavoidable element of working in organizations and happens for all sorts of reasons. Some leaders don't believe it's valuable to explain their thinking to others, because they see themselves as the one important decision-maker.

Other times, your leader doesn't agree with a policy they've been instructed to roll out. Adopting "high-hype" technologies, like blockchain during the crypto boom, often happens through top-down direction from company leadership. Engineering might disagree with the decision, but is obligated to align with it. Such leaders find that it's hard to explain a strategy that they themselves don't understand.

This is a frustrating situation. What I've found most effective is writing a strategy of my own—one that acknowledges the broader strategy I disagree with in its diagnosis as a static, unavoidable truth. From there, I can make practical decisions that recognize the context, even if it's not a context I'd have selected for myself. I generally don't share this version unless a colleague raises the concern that they don't understand my decision making, at which point I talk them through the thinking in my private strategy.

Summary

I started this chapter by acknowledging that the steps to building engineering strategy are a theory of strategy, one that can get messy in practice. Now you know why strategy documents often come across as overly pristine—because they're trying to communicate clearly about a complex topic.

You also know how to navigate the many ways reality pulls you away from perfect strategy, such as unrealistic timelines, higher-altitude strategies invalidating your own strategy work, working in a chaotic environment, and dealing with stakeholders who refuse to align with your strategy. Finally, sometimes strategy work done by others is really just unsupported policy, with neither a diagnosis nor an operational approach. That's all stuff you're going to run into and overcome on your path to doing good strategy work.

PART | III

Refinement Tools

Perhaps the most important step in building an engineering strategy is refinement. Since Chapter 8 has already given you an overview of strategy refinement, Part III of this book goes into much greater detail about three core mapping techniques: strategy testing, systems modeling, and Wardley mapping.

As we work through them, keep in mind that there are many other techniques out there. This section covers those that I've found most useful; an excellent resource is Eben Hewitt's *Technology Strategy Patterns* (O'Reilly, 2018). You can also find notes I made about that book on my blog (*https://lethain.com/notes-on-the-technology-strategy-patterns*).

13

Strategy Testing for Iterative Refinement

If I could popularize only one idea about technical strategy, it would be this: prematurely rolling out a strategy prevents you from evaluating whether the strategy is effective. Pressure changes people's behavior in profound ways, and they often make those changes to create the impression that they're complying with your strategy while minimizing changes to the status quo (if you're an executive) or getting your strategy repealed (if you're not an executive). Neither is particularly helpful.

While some strategies are obviously wrong from the beginning, it's much more common to see reasonable strategies fail because they didn't get the small details right. Premature pressure is one common symptom of a more general phenomenon: most strategies are developed in a waterfall model, finalizing their approach before incorporating the lessons that reality teaches when you attempt the strategy in practice.

One effective way to avoid the waterfall strategy trap is explicitly testing your strategy to refine the details. This chapter describes the mechanics of strategy testing, including:

- When it's important to test strategy (and when it isn't)
- How to test strategy
- When you should stop testing
- Roles in strategy testing
- Metrics and meetings for strategy testing
- How to identify an untested strategy
- What to do when a strategy has progressed too far without testing

Many of the ideas in this chapter came together while I was working with Shawna Martell (*https://oreil.ly/N4No1*), Dan Fike (*https://oreil.ly/9mJYE*), Madhuri Sarma (*https://oreil.ly/RUtUk*), and many others in Carta Engineering.

When to Test Strategy

Strategy testing is ensuring that a strategy will accomplish its intended goal at a cost that you're willing to pay. This means it needs to happen before the strategy is implemented—usually in its early development stages.

Here are a few examples of when to test common strategy topics:

- If you're integrating a recent acquisition, your testing might focus on getting a single API integration working before you finalize the overall approach.
- For a developer productivity strategy that requires typing in a Python codebase, you might start by having an experienced team member type an important module.
- For a service migration, you might attempt to migrate one simple component (to test migration tooling) and one highly complex component (to test integration complexity) before moving to a broader rollout.

In every case, the two most important pieces are testing *before* finalizing the strategy, and testing *narrowly,* with a focus on the underlying mechanics of the approach. Avoid getting caught up in solving broad problems, like motivating adoption or addressing conflicting incentives.

This isn't to say that you need to test *every* strategy. A few common cases where you might *not* want to test a strategy are:

- When you're dealing with a permissive strategy (see Chapter 4) that's very cheap to apply, testing isn't always important; indeed, you can treat most highly permissive strategies as tests of whether it would be effective to implement a similar but less permissive strategy in the future.
- Sometimes testing isn't viable. For example, a hiring strategy where you shift hiring into certain regions isn't something you can test in most cases; it's something you might need to run for several years to get any meaningful signal on results.
- There are also cases where you have such high conviction in a given strategy that it's not worth testing, perhaps because you've already done

something nearly identical at the same company. Hubris comes before the fall, so I'm generally skeptical of this category.

That said, you should try very hard to find a way to test every strategy. You certainly should *not* try hard to convince yourself that testing a strategy isn't worthwhile. Testing is so, so much cheaper than implementing a bad strategy that it's almost always a good investment of time and energy.

How to Test Strategy

For a valuable step that's so often skipped, strategy testing is relatively straightforward. The approach I've found effective begins with identifying the narrowest, deepest available slice of your strategy and iterating on applying your strategy to that slice until you're confident the approach works well. For example, if you're testing a new release strategy for your Product Engineering organization, you might decide to do exactly one important release following the new approach.

As you iterate, identify metrics that help you verify the approach is working. These metrics should measure not adoption, but the impact of the change: for example, metrics showing that the new release process reduces customer impact or drives more top-of-funnel visitors.

Operate from the belief that people mean well, and that strategy failures are most likely due to excess friction and ergonomics that make adoption difficult. For example, if people aren't using the release tooling, you might assume that it's too complex; definitely *don't* assume that they're just too resistant to change.

Keep refining until you're positive that your strategy's details work in practice—or that they don't, and thus you need to approach the strategy from a new direction. For example, if the metrics you previously identified show that the new process has significantly reduced the customer impact of the new release, that's a clear sign that you need to change course.

The most important details are the things you should *not* do:

- Don't go broad in areas where impact *feels* higher but iteration cycles are slower.
- Don't get so caught up in *forcing* people to adopt the new approach that you're distracted from improving the underlying mechanics.
- Don't get so attached to your current approach that you can't accept that it might not be working. Strategy testing is only valuable because many strategies don't work as intended, and it's much cheaper to learn that early.

Testing Roles: Sponsors and Guides

Sometimes the strategy-testing process is led by one individual. However, it's more common for these responsibilities to be split between two roles: a sponsor who provides organizational authority and a guide who coordinates the day-to-day work of validating the approach.

The *sponsor* might be an executive or (at a smaller company) a principal engineer. The sponsor is responsible for:

- Making quick decisions when necessary to avoid getting stuck in the development stages
- Pushing past historical decisions and old beliefs that prevent meaningful testing
- Marshaling support across the organization
- Storytelling to stakeholders, especially the executive team, to keep funding flowing
- Preventing people from overloading the strategy (to make it solve *their* semirelated problem)
- Setting the pace to avoid stalling out
- Identifying when the energy is dropping
- Identifying when to change to the next phase of strategy building (such as from development to implementation)

The *guide* could be an engineering manager, a technical program manager, or (at a larger company) a principal engineer. The guide is responsible for:

- Translating the strategy into particulars, especially when testing gets stuck
- Identifying and addressing slowdowns and blockers
- Escalating issues to sponsor as frequently as needed
- Tracking goals and workstreams
- Maintaining the pace set by the sponsor

In terms of filling these roles, I've learned a few lessons over time. For sponsors, what matters the most is that they're genuinely authorized by the company to make the decisions they're making, and that they care enough about the impact that they're willing to make difficult decisions quickly. A sponsor is only meaningful to the extent that they're available to rapidly resolve any issues the guide escalates to them. If they aren't available for escalations or don't resolve them quickly, they're a poor sponsor.

For a guide, you need someone who can execute at the sponsor's pace without getting derailed by various organizational messes and who has good, nuanced judgment relevant to the strategy being tested. The worst guides are ideological (they reject the results of testing) or easily derailed. You're likely testing *because* there's friction somewhere, so someone who can't navigate friction is going to fail by default.

Meetings and Metrics

The only absolute requirement for the strategy-testing phase is that the sponsor, guide, and any other key folks working on the strategy *must meet every single week*. Within that meeting, you'll iterate on which metrics capture the current areas you're trying to refine, discuss what you've learned from prior metrics or data, and schedule one-off follow-ups to ensure you're making progress.

The best version of this meeting is heavy on debugging and light on presentation. Look with some suspicion at any week where you're not learning something that informs subsequent testing or making a decision that modifies your approach to testing. It might mean that you've underresourced the testing effort or that your testing approach is too ambitious, but it's a meaningful signal that testing isn't showing enough promise to maintain attention.

If all of this seems like an overly large commitment, I'd push you to consider your strategy altitude to adjust the volume or permissiveness of the strategy you're working on. If a strategy isn't worth testing, then it's either already quite good (which should be widely evident) or only worth rolling out in a highly permissive format.

Identifying Untested Strategies

While not all strategies *must* be refined by a testing phase, essentially all failing strategies skip the testing phase to move directly into implementation. Strategies that skip testing *sound right*, but don't accomplish much. For instance, fully standardizing authorization and authentication across your company on one implementation *sounds right*, but can still fail—for example, if each team is responsible for its own approach to determining the standard.

One particularly obvious pattern is something I describe as "pressure without a plan." This is a strategy that *sounds right* but lacks concrete details.

Service migrations are particularly prone to this—perhaps due to apocryphal descriptions of Amazon's service migration in the 2000s, which is often summarized as a top-down, zero-details mandate to switch away from the monolith.

Identification comes down to understanding two things. First, *are there numbers that show the strategy is driving the desired impact?* For example, tracking API requests to the new authentication service as a percentage of all authentication requests is more meaningful than a spreadsheet tracking whether each team has formally committed to moving to the new service. Try to avoid proxy metrics when possible; look at the actual thing that matters.

Second, if the numbers aren't moving, *is there a clear mechanism for debugging and solving those issues, and is this team actually making progress?* For example, a team supporting adoption of a new authentication service might look slow as it designs an approach to migrating existing services to fit the new service's design, but it's still making progress as long as it's uncovering a path forward.

Because the numbers aren't moving, you need to find a different source of meaningful evidence to validate that progress is happening. Generally, the best bet is new software running in a meaningful environment (for product code, that would be the production environment). It's also useful to talk with skeptics or veterans of failed integrations, but be cautious of debugging exclusively with skeptics. They're almost always right, but often aren't describing current problems.

Unless the answer to one of these questions is *obviously yes*, then it's very likely that you've found a strategy that hasn't been tested.

Recovering from Skipped Testing

Once you've recognized a strategy that skipped testing and is now struggling, the next question is what to do about it. The strategy doc "Should We Decompose Our Monolith?" (Document 20-1) looks at recovering from a failing service migration, and is lightly based on my experience dealing with similarly stuck service migrations at both Calm and Carta. The answer to a stuck strategy is always to write a new strategy, and *don't* skip testing this time.

Typically, this means explicitly pausing the struggling strategy while you run a new testing phase. This is painful to do, because the people invested in the current strategy will be upset with you—but there will always be people who disagree with any change. In the long term, the only thing that makes most people happy is a successful strategy, and anything that delays progress toward that is a poor investment.

Sometimes it is difficult to pause a struggling strategy *officially*, in which case you have to look for an indirect mechanism to pause it *implicitly*. For example, delaying new services while you take a month to invest in improving service provisioning might give you enough breathing room to test the missing mechanisms from your strategy, without anyone losing face over a failing migration. It would be nice to always be able to say these things out loud, but managing personalities is an enduring leadership challenge; even when you're an executive, you just have a different set of messy stakeholders.

Summary

Testing doesn't determine whether a strategy might be good. It exposes the missing details required to translate a directionally accurate strategy into a strategy that *works*. After reading this chapter, you know how sponsors and guides lead that translation process. You can set up and run the necessary meetings to test a strategy and also put together metrics to determine if the strategy is ready for a broader rollout.

Systems Modeling

While I was probably late to learn the concept of strategy testing, I might have learned about systems modeling too early, stumbling on Donella Meadows's *Thinking in Systems: A Primer* (Chelsea Green, 2008) before I had a clear set of problems to apply its techniques against. Fortunately, I remembered those lessons as I began my software career, and over time I've discovered a number of ways to use systems modeling. While systems modeling isn't perfect, it remains the most effective, flexible tool I've found to debug complex problems.

This chapter starts with a two-minute primer on the basics of systems modeling, then covers how to implement these approaches with examples from a number of systems models created to refine the strategies discussed throughout this book. It ends with resources for those looking for a deeper exploration. I'll cover:

- When systems modeling is (or isn't) the right technique
- Tooling
- How to build a systems model
- How to document and communicate what you learn from a systems model
- What systems modeling can and can't do

After working through this chapter's overview of systems modeling, you can see the approaches implemented in a number of systems models created to refine the strategies throughout this book. The theory of systems modeling is certainly interesting, but hopefully seeing real models in support of concrete engineering strategies will be even more useful.

A Two-Minute Primer

If you want an exceptional introduction to systems thinking, there's no better place to go than *Thinking in Systems*. If you want a worse, but shorter, introduction, see my essay "Introduction to Systems Thinking" (*https://lethain.com/systems-thinking*), which is also available in my book *An Elegant Puzzle: Systems of Engineering Management* (Stripe Press, 2019).

If you want something *even shorter*, Figure 14-1 is the briefest summary I can manage.

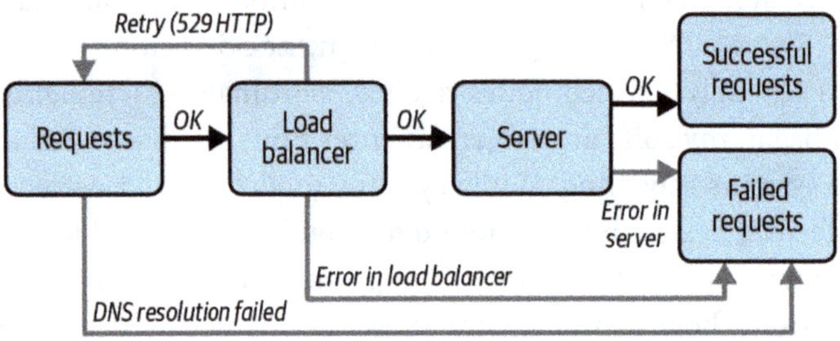

Figure 14-1. Requests succeeding and failing between a user, load balancer, and server

In systems modeling, anything that can accumulate is called a *stock*. For example, each of the boxes in the systems model shown in Figure 14-1 (Requests, Server, and so on) represents a stock. Changes to stocks are called *flows*. Every arrow between stocks (like "OK" or "Error in server") represents a flow.

Systems modeling is the practice of using various configurations of stocks and flows to understand circumstances and behaviors that might otherwise be surprising or too slow to understand from measurement. For example, you can use this model to explore the tradeoffs between a load balancer that caps throughput to a load-sensitive service behind it and one that does not, as shown in Figure 14-2.

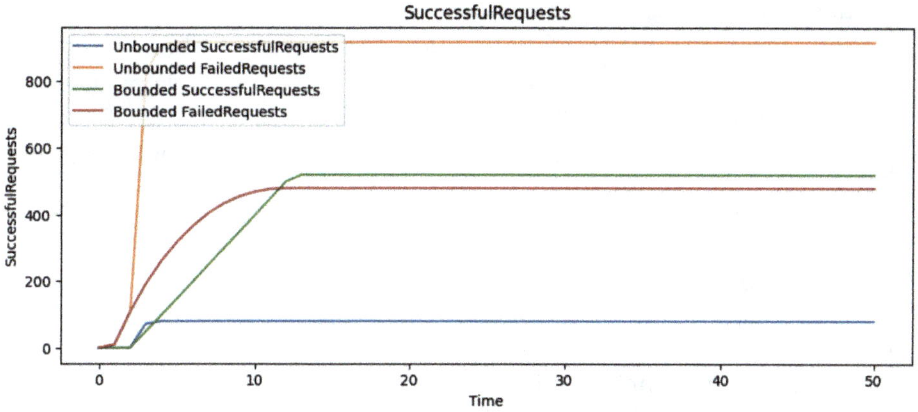

Figure 14-2. Successful and errored requests in two different scenarios

Without a model, you might get into a philosophical debate about how ridiculous it is that the downstream server is load-sensitive. With the model, it's immediately obvious that the downstream server is worth protecting, even if it is concerningly sensitive. This is what models do: they create a cheap way to understand reality when fully understanding it would be too cumbersome.

More Systems Thinking Resources

- *Thinking in Systems: A Primer* by Donella Meadows (Chelsea Green, 2008)
- *Business Dynamics: Systems Thinking and Modeling for a Complex World* by John D. Sterman (McGraw-Hill, 2000)
- *An Introduction to Systems Thinking* by Barry Richmond (Isee Systems, 2004)

When Is Systems Modeling Useful?

Although refinement is an important step in developing any strategy, some refinement techniques work better for any given strategy. Systems modeling is extremely useful in three distinct scenarios:

When you're unsure where the leverage points might be in a complex system
: Modeling allows you to cheaply test which levers might be meaningful. For example, modeling Uber's strategy for onboarding new drivers (Document 17-4) showed that improving onboarding was less important than reengaging departed drivers.

When you have significant data to compare against
: Having lots of data allows you to focus on the places where the real data and your model are in tension. For example, I was able to model the impact of hiring on Uber's engineering productivity (*https://lethain.com/productivity-in-the-age-of-hypergrowth*), then compare that with internal data.

When stakeholders' disagreements are based on their unstated intuitions
: Models can turn those intuitions into something structured that can be debated more effectively.

In all three categories, modeling makes it possible to iterate your thinking much faster than running a live process or technology experiment with your team. I sometimes hear concerns that modeling slows things down, but this is just an issue of familiarity. Once you get some practice, modeling can be faster than asking for advice from industry peers. The models I developed for this book took less than an hour each. (With one notable exception: modeling LLMs' impacts on developer experience took much longer, because I deliberately used an impractical tool to reveal the importance of good tooling.)

Additionally, systems modeling often exposes counterintuitive dimensions to the problem you're working on. For example, my experience with the LLM model suggests that effective LLMs might cause us to spend *more* time writing and testing code, but *less* time fixing issues discovered after that code goes to production. You might imagine they'd reduce testing time, but the model shows that reducing testing time is only valuable to the extent that the issues identified in production remain at worst constant. If any issues found in production increase, then reducing testing time does not contribute to increased productivity.

Modeling without praxis creates unsubstantiated conviction: true understanding comes from applying ideas to real situations. However, in combination with learning from applying your models, I've encountered few other techniques that can similarly accelerate learning.

That doesn't mean that systems modeling is always the ideal refinement technique. If you're already sure about your general approach and want to refine the narrow details, then strategy testing is a better option. If you're trying to understand the evolution of a wider ecosystem, you may prefer Wardley mapping.

Tooling

While the idea is quite intuitive, the *tools* of systems modeling are a real obstacle to wider adoption. The tooling ecosystem for systems modeling has been fragmented for some time, perhaps because many of the tools that were popular early on were quite expensive. A mix of complex requirements, patent consolidation, and a perceived small market size have also discouraged a modern solution from consolidating the tooling market.

Earlier, I mentioned that systems modeling is extremely quick, but that many folks find it slow and laborious. Part of that is an issue of practice, but I suspect that tooling quality is at least as big a part of the challenge. In the LLM impact model in Chapter 17, I went through the steps of building the model in an increasingly messy spreadsheet. This was slow, challenging, and extremely brittle. Even after finishing the model, I couldn't extend it effectively to test new ideas, and I inadvertently introduced a number of bugs into the implementation.

Going in the opposite direction, I explored some potentially simpler toolchains than the one I typically rely on, including SageModeler (*https://oreil.ly/9c2Gt*) and Insight Maker (*https://insightmaker.com*). There are many of these introductory toolchains for systems modeling, but I generally find that they're either constrained in their capabilities, have a fairly high learning curve, or make it difficult to share your model with others.

In the end, I wound up back at a toolchain I wrote some years ago: `lethain/systems` (*https://github.com/lethain/systems*). It's far from perfect, but I think it's a relatively effective mechanism for demonstrating systems modeling for a few reasons:

- It's a quick way to create and iterate on models.
- It's an easy way to share models.
- It leaves relatively little surface area for bugs in your models.
- It's a free, open source, and self-hosted toolchain.
- It integrates well with the Jupyter ecosystem for diagramming, modeling, and so on.

You should absolutely pick *any* tool that feels right to you and practice with it until you feel confident modeling scenarios quickly. After that, I wouldn't recommend spending too much time thinking about tools at all: the most important thing is to build models and learn from them quickly, and almost any tool will be sufficient for that goal with some deliberate practice.

How to Model

Learning to model systems takes practice, so I'll approach the details of learning to model from two directions: first, by documenting a general approach; second, by providing breadcrumbs for deeper exploration of the models developed in this book.

The systems modeling structure I find effective is as follows:

1. Sketch the stocks and flows on paper or in a diagramming application (like Excalidraw (*https://excalidraw.com*), Figma, or Whimsical). Use whatever you're comfortable with.
2. Reason about how you would expect a potential change to shift the flows through the diagram. Which flows do you expect to go up and which go down, and how would that movement help you evaluate whether your strategy is working?
3. Model the stocks and flows in your spreadsheet tool of choice. Start by modeling the flows from left to right (the "happy path" flows). Once you have that fully working, then start modeling the right-to-left flows (the "exception path" flows).
4. Exercise the model by experimenting with a number of different starting values and determining how the rates influence the model's values. This is essentially performing sensitivity analysis (*https://oreil.ly/GqJR-*).
5. Document your work in a standalone writeup. You can then link to that writeup from any other strategies that benefit from a given model's insights. You might link to any section of your strategy, depending on what topic the particular model explores. I recommend decoupling models from specific strategies, as *generally* the details of any given model are a distraction from understanding a strategy. It's best to avoid that distraction unless a reader is surprised by the conclusion, in which case the link lets them drill into the details.

This is the sequence of steps I generally follow, and I'd encourage you to do the same, but you should adapt them to solve the particular problems at hand. Over time, most of these steps—excluding documentation—turn into a single iterative process. I document everything after several iterations.

Deeper Exploration

Now that we've covered the overarching approach to systems modeling, here are the breadcrumbs to specific models that go deeper on particular elements:

- Document 17-4 explores how the driver lifecycle at Theoretical Ride Sharing might be improved with LLMs and introduces using the `lethain/systems` library (*https://github.com/lethain/systems*) for modeling.
- Document 17-2 looks at how LLMs might impact developer experience at Theoretical Ride Sharing, and demonstrates (the downsides of) modeling with a spreadsheet.
- Document 18-1 studies the financial consequences of various policies for how we backfill departed engineers in an engineering organization, and introduces further `lethain/systems` features (*https://github.com/lethain/systems*).
- Document 16-2 determines whether it's possible to optimize an existing service provisioning workflow or if it instead needs to be replaced with a self-service workflow.

Beyond these models, you can find other systems models that I've written in my blog's systems-thinking category (*https://lethain.com/tags/systems-thinking*).

How to Document a Model

Communicating with models in a professional setting is challenging. The core problem is that there are many distinct groups of model readers. Some will lack familiarity with the tooling you use to develop models. Others will try to refine—or invalidate—your model by digging into the details.

I navigate those mismatches by focusing first on the audience that is least likely to dig into the model. I still want to keep all the details handy—ideally in the rawest form possible, to allow others to manipulate the model themselves—but that's very much my secondary goal when documenting a model.

I recommend the following order, which I used for the models in this book:

- Learning section, with charts showing what the model has taught you
- Sketch and explain the stocks and flows
- Reason about what the sketch itself teaches you

- Explain how you developed the model, with an emphasis on any particularly complex portions
- Exercise the model by testing how changing the flows and stocks leads to different outcomes

If you remember nothing else, remember this: most people don't care how you built the model—they just want the insights. Your document should reflect that reality. Give them the insights early, and assume no one will trust your model nearly as much as you do. Models are an *input* into a strategy, but never a reliable sole backer.

What Systems Modeling Isn't

Although I find systems modeling a uniquely powerful way to accelerate learning, I've also encountered many practitioners who believe that their models *are* reality rather than *reflecting* reality. Over time, I've developed a short list of cautions to help would-be modelers avoid overcommitting to their model's insights:

When your model and reality conflict, reality is always right
: At Stripe, we developed a model to guide our reliability strategy (*https://lethain.com/modeling-reliability*). The model was intuitively quite good, but its real-world results were mixed. Our attachment to our early model distracted us: we spent too much time collecting and classifying data and were slow to engage with the most important problems: maximizing the impact of scarce mitigation bandwidth, and growing that mitigation bandwidth. We'd have been more impactful if we'd engaged directly with the lessons reality was teaching us rather than looking for reasons to disregard them.

Models are immutable, but reality isn't
: I once joined an organization that was investing tremendous energy into hiring, yet struggling to hire. Their intuitive model pushed them to spend years investing into optimizing the top of their funnel, and later steered them to improve the closing process. What they weren't able to detect was that the largest hurdle in their hiring process was a misalignment among their own interviewers' expectations (*https://lethain.com/getting-to-yes*).

Every model omits information; some omit critical information
: The service migration at Uber (Document 16-1) is a great example: modeling clarified that we *had* to adopt a more aggressive approach to succeed. We did succeed, but the model didn't study the consequences of completing

the migration, which included a very challenging development environment. The model captured everything my team cared about as the team responsible for running the migration, but did nothing to evaluate whether the migration was a good idea overall.

In each of those situations, two things are true: the model was extremely valuable, and the model subtly led us astray. We would have been led astray even without a model. The key thing to remember isn't that models are inherently misleading: it's that the real risk is being overly confident about your model. Modeling is a powerful tool to use in tandem with judgment—not a replacement for judgment.

Summary

Systems modeling isn't perfect. As noted previously, if you've already determined your strategy and want to refine the details, strategy testing is probably a better choice. If you're trying to understand the dynamics of an evolving ecosystem, try Wardley mapping.

However, if you have the general shape but lack conviction on how the pieces fit together, systems modeling is a remarkable tool. After this chapter, you know how to select appropriate tooling and use that tooling to model your problem. In Part IV of this book, I'll model a handful of detailed problems to provide concrete examples of applying this technique.

Wardley Maps

Of the three core strategy-refinement techniques, this is the technique that I've personally used the least. Despite that, I decided to include it in this book because it highlights how many different techniques can be used for refining strategy, and how it's never too late to keep expanding your toolkit.

Whereas techniques like systems thinking and strategy testing often zoom in, Wardley mapping is remarkably effective at zooming out. It's particularly effective at looking at the broader ecosystems in which your organization exists.

This chapter starts with a 10-minute primer on Wardley mapping, then provides:

- Tool recommendations
- When Wardley maps are an ideal strategy refinement tool, and when they're not
- The process I use to map
- How to integrate a Wardley map into your strategy creation process
- Breadcrumbs to example Wardley maps
- How to document a Wardley map in the context of a strategy writeup

After working through this chapter and digging into some of this book's examples of Wardley maps, you'll have a good background to start your own mapping practice.

Wardley Mapping: A 10-Minute Primer

Wardley maps are a technique to ensure your strategy is grounded in reality—or, as mapping practitioners would say, for creating situational awareness. It was created by Simon Wardley in 2005, and if you have a few days, you might want to start by reading Wardley's book on the topic, *Wardley Maps* (*https://oreil.ly/MEXtt*), available online for free on Medium. If you only have 10 minutes, then this section should be enough to get you up to speed on reading Wardley maps.

As a practical example, I'll walk you through how to create a Wardley map that aims to understand a knowledge-base management product (along the lines of a wiki, like Confluence or Notion). We'll start from the map shown in Figure 15-1.

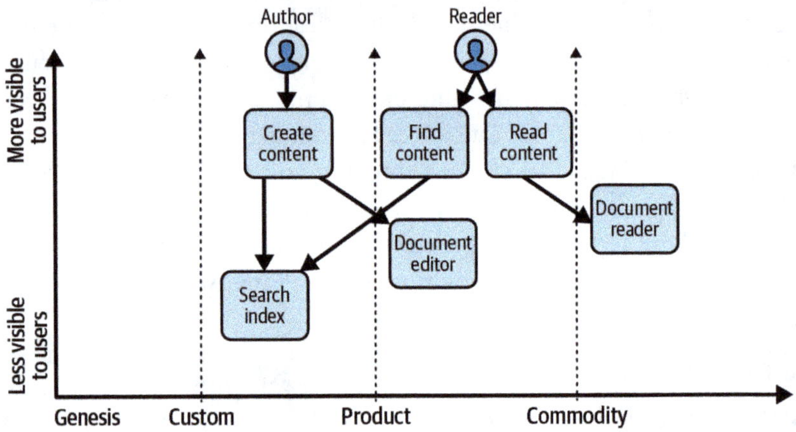

Figure 15-1. Wardley map for a knowledge-base management application

You need to know three foundational concepts to read a Wardley map: its components, its x-axis, and its y-axis.

COMPONENTS OF A WARDLEY MAP

Maps are populated with three kinds of components: users, needs, and capabilities. *Users* exist at the top, and represent a cohort of users who will use your product. Each kind of user has a specific set of *needs*, generally tasks that they need to accomplish. Fulfilling each need requires certain capabilities. Any box connecting directly to a user is a need.

Any box connecting to a need is a *capability*. A capability can be connected to any number of needs, but can never connect directly to a user; they connect to users only indirectly, via needs.

X-AXIS

The x-axis is divided into four segments, representing how commoditized a capability is. On the far left is *genesis*, which represents a brand-new capability that hasn't existed before. On the far right is *commodity*, something so standard and expected that it's unremarkable, like turning on a switch causing electricity to flow. In between are *custom* and *product*, the two categories where most items fall on the map. *Custom* represents something that requires specialized expertise and operation to function, such as a web application that requires software engineers to build and maintain. *Product* represents something that can generally be bought.

In this map, document reading is commoditized: it's unremarkable if your application allows its users to read content. On the other hand, document editing is somewhat on the border of product and custom. You might integrate an existing vendor for document editing needs or you might build a tool yourself, but in either case, document editing is less commoditized than document reading.

Y-AXIS

The y-axis represents *visibility to the user*. In this map, reading documents is something that is extremely visible to the user. On the other hand, even though users depend on new documents being indexed for search, they generally have no visibility into the indexing process and often don't even know that you have a search index to begin with.

Although maps can get quite complex, those three concepts are generally sufficient to allow you to decode one.

In addition to mapping the current state, Wardley maps are also excellent for exploring how circumstances might change over time. To illustrate that, let's look at a second iteration of our map (Figure 15-2). Pay particular attention to the red arrow, which indicates capabilities that are expected to change in the future.

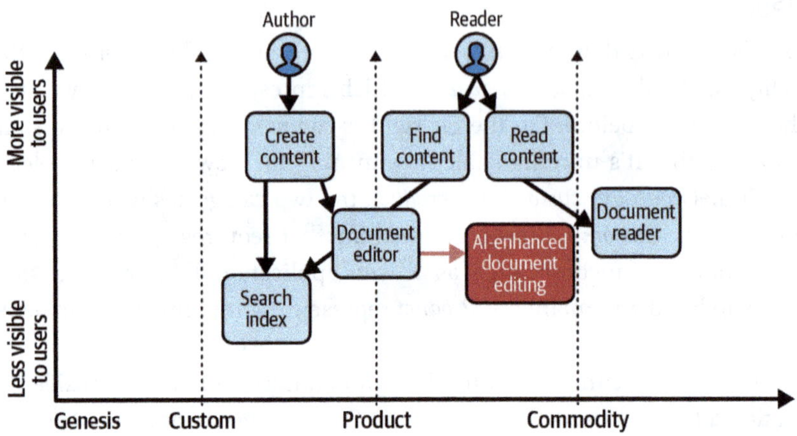

Figure 15-2. Mapping AI-enhanced document editing as the future state of document editing

The updated map now indicates that the current document-creation experience will be superseded by an AI-enhanced editing process. Critically, it also predicts that the AI-enhanced process will be more commoditized than the current authoring experience, perhaps because the enhancement will be driven by commoditized foundational models from providers like Anthropic and OpenAI. Building on that, the only place left in the map for meaningful differentiation is in search indexing. Either the knowledge-base company needs to accept the implication that it will increasingly be a search company, or it needs to expand the set of user needs it serves to find a new avenue for differentiation.

Some maps show the evolution of a given capability using a *pipeline*, a box that describes a series of expected improvements in a capability over time (Figure 15-3).

Now, instead of simply indicating that the authoring experience may be replaced by an AI-enhanced capability over time, the map expresses a sequence of steps. From the starting place of a typical editing experience, the next expected step is AI-assisted creation, and then finally AI-led creation, where the author only provides high-level direction to a machine-learning–powered agent.

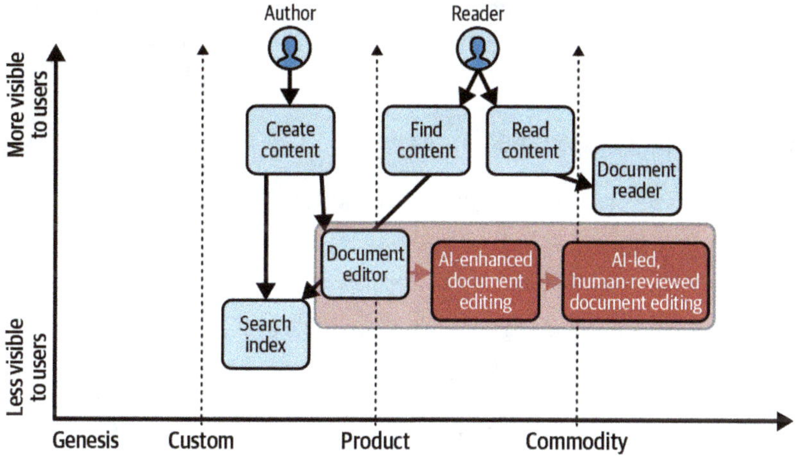

Figure 15-3. A pipeline showing the evolution of document editing

For completeness, it's also worth mentioning that some Wardley maps will have an *overlay*, which is a box to group capabilities or requirements together by some common denominator, as shown in Figure 15-4. This usually happens to indicate the teams responsible for various capabilities, but the technique can be used to emphasize any interesting element of a map's topology.

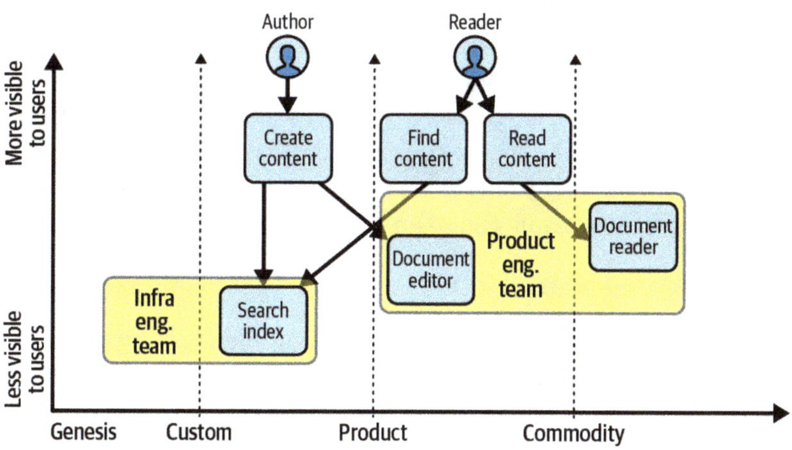

Figure 15-4. A map overlay showing which teams own which capabilities

Maps you encounter in the wild might appear significantly more complex than these initial examples, but they'll be composed of the same fundamental elements.

More Wardley Mapping Resources

- *The Value Flywheel Effect* (*https://oreil.ly/WR2NB*) by David Anderson
- *Wardley Maps* (*https://oreil.ly/MEXtt*) by Simon Wardley on Medium, also available as a PDF (*https://oreil.ly/sXhPw*)
- Learn Wardley Mapping (*https://oreil.ly/xiDdy*) by Ben Mosior
- WardleyMaps.com's resources (*https://oreil.ly/HK3HK*) and @WardleyMaps on YouTube (*https://oreil.ly/sclmb*)

Tools for Wardley Mapping

You learned in Chapter 14 that systems modeling has a serious tooling problem, which often prevents would-be adopters from developing their systems modeling practice. Fortunately, Wardley mapping doesn't suffer from that problem. You can simply print out a Wardley map and draw on it by hand. You can also use OmniGraffle, Miro, Figma, or whatever diagramming tool you're already familiar with. There are more focused tools as well; Ben Mosior has pulled together an excellent writeup on Wardley mapping tools as of 2024 (*https://oreil.ly/Nns2O*).

I'd strongly encourage you to start with Mapkeep (*https://mapkeep.com*), which is a simple, free, and intuitive tool for your initial mapping needs. After you've gotten some practice, you may want to move back into your familiar diagramming tool to make it easier to collaborate with colleagues. Initially, though, prioritize the simplest tool you can, to avoid losing learning momentum as you deal with configuration, setup, and so on.

When Are Wardley Maps Useful?

All successful strategy begins with understanding the constraints and circumstances within which the strategy needs to work. Wardley mapping labels that understanding as situational awareness, and creating situational awareness is the foremost goal of mapping.

Situational awareness is always useful, but it's particularly essential in highly dynamic environments, where the industry around you, the competitors you're selling against, and/or the capabilities powering your product are shifting rapidly. In the past several decades there have been a number of these dynamic contexts, including the rise of web applications, the proliferation of mobile devices, and the expansion of machine learning techniques.

When you're in such environments, it's obvious that the world is changing rapidly. What's sometimes easy to miss is that any strategy that needs to last longer than a year or two is built on an evolving foundation, even if things seem very stable at the time. For example, in the early 2010s, startups like Facebook, Uber, and Digg were all operating in physical datacenters with their own hardware. Over the next five years, as cloud-based infrastructure rapidly expanded, having a presence in a physical datacenter went from the default approach for startups to a relatively unconventional solution. Any strategy written in 2010 that imagined the world of hosting as static was destined to be invalidated.

No tool is universally effective, and that's true here as well. While Wardley maps are extremely helpful at helping people understand broad change, they're less helpful in the details. If you're looping to optimize your onboarding funnel, then something like systems modeling or strategy testing is likely going to serve you better.

How to Wardley Map

Learning Wardley mapping is a mix of reading others' maps and writing your own. I'd recommend skimming all of the maps collected in the following section as well. In this section are the concrete steps I encourage you to follow as you create your first map:

Step 1. Commit to starting small and iterating
: Simple maps are the foundations of complex maps. Even the smallest Wardley map will have enough detail to reveal something interesting about the environment you're operating in. Conversely, if your map is complex from the start, it's easy to get caught up in all of its imperfections. At worst, this will cause you to lose momentum in creating the map; at best, it will accidentally steer your attention rather than facilitating discovery of which details are important to focus on.

Step 2. List users, needs, and capabilities
: Identify the first one or two users for your product by function. In the knowledge management example earlier in this chapter, your two initial users might be an author and a reader. From there, identify those users' needs, such as authoring content, finding content, and providing feedback on which content is helpful. Finally, write down the underlying technical

capabilities necessary to support those needs, like indexing content in a search index or creating a customer-support process to deal with frustrated users.

Remember to start small! On your first pass, it's fine to focus on a single user. As you iterate on your map, bring in more users, needs, and capabilities until the map conveys something useful. Tooling for this can be a piece of paper or wherever you keep notes.

Step 3. Establish value chains

Take your list and then connect each of the components into chains, from user to need to capability. For example, you'd connect the reader of the knowledge-base example to the need to discover content. Then you could connect that need to the capability to index for search. That sequence, from reader to discovering content to search index, represents one value chain.

Convergence across chains is a good thing. As your chains get more comprehensive, any given capability is likely to be referenced by multiple different needs. Similarly, it's expected that multiple users might have a shared need.

Step 4. Plot your value chains on a Wardley map

You can do this using any of the tools discussed in the section "Tools for Wardley Mapping" on page 128, including a piece of paper. Because you have already created the value chains, what you're focused on in this step is placing each component relative to its visibility to users and maturity. Higher up is more visible to the user, lower down is less visible; leftward represents more custom solutions, rightward represents most commoditized solutions.

Step 5. Study the current state of the map

With the value chains plotted, your map will begin to reveal where your organization's attention should be focused and what complexity you can delegate to vendors. Jot down any realizations you have as you study this topology.

Step 6. Predict how the map will evolve

Create a second version of your map that includes your predicted changes. (Keep the previous version so you can better see the evolution of your thinking!)

It can be helpful to create multiple maps that contemplate different scenarios. Thinking about the knowledge-base example, you might first contemplate a future where AI-powered tools become the dominant mechanism for authors creating content. Then you could explore another future where AI has been regulated out of most tools, and imagine how that would shape your approach differently.

Your time frame for these changes will vary, depending on the environment you're mapping. Always prefer a time frame that makes it easy to believe the changes will happen—whether that's five years or one. If you're caught up wondering whether change might take longer than a certain time frame, simply extend your time frame to sidestep that issue.

Step 7. Study the future state of the map

Now that you've predicted the future, study this new map. Write down any unexpected implications of this evolution, and note how you may need to adjust your approach as a result.

Step 8. Share the map with others for feedback

It's impossible for anyone to know everything, which is why the best maps tend to be communal creations. That's not to suggest that you should perform every step in a broad community or that your map should be the consensus of a working group. Instead, you should test your map against other people. See what they find insightful and what they find artificial in it, and include that in your map's topology.

Step 9. Document what you've learned

I'll discuss this more next, in the section on documentation. You should also connect your Wardley map writeup with your overall strategy document, typically in the *Refine* or *Explore* sections.

One downside of presenting steps for doing something is that the sequence can become a fixed recipe. The method presented here is far from the canonical way. These are simply the steps that I've found most useful, and I'd encourage you to try them if mapping is a new tool in your toolkit. Start here, then experiment with other approaches until you find the best approach for you and the strategies that you're working on.

Breadcrumbs for Wardley Map Examples

With the foundation in place, the best way to build on Wardley mapping is to write your own maps. The second-best way is to read existing maps that others have made, a number of which exist within Part IV of this book. For instance, Chapter 17 studies the evolution of the LLM ecosystem, and how that will impact product engineering organizations attempting to validate and deploy new paradigms like agentic workflows and retrieval augmented generation.

In addition to the maps within this book, I also label maps that I created on my blog using the Wardley category (*https://lethain.com/tags/wardley*). For example, "Measuring developer experience, benchmarks, and providing a theory of improvement" (*https://lethain.com/measuring-developer-experience-benchmarks-theory-of-improvement*) explores how Wardley mapping has helped me refine my understanding of how the developer experience ecosystem will evolve over time.

How to Document a Wardley Map

As explored in Chapter 11, it's always tempting to structure documents around the creation process. However, it's essentially always better to write in two steps. First develop a writing-optimized version that's focused on facilitating your thinking. Then rework it into a reading-optimized version that supports both readers who are interested in the details and those who are not.

The process in the previous section is the writing-optimized version. For a reading-optimized version, I recommend three sections:

How things work today
: This section should begin with a map of the current environment, explain any interesting rationales or controversies behind placements on the map, and highlight the most interesting parts.

Transition to future state
: This section should start with a second map showing the transition from the current state to a projected future state. It's very reasonable to have multiple distinct maps, each of which considers one potential evolution or one step of a longer evolution.

Users and value chains
: Users and value chains are the first place you start when creating a Wardley map, but generally the least interesting part of explaining that map's implications. This isn't because the value chains are unimportant—it's because the map itself tends to implicitly explain the value chain enough that you can move directly to focusing on the map's most interesting implications.

For a sufficiently complex map, you could certainly split users and value chains into two sections, but generally, covering users and value chains in one joint section rather than separately eliminates redundancy.

> This is a good example of the difference between reading and writing: splitting these two topics helps writers clarify their thinking, but muddles the experience of reading.

This ordering may seem too brief or a bit counterintuitive for you, as the person who has the full set of details, but my experience is that it will be simpler to read for most readers. That's because most readers read until they agree with the conclusion, then stop reading, and are only interested in the details if they disagree with the conclusion.

This format is also fairly different from the format I recommend for documenting systems models. That is because systems model diagrams exclude much of the relevant detail, showing the relationship between stocks but not showing the magnitude of the flows. You can only fully understand a systems model by seeing both the diagram and a chart showing the model's output. Wardley maps, on the other hand, tend to be more self-explanatory, and often can stand on their own with relatively less written description.

What About Doctrines and Gameplay?

This book's components of strategy, as laid out in Chapter 5, are most heavily influenced by Richard Rumelt's approach. Simon Wardley's approach to strategy, built around Wardley mapping, could be viewed as a competing lens. For each problem that Rumelt's system solves, there is a Wardley solution as well. Thus, I think it's worth mentioning some of the components I haven't included and why I left them out.

The two most important components I've not discussed thus far are Wardley's ideas of doctrine (*https://oreil.ly/pGYHM*) and gameplay (*https://oreil.ly/ILSLT*). *Doctrine*, as Wardley uses it, refers to universally applicable practices like knowing your users, biasing toward data, and designing for constant evolution. *Gameplay* is similar to doctrine, but context-dependent rather than universal. Some examples of gameplay are talent raiding (hiring from knowledgeable competitors), bundling (selling products together rather than separately), and exploiting network effects.

I decided not to spend much time on doctrine and gameplay because I find them lightly specialized for the needs of business strategy, and consequently a bit messy to apply to the engineering strategy problems that this book is most interested in solving.

I don't personally view Rumelt's approach and Wardley's approaches as competing efforts. What's most valuable to me is to have a broad toolkit and pull in the tools that feel most applicable to the problems at hand. I find Wardley maps exceptionally valuable for enhancing exploration, diagnosis, and refinement in some problems. In other problems, typically those that are of a shorter duration or more internally oriented, I find the Rumelt playbook more applicable. In all problems, I find the combination more valuable than anchoring in one camp's perspective.

Summary

No refinement technique will let you reliably predict the future, but Wardley mapping is very effective at helping you plot out the various potential futures in which your strategy might need to operate. With those futures in mind, you can tune your strategy to excel in those that are most likely, and to weather the less desirable ones.

It took me years to dive into Wardley mapping. Once I finally did, it was simpler than I'd feared, and now I find myself creating Wardley maps somewhat frequently. The next time you're working on a strategy that's impacted by the ecosystem evolving around it, try your hand at mapping—and soon you'll start to build your own collection of maps (*https://lethain.com/tags/wardley*).

PART | IV

Case Studies

Chapter 1 started with a commitment to grounding its approach in concrete case studies. In this section, I'm living up to that commitment by presenting 10 real-world strategies I've directly worked on or observed. These strategies take the somewhat abstract concepts I've covered thus far and materialize them into concrete ideas, hopefully making them easier to grasp and apply.

The first five strategies are selected to show a varied mix of refinement techniques and operational mechanisms. The next five strategies are organized by the companies in which they were implemented. If you work through these case studies and find yourself wanting more, the Appendix includes suggestions for further study.

16

Service Migration Strategy

In early 2014, I joined Uber as an engineering manager for the Infrastructure team. We were responsible for a wide range of tasks, including provisioning new services. While the overall team I led grew significantly over time, the subset working on service provisioning never grew beyond four engineers.

Those four engineers successfully migrated 1,000+ services onto a new, future-proofed service platform. More importantly, that small team did it while absorbing the majority, although certainly not the entirety, of the migration workload rather than spreading it across the 2,000+ engineers working at Uber at the time. Their strategy serves as an interesting case study of how a team can drive strategy, even without any executive sponsor, by focusing on solving a pressing user problem—and providing effective ergonomics while doing so.

Reading These Documents

The documents in this chapter are recreations intended to capture my time at Uber, and they are written from the perspective of 2014. Read them as internal documents, written from the service provisioning team's perspective. They are:

Document 16-1: Service Migration Strategy
: The Infrastructure team's approach to facilitating migration out of Uber's Python monolith.

Document 16-2: Service Onboarding Model
: A systems model of why service provisioning was going slowly.

Document 16-3: Wardley Mapping the Service Orchestration Ecosystem
: A Wardley map of how we predicted service orchestration would evolve.

You can find the full implementation of the service onboarding systems model on GitHub (*https://github.com/lethain/eng-strategy-models/blob/main/UberServiceOnboarding.ipynb*).

If you're reading these documents with the goal of applying the strategies they put forward, start at the top and read to the end. If, on the other hand, your main goal is to understand the thinking behind them, read the sections in reverse order, starting with *Explore*, then *Diagnose*, and so on. Chapter 11 explains this approach to separating reading from thinking and details the general structure of strategy documents. Chapters 14 and 15 provide similar guides to reading and writing systems models and Wardley maps, respectively. Read on for the documents themselves. My commentary appears in the footnotes.

Document 16-1: Service Migration Strategy: Uber

POLICY AND OPERATION

We've adopted these guiding principles for extending Uber's service platform:[1]

- *Constrain manual provisioning allocation to maximize investment in self-service provisioning.* The service provisioning team will maintain a fixed allocation of one full-time engineer on manual service-provisioning tasks. We will move the remaining engineers to work on automation to speed up future service provisioning. This will degrade manual provisioning in the short term, but the alternative is permanently degrading provisioning by the influx of new service requests from newly hired product engineers.
- *Self-service must be safely usable by a new hire without Uber context.* It is possible today to make a Puppet or Clusto change while provisioning a new service that negatively impacts the production environment. This must not be true in any self-service solution.
- *Move to structured requests, and out of tickets.* Missing or incorrect information in provisioning requests creates significant delays in provisioning. Further, collecting this information is the first step of moving to a self-service process. As such, we can get paid twice by reducing errors in manual provisioning while also creating the interface for self-service workflows.

1 Relative to the default structure, this document makes one tweak: folding the *Operation* section in with *Policy*.

- *Prefer initializing new services with good defaults rather than requiring user input.* Most new services are provisioned for new projects with strong timeline pressure but little certainty on their long-term requirements. These users cannot accurately predict their future needs, and expecting them to do so creates significant friction.

  Instead, the provisioning framework should suggest good defaults, and make it easy to change the settings later when users have more clarity. The gate from development environment to production environment is a particularly effective one for ensuring settings are refreshed.

We are materializing those principles into this sequenced set of tasks:

1. Create an internal tool that coordinates service provisioning, replacing the process where teams request new services via Phabricator tickets. This new tool will maintain a schema of required fields that must be supplied, with the aim of eliminating the majority of back and forth between teams during service provisioning.
2. In addition to capturing necessary data, this will also serve as our interface for automating various steps in provisioning without requiring future changes in the workflow to request service provisioning.
3. Extend the internal tool to generate Puppet scaffolding for new services, reducing the potential for errors in two ways. First, the data supplied in the service provisioning request can be directly included in the rendered template. Second, this will eliminate most human tweaking of templates, where typos can create issues.
4. Port allocation poses a particularly high risk, as reusing a port can break routing to an existing production service. As such, this will be the first area we fully automate, with the provisioning service supplying the allocated port rather than requiring requesting teams to provide an already allocated port. Doing this will require moving the port registry out of a Phabricator wiki page and into a database, which will allow us to guard access with a variety of checks.

5. Manual assignment of new services to servers often leads to new services being allocated to already heavily utilized servers. We will replace the manual assignment with an automated system, and do so with the intention of migrating to the Mesos/Aurora cluster once it is available for production workloads.

Each week, we'll review the size of the service provisioning queue, along with the service provisioning time, to assess whether the strategy is working or needs to be revised.[2]

REFINE

In order to refine our diagnosis, we've created a systems model for service onboarding (Figure 16-1). This will allow us to simulate a variety of different approaches to our problem, and determine which approach, or combination of approaches, will be most effective.

As we exercised the model, it became clear that:

1. We are increasingly falling behind.
2. Hiring onto the service provisioning team is not a viable solution.
3. Moving to a self-service approach is our only option.

2 Although I didn't have a name for this practice in 2014 when we created and implemented this strategy, the preceding section captures an important reality of team-led bottom-up strategy: when you don't have the authority to mandate compliance, you have to get the details right. The best way to do that is a prolonged strategy testing phase. Indeed, because compliance is rooted in effectiveness, my experience is that nonexecutive strategy developers can never stop refining their approach.

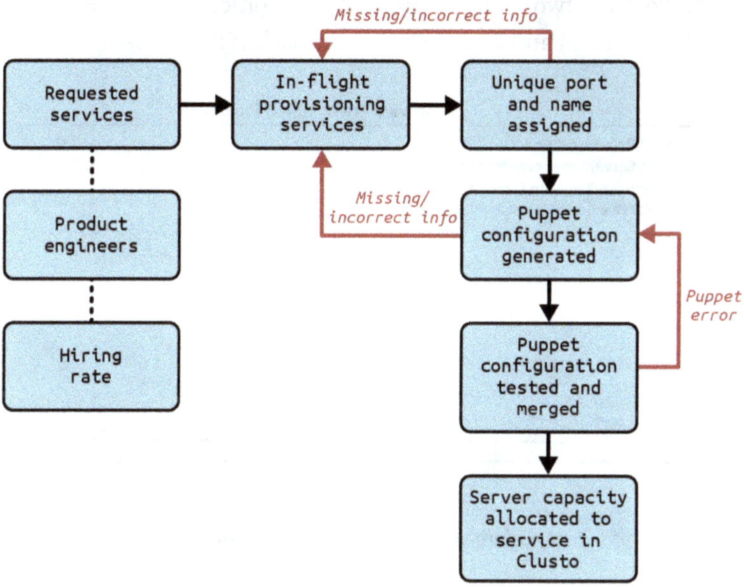

Figure 16-1. Systems model of provisioning services at Uber circa 2014

While the model writeup justifies each of those statements in more detail, we'll include two charts here. The first chart (Figure 16-2) shows the status quo, where new service-provisioning requests, labeled as `Initial RequestedServices`, quickly accumulate into a backlog.

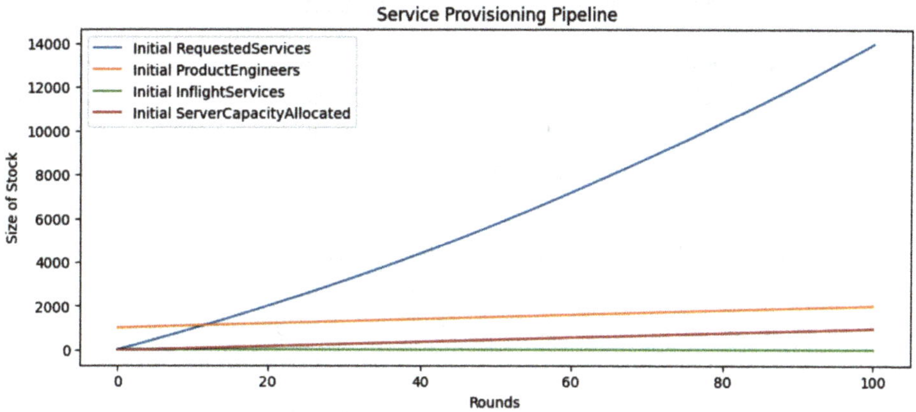

Figure 16-2. Service provisioning model without error states

Second, we have two charts comparing the outcomes between the current status quo (Figure 16-2) and a self-service approach (Figure 16-3).

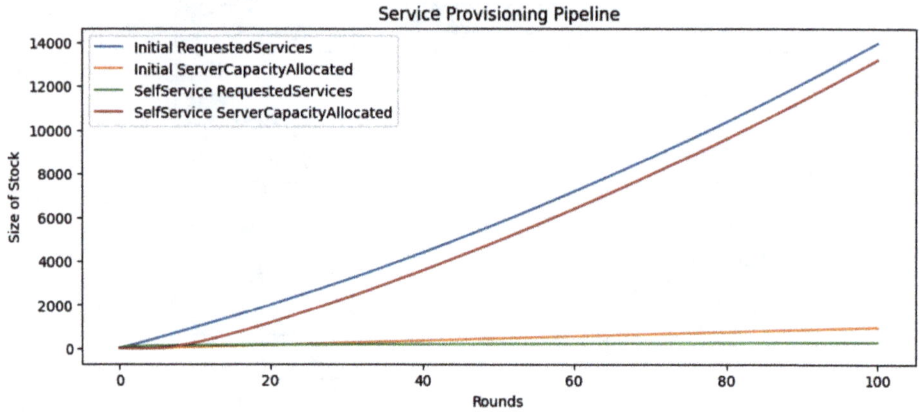

Figure 16-3. Impact of self-service provisioning on provisioning rate

In that chart, you can see that the service provisioning backlog in the self-service model remains steady, as represented by the `SelfService Requested Services` line. Of the various attempts to find a solution, none of the others showed promise, including eliminating all errors in provisioning and increasing the team's capacity by 500%.

DIAGNOSE

We've diagnosed the current state of service provisioning at Uber as:

- Many product engineering teams are aiming to leave the centralized monolith, which is generating two to three service provisioning requests each week. We expect this rate to increase roughly linearly with the size of the product engineering organization.

  Even if we disagree with this shift to additional services, there's no team responsible for maintaining the extensibility of the monolith, and working in the monolith is the number one source of developer frustration, so we don't have a practical counter proposal to offer engineers other than provisioning a new service.
- The engineering organization is doubling every six months. Consequently, a year from now, we expect eight to twelve service provisioning requests every week.

- Within infrastructure engineering, there is a team of four engineers responsible for service provisioning today. While our organization is growing at a similar rate as product engineering, none of that additional headcount is being allocated directly to the team working on service provisioning. We do not anticipate this changing.

  Some additional headcount is being allocated to Service Reliability Engineers (SREs) who can take on the most nuanced, complicated service provisioning work. However, their bandwidth is already heavily constrained across many tasks, so relying on SREs is an insufficient solution.
- The queue for service provisioning is already increasing in size as things stand today. Barring some change, many services will not be provisioned in a timely fashion.
- Today, provisioning a new service takes about a week, with numerous round trips between the requesting team and the provisioning team. Missing and incorrect information between teams is the largest source of delay in provisioning services.
- If the provisioning team has all the necessary information and it's accurate, then a new service can be provisioned in about three to four hours of work across configuration in Puppet, metadata in Clusto, allocating ports, assigning the service to servers, and so on.
- There are few safeguards on port allocation, server assignment, and so on. It is easy to inadvertently cause a production outage during service provisioning unless done with attention to detail.

  Given our rate of hiring, training the engineering organization to use this unsafe toolchain is an impractical solution: even if we train the entire organization perfectly today, there will be just as many untrained individuals in six months. Further, product engineering leadership has no interest in their team being diverted to service-provisioning training.
- It's widely agreed across the infrastructure engineering team that essentially every component of service provisioning should be replaced as soon as possible, but there is no concrete plan to replace any of the core components. Further, there is no team accountable for replacing these components, which means the service provisioning team will either need to work around the current tooling or replace that tooling ourselves.

- It's urgent to unblock development of new services, but moving those new services to production is rarely urgent, and occurs after a long internal development period. Evidence of this is that requests to provision a new service generally come with significant urgency and internal escalations to management. After the service is provisioned for development, there are relatively few urgent escalations other than one-off requests for increased production capacity during incidents.
- Another team within infrastructure is actively exploring adoption of Mesos and Aurora, but there's no concrete timeline for when this might be available for our usage. Until they commit to supporting our workloads, we'll need to find an alternative solution.

EXPLORE

Uber's server and service infrastructure today is composed of a handful of pieces. First, we run servers on-prem within a handful of colocations. Second, we describe each server in Puppet manifests to support repeatable provisioning of servers. Finally, we manage fleet and server metadata in a tool named Clusto, originally created by Digg, which allows us to populate Puppet manifests with server and cluster appropriate metadata during provisioning. In general, we agree that our current infrastructure is nearing its end of lifespan, but it's less obvious what the appropriate replacements are for each piece.

There's significant internal opposition to running in the cloud, up to and including our CEO, so we don't believe that will change in the foreseeable future. We do, however, believe there's opportunity to change our service definitions from Puppet to something along the lines of Docker, and to change our metadata mechanism toward a more purpose-built solution like Mesos/Aurora or Kubernetes.

As a starting point, we find it valuable to read "Large-Scale Cluster Management at Google with Borg" (*https://oreil.ly/95B_Q*), which informed some elements of the approach to Kubernetes, and "Mesos: A Platform for Fine-Grained Resource Sharing in the Data Center" (*https://oreil.ly/6HQID*), which describes the Mesos/Aurora approach.[3]

3 If you're wondering why there's no mention of the article "Borg, Omega, and Kubernetes" (*https://oreil.ly/qEAdV*), that's because it wasn't published until 2016, after this strategy was developed.

Within Uber, we have a number of ex-Twitter engineers who can speak with confidence to their experience operating with Mesos/Aurora at Twitter. We have been unable to find anyone to speak with that has production Kubernetes experience operating a comparably large fleet of 10,000+ servers, although presumably someone is operating—or close to operating—Kubernetes at that scale.

Our general belief of the evolution of the ecosystem at the time is supported by our Wardley mapping exercise on service orchestration (Figure 16-4).[4]

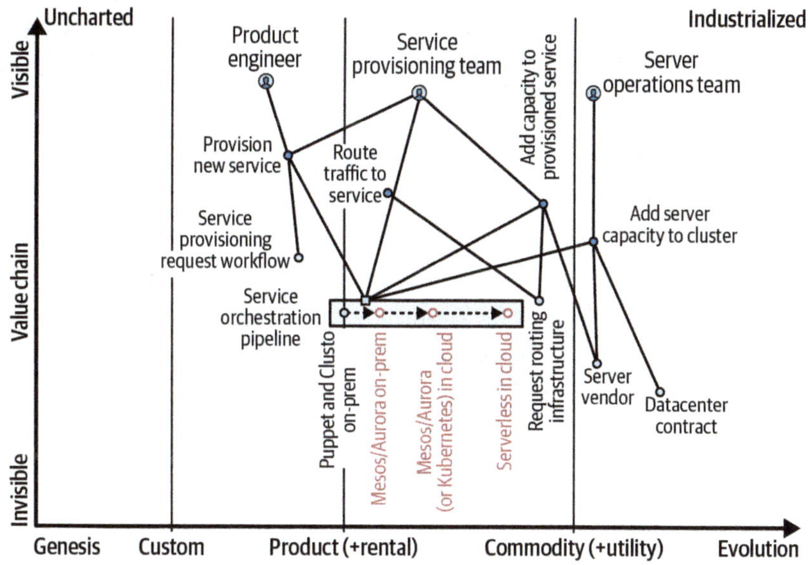

Figure 16-4. Wardley map of service orchestration

One of the unknowns today is how the evolution of Mesos/Aurora and Kubernetes will look in the future. Kubernetes seems promising with Google's backing, but there are few if any meaningful production deployments today. Mesos/Aurora has more community support and more production deployments, but the absolute number of deployments remains quite small, and there is no large-scale industry backer outside of Twitter.

4 Wardley mapping is introduced in Chapter 15 as one of the techniques for strategy refinement, but it can also be a useful technique for exploring a dynamic ecosystem—like service orchestration in 2014. Assembling each strategy requires exercising judgment on how to compile the pieces together most usefully, and in this case I found that the map fit most naturally with the rest of *Explore* rather than in the more operationally focused *Refine* section.

Even further out, there's considerable excitement around "serverless" frameworks, which seem like a likely future evolution, but canvassing the industry and our networks, we've been unable to find enough real-world usage to make an active push toward this destination today.

Document 16-2: Service Onboarding Model

At the core of Uber's service migration strategy (2014) is understanding the service onboarding process, and identifying the levers to speed up that process. Here we'll develop a systems model representing that onboarding process, and exercise the model to test a number of hypotheses about how to best speed up provisioning.

In this document, we'll cover:

- Where the model of service onboarding suggested we focus on efforts.
- Developing a system model using the `lethain/systems` package on GitHub (*https://github.com/lethain/systems*). That model is available in the `lethain/eng-strategy-models` repository (*https://github.com/lethain/eng-strategy-models/blob/main/UberServiceOnboarding.ipynb*).
- Exercising that model to learn from it.

Let's figure out what this model can teach us.

LEARNINGS

Even if we model this problem with a 100% success rate (i.e., no errors at all), as in Figure 16-5, the backlog of requested new services continues to increase over time. This clarifies that the problem to be solved is not the service provisioning team's efficiency in running their current process, but rather that the fundamental approach is not working.

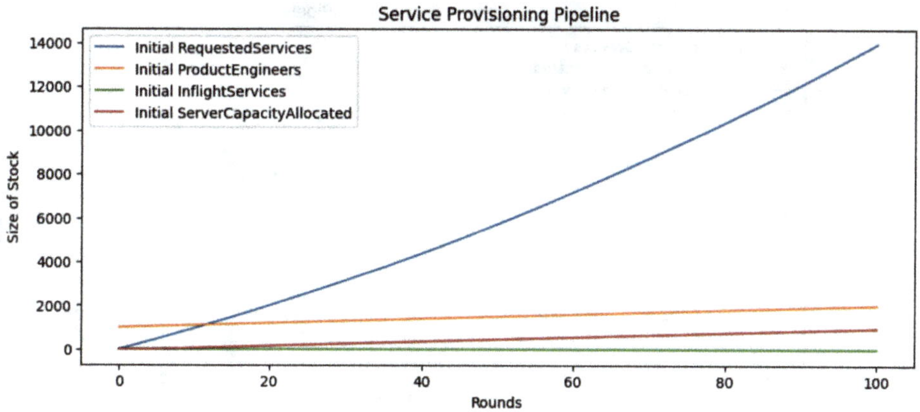

Figure 16-5. Service provisioning model without error states

Although hiring is tempting as a solution, our model (Figure 16-6) suggests it is not a particularly valuable approach in this scenario. Even increasing the Service Provisioning team's staff allocated to manually provisioning services by 500% doesn't solve the backlog of incoming requests.

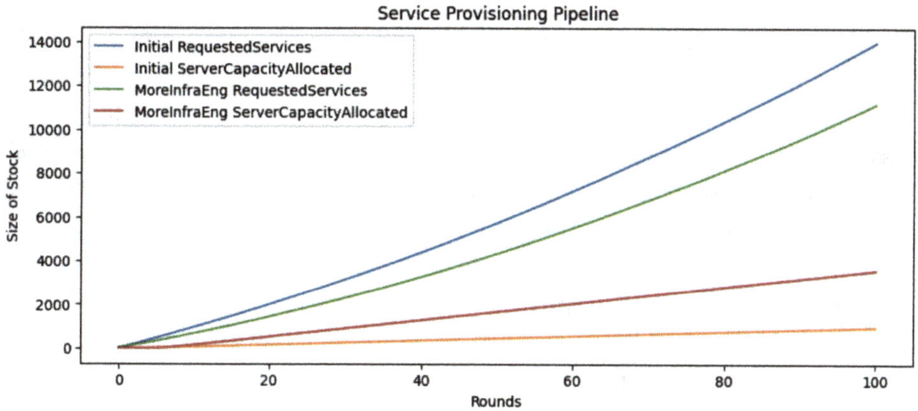

Figure 16-6. Impact of infrastructure engineering hiring on service provisioning

If reducing errors doesn't solve the problem, and increased hiring for the team doesn't solve the problem, then we have to find a way to eliminate manual service provisioning entirely. The most promising candidate is moving to a self-service provisioning model, which our model shows solves the backlog problem effectively (shown in Figure 16-7).

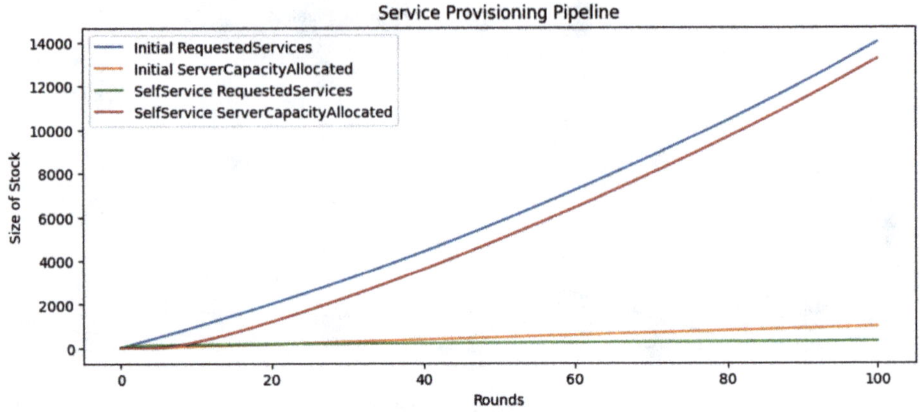

Figure 16-7. Impact of self-service provisioning on provisioning rate

Refining our earlier statement, additional hiring may benefit the team if we are able to focus those hires on building self-service provisioning, and if we're able to ramp up their productivity (*https://lethain.com/productivity-in-the-age-of-hypergrowth*) faster than the increase of incoming service provisioning requests.

SKETCH

Our initial sketch of service provisioning (Figure 16-8) is a simple pipeline starting with `Requested services` and moving step by step through to `Server capacity allocated to service in Clusto`. Some of these steps are likely much slower than others, but it gives a sense of the stages and where things might go wrong. It also gives us a sense of what we can measure to evaluate if our approach to provisioning is working well.

One element in Figure 16-8 worth mentioning is the dotted lines from `Hiring rate` to `Product engineers` and from `Product engineers` to `Requested services`. These are called *links*, which are stocks that influence another stock but don't flow directly into it.[5]

5 A purist would correctly note that links should connect to *flows* rather than stocks. That is true! However, as we'll encounter when we convert this sketch into a model, there are actually several counterintuitive elements here that are necessary to model this system but make the sketch less readable. As a modeler, you'll frequently encounter these sorts of tradeoffs, and you'll have to decide what choices best serve your needs in the moment.

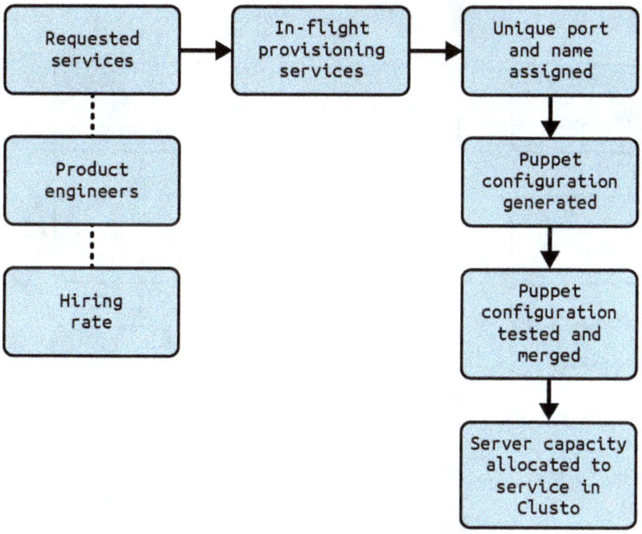

Figure 16-8. Systems model of provisioning services

The biggest missing element of the initial model is error flows, where things can sometimes go wrong in addition to sometimes going right. There are many ways things can go wrong, but we're going to focus on modeling a few error flows in particular:

1. `Missing/incorrect information` occurs twice in this model, and throws a provisioning request back into the initial provisioning phase where information is collected. When this occurs during port assignment, this is a relatively small trip backward. However, when it occurs in Puppet configuration, this is a significantly larger step backward.
2. `Puppet error` occurs in the second to final stock, `Puppet configuration tested and merged`. This sends requests back one step in the provisioning flow.

Updating our sketch to reflect these flows, we get a fairly complete, and somewhat nuanced, view of the service provisioning flow (Figure 16-9).

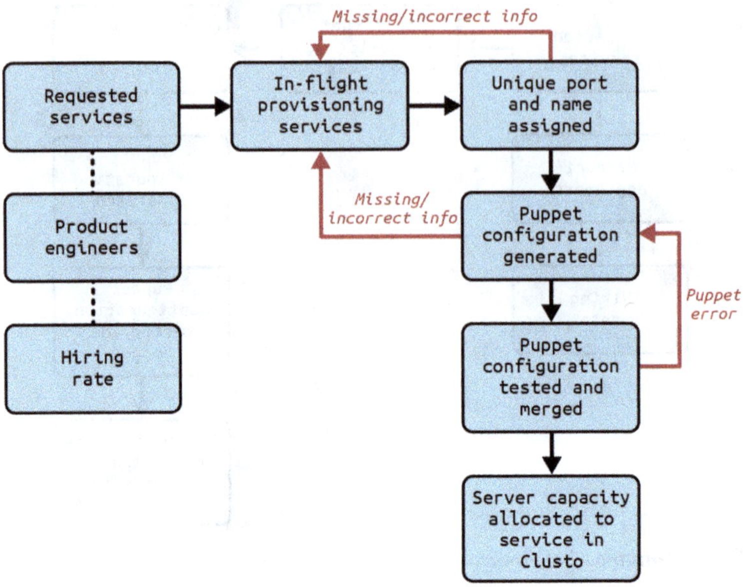

Figure 16-9. Model of provisioning services with error transitions

Note that the combination of these two flows introduces the possibility of a service being almost fully provisioned, but then traveling from Puppet testing back to Puppet configuration due to `Puppet error`, and then backward again to the initial step due to `Missing/incorrect information`. This means nearly all provisioning progress can be lost if things go wrong.

There are more nuances we could introduce, but there's already enough complexity here for us to learn quite a bit from this model.

REASON

Studying our sketches, a few things stand out:

1. The hiring of product engineers is going to drive up service provisioning requests over time, but there's no counterbalancing hiring of infrastructure engineers to work on service provisioning. This means there's an implicit, but very real, deadline to scale this process independently of the size of the infrastructure engineering team.

   Even without building the full model, it's clear that we have to either stop hiring product engineers, turn this into a self-service solution, or find a new mechanism to discourage service provisioning.

2. The size of error rates is going to influence results a great deal, particularly those for `Missing/incorrect information`. This is probably the most valuable place to start looking for efficiency improvements.
3. Missing information errors are more expensive than the model implies, because they require coordination across teams to resolve. Conversely, Puppet testing errors are probably cheaper than the model implies, because they should be solvable within the same team and consequently benefit from a quick iteration loop.

Now we need to build a model that helps guide our inquiry into those questions.

MODEL

You can find the full implementation of this model on GitHub (*https://github.com/lethain/eng-strategy-models/blob/main/UberServiceOnboarding.ipynb*) if you want to see the entirety rather than these emphasized snippets.

First, let's get the success states working:

```
HiringRate(10)
ProductEngineers(1000)
[PotentialHires] > ProductEngineers @ HiringRate

[PotentialServices] > RequestedServices(10) @ ProductEngineers / 10
RequestedServices > InflightServices(0, 10) @ Leak(1.0)
InflightServices > PortNameAssigned @ Leak(1.0)
PortNameAssigned > PuppetGenerated @ Leak(1.0)
PuppetGenerated > PuppetConfigMerged @ Leak(1.0)
PuppetConfigMerged > ServerCapacityAllocated @ Leak(1.0)
```

As we run this model, we can see from Figure 16-10 that the number of requested services grows significantly over time. This makes sense, as we're only able to provision a maximum of 10 services per round.

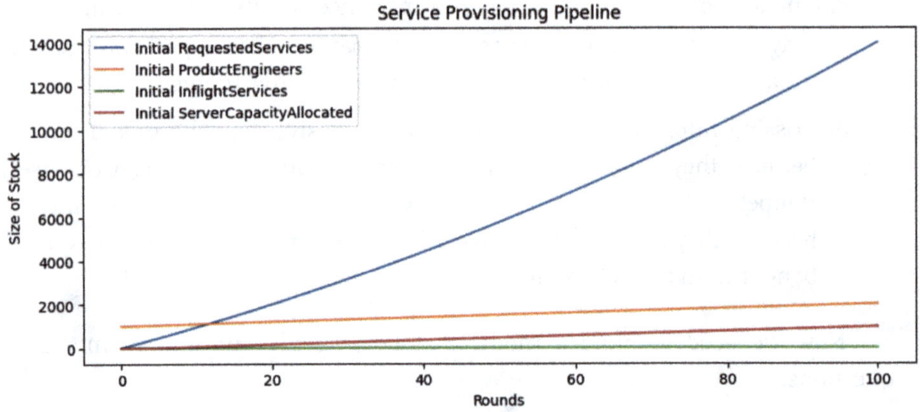

Figure 16-10. Service provisioning model without error states

However, it's also the best case, because we're not capturing the three error states:

1. Unique port and name assignment can fail because of missing or incorrect information.
2. Puppet configuration can also fail due to missing or incorrect information.
3. Puppet configurations can have errors in them, requiring rework.

Let's update the model to include these failure modes, starting with unique port and name assignments. The error-free version looks like this:

```
InflightServices > PortNameAssigned @ Leak(1.0)
```

Now let's add in an error rate, where 20% of requests are missing information and return to inflight services stock:

```
PortNameAssigned > PuppetGenerated @ Leak(0.8)
PortNameAssigned > RequestedServices @ Leak(0.2)
```

Then let's do the same thing for Puppet configuration errors:

```
# original version
PuppetGenerated > PuppetConfigMerged @ Leak(1.0)

# updated version with errors
PuppetGenerated > PuppetConfigMerged @ Leak(0.8)
PuppetGenerated > InflightServices @ Leak(0.2)
```

Finally, we'll make a similar change to represent errors made in the Puppet templates themselves:

```
# original version
PuppetConfigMerged > ServerCapacityAllocated @ Leak(1.0)

# updated version with errors
PuppetConfigMerged > ServerCapacityAllocated @ Leak(0.8)
PuppetConfigMerged > PuppetGenerated @ Leak(0.2)
```

Even with relatively low error rates, we can see from Figure 16-11 that the throughput of the system overall has been meaningfully impacted by introducing these errors.

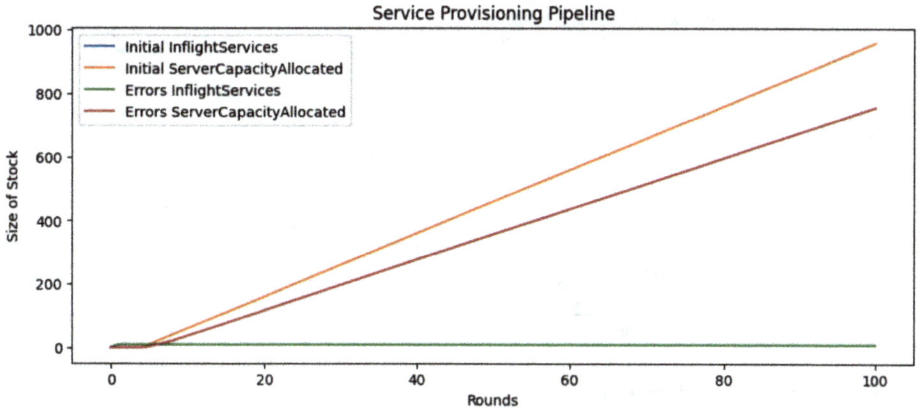

Figure 16-11. Service provisioning model with error states

Now that we have the foundation of the model built, it's time to start exercising the model to understand the problem space a bit better.

EXERCISE

We already know the errors are impacting throughput, but let's start by narrowing down which errors matter most by increasing the error rate for each of them independently and comparing the impact.

To model this, we'll create three new specifications, each of which increases one error from a 20% error rate to a 50% error rate, and see how the overall throughput of the system is affected:

```
# test 1: port assignment errors increased
PortNameAssigned > PuppetGenerated @ Leak(0.5)
PortNameAssigned > RequestedServices @ Leak(0.5)
```

```
# test 2: puppet generated errors increased
PuppetGenerated > PuppetConfigMerged @ Leak(0.5)
PuppetGenerated > InflightServices @ Leak(0.5)

# test 3: puppet merged errors increased
PuppetConfigMerged > ServerCapacityAllocated @ Leak(0.5)
PuppetConfigMerged > PuppetGenerated @ Leak(0.5)
```

Comparing the impact of increasing the error rates from 20% to 50% in each of the three error loops, we can get a sense of the model's sensitivity to each error (Figure 16-12).

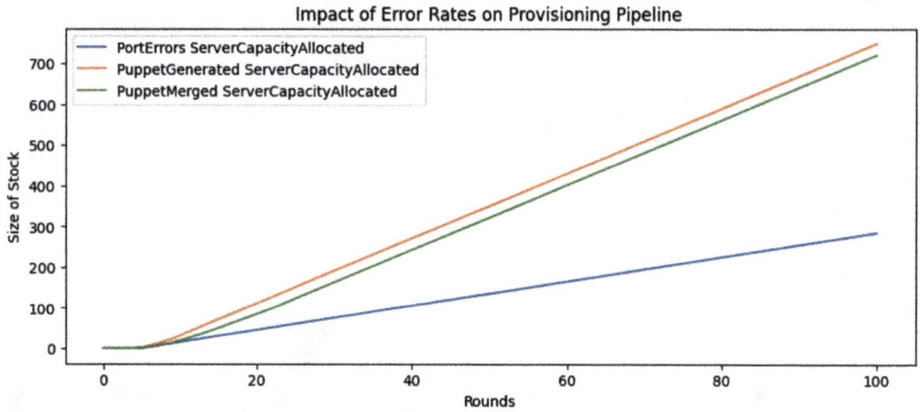

Figure 16-12. Impact of error rates across stages of provisioning

The chart in Figure 16-12 captures why exercising is so impactful: we'd assumed during sketching that errors in Puppet generation would matter the most because they caused a long trip backward, but it turns out a very high error rate early in the process matters even more because there are still multiple other potential errors later on that compound on its increase.

Next, we can get a sense of the impact of hiring more people onto the service provisioning team to manually provision more services, which we can model by increasing the maximum size of the inflight services stock from 10 to 50:

```
# initial model
RequestedServices > InflightServices(0, 10) @ Leak(1.0)

# with 5x capacity!
RequestedServices > InflightServices(0, 50) @ Leak(1.0)
```

Unfortunately, we can see in Figure 16-13 that even increasing the team's capacity by 500% doesn't solve the backlog of requested services.

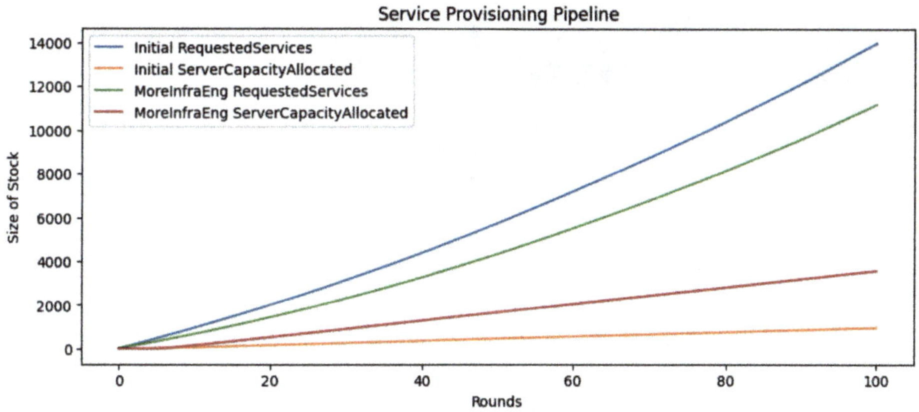

Figure 16-13. Impact of infrastructure engineering hiring on service provisioning

There's some impact, but not that much, and the backlog of requested services remains extremely high. We can conclude that more infrastructure hiring isn't the solution we need, but let's see if moving to self-service is a plausible solution.

We can simulate the impact of moving to self-service by removing the maximum size from inflight services entirely:

```
# initial model
RequestedServices > InflightServices(0, 10) @ Leak(1.0)

# simulating self-service
RequestedServices > InflightServices(0) @ Leak(1.0)
```

Figure 16-14 shows that this finally solves the backlog.

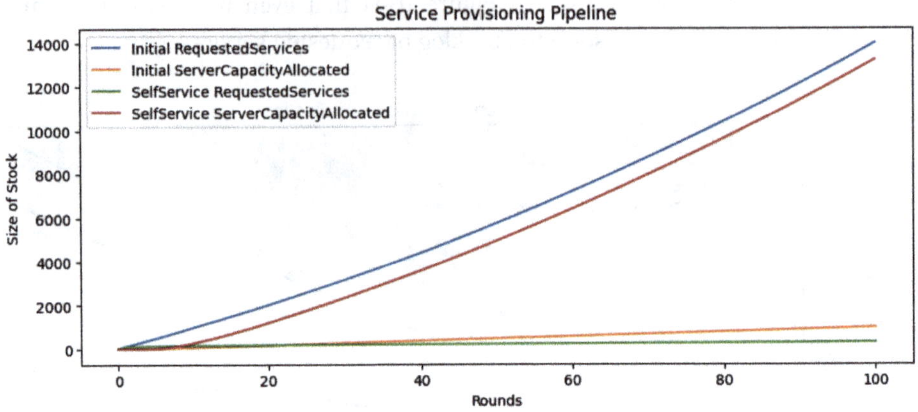

Figure 16-14. Impact of self-service provisioning on provisioning rate

At this point, we've exercised the model a fair amount and have a good sense of what it wants to tell us. We know which errors are most important to address early, and we also know that we need to make the move to a self-service platform sometime soon.

Document 16-3: Wardley Mapping the Service Orchestration Ecosystem

In Uber's 2014 service migration strategy (Document 16-1), we explored how to navigate the move from a Python monolith to a services-oriented architecture while also scaling with user traffic that doubled every six months.

The Wardley map in Figure 16-15 explores how orchestration frameworks were evolving during that period to be used as an input into determining the most effective path forward for Uber's Infrastructure Engineering team.

HOW THINGS WORK TODAY

There are three primary internal teams involved in service provisioning. The Service Provisioning team abstracts applications developed by Product Engineering from servers managed by the Server Operations team. As more servers are added to support application scaling, this is invisible to the applications themselves, freeing Product Engineers to focus on what the company values the most: developing more application functionality.

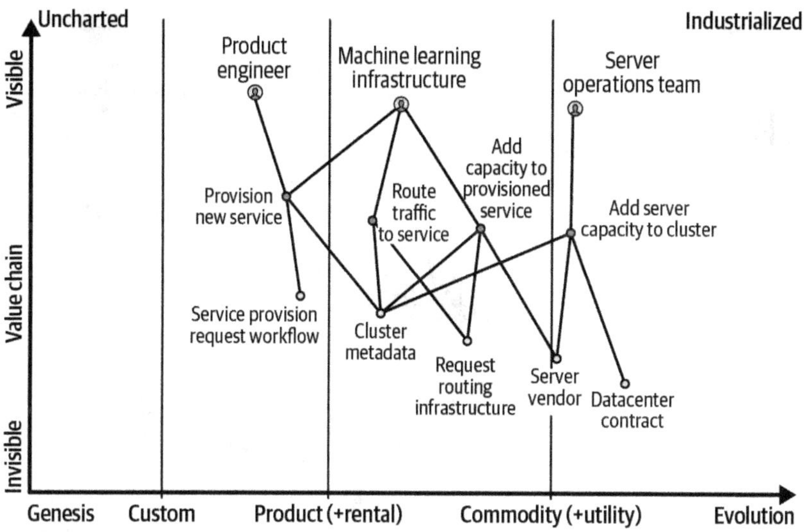

Figure 16-15. Wardley map for service orchestration

The challenges within the current value chain are cost-efficient scaling, reliable deployment, and fast deployment. All three of those problems anchor on the same underlying problem of resource scheduling. We want to make a significant investment into improving our resource scheduling, and we believe that understanding the industry's trend for resource scheduling underpins making an effective choice.

TRANSITION TO FUTURE STATE

Most interesting cluster orchestration problems are anchored in cluster metadata and resource scheduling. Request routing, whether through DNS entries or allocated ports, depends on cluster metadata (see Figure 16-16). Mapping services to a fleet of servers depends on resource scheduling managing cluster metadata. Deployment and autoscaling both depend on cluster metadata.

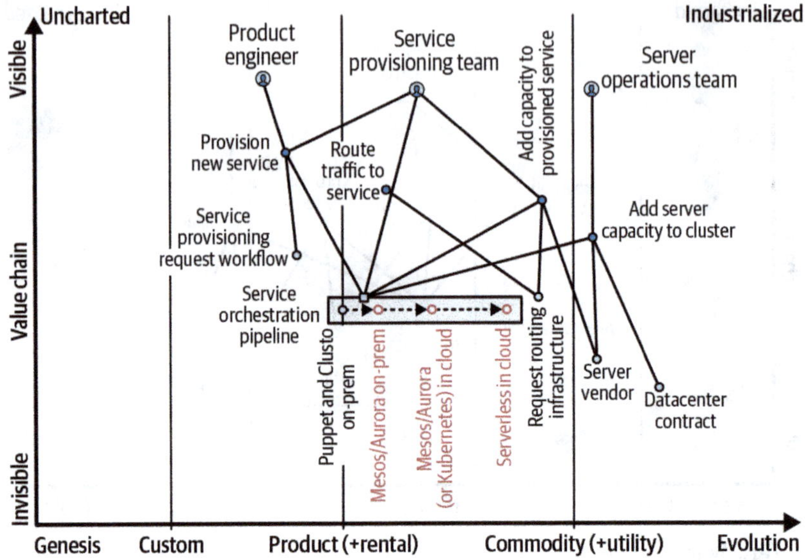

Figure 16-16. Pipeline showing progression of service orchestration over time

This is also an area where we see significant changes occurring today in 2014.

Uber initially solved this problem using Clusto, an open source tool released by Digg with goals similar to HashiCorp's Consul (*https://www.consul.io*) but with limited adoption. We also used Puppet (*https://www.puppet.com*) for configuring servers, alongside custom scripting. This has worked, but has required custom, ongoing support for scheduling. The key question we're confronted with is whether to build our own scheduling algorithms (e.g., bin packing (*https://oreil.ly/qhbYe*)) or adopt a different approach. It seems clear that the industry intends to directly solve this problem via two paths: relying on cloud providers for orchestration (Amazon Web Services, Google Cloud Platform, etc.) and through open source scheduling frameworks such as Mesos and Kubernetes.

Industry peers with more than five years of infrastructure experience are almost unanimously adopting open source scheduling frameworks to better support their physical infrastructure. This will give them a tool to perform a bridged migration from physical infrastructure to cloud infrastructure.

Newer companies with less existing infrastructure are moving directly to the cloud and avoiding the orchestration problem entirely. The only companies not adopting one of these two approaches are extraordinarily large and complex (think Google or Microsoft) or allergic to making any technical change at all.

From this analysis, it's clear that continuing our reliance on Clusto and Puppet is going to be an expensive investment that's not particularly aligned with the industry's evolution.

USER AND VALUE CHAINS

The map in Figure 16-16 explores the orchestration ecosystem within a single company, with an emphasis on what did, and did not, stay the same from roughly 2008 to 2014. It attends to three users in particular:

1. Product Engineers are focused on provisioning new services, and then deploying new versions of that service as they make changes. They operate their own service and are entirely unaware of anything beneath the orchestration layer (including any servers).
2. The Service Provisioning team invests their energy in provisioning new services, orchestrating resources for those services, and routing traffic to those services. This team acts as the bridge between the Product Engineers and the Server Operations team.
3. The Server Operations team prioritizes adding server capacity to be used for orchestration. They work closely with the Service Provisioning team and have no contact with the Product Engineers.

It's worth acknowledging that, in practice, these are artificial aggregates of multiple underlying teams. For example, routing traffic between services and servers is typically handled by a Traffic or Service Networking team. However, these omissions are intended to clarify the distinctions relevant to the evolution of orchestration tooling.

Summary

In Chapter 23, I'll show you a rubric to evaluate the service provisioning strategy described in these three documents. In particular, that chapter will introduce the concept of strategy phases, which allow you to concretely talk about a strategy that works extremely well initially, but runs into issues later.

I developed the concept of strategy phases specifically to deal with the legacy of the Uber service migration described in this chapter. This strategy worked exceptionally well, solving a series of complex problems with a very small team. It also, unfortunately, facilitated the introduction of a very difficult developer experience for the engineers building on top of the service architecture they facilitated. Although this was indeed a downside of this approach, strategy is ultimately a study of tradeoffs, and acknowledging these challenges is part of why looking at real strategy documents is so much more valuable than reading press releases.

17

LLM Adoption Strategy

Whether you're a product engineer, a product manager, or an engineering executive, you've probably been pushed to consider using LLMs to extend your product or enhance your processes. LLM capabilities transitioned into the mainstream starting around 2023, and even though most integrations appear superficial, many companies worry that they're falling behind.

That context makes LLM adoption a great topic for a strategy case study. This chapter contains engineering strategy documents written to determine how a hypothetical company I'll call Theoretical Ride Sharing should adopt LLMs. Theoretical has 2,000 employees, 300 of whom are software engineers. The company has raised $400 million. It's doing $50 million in annual revenue and operating in 200 cities across North America and Europe. Theoretical is a ride-sharing business, similar to Uber or Lyft, but its innovation is to use larger vehicles—essentially, reinventing public transit.

Reading These Documents

The documents in this chapter are:

Document 17-1: How Should We Adopt Large Language Models?
: This strategy document considers how adopting LLMs might impact the company's developer experience.

Document 17-2: Modeling LLMs' Impact on the Developer Experience
: A systems model of the software development process at this company.

Document 17-3: Wardley Mapping the LLM Ecosystem
: This map of the LLM space focuses on how product companies should address the proliferation of model providers, such as Anthropic, Google, and OpenAI, and LLM product patterns like agentic workflows and retrieval-augmented generation (RAG). It also discusses running evaluations to maintain performance as models change.

Document 17-4: Modeling Driver Onboarding
: This model looks at whether LLMs might improve a core product and business problem: maximizing active drivers on the company's ride-sharing platform.

If you're reading these documents with the goal of applying the strategies they put forward, start at the top and read to the end. If, on the other hand, your main goal is to understand the thinking behind them, read the sections in reverse order, starting with *Explore*, then *Diagnose*, and so on. For more on this structure, see Chapter 11.

As with the other chapters in Part IV, "Case Studies", this chapter reproduces a set of documents, provides context and commentary in footnotes, and concludes by drawing out some key takeaways.

Document 17-1: How Should We Adopt Large Language Models?

POLICY

Our combined policy for using LLMs at Theoretical Ride Sharing is:[1]

- *Develop an LLM-backed process for reactivating departed and suspended drivers in mature markets.* Through modeling our driver lifecycle, we determined that improving onboarding time will have little impact on the total number of active drivers. Instead, we are focusing on mechanisms to reactivate departed and suspended drivers, which is the only opportunity to meaningfully impact active drivers.

  Report on progress monthly in *Exec Weekly Meeting*, coordinated in `#exec-weekly`.

1 Relative to the default structure, this document has been refactored in two ways to improve readability: first, *Operation* has been folded into *Policy*; second, *Refine* has been embedded in *Diagnose*.

- *Start with Anthropic.* We use Anthropic models, which are available through our existing cloud provider via AWS Bedrock (*https://oreil.ly/yK3nL*). To avoid maintaining multiple implementations, where we view the underlying foundational model quality to be somewhat undifferentiated, we are not looking to adopt a broad set of LLMs at this point. This is anchored in our Wardley map of the LLM ecosystem (Document 17-3).

  Exceptions will be reviewed by the *Machine Learning Review* in `#ml-review`.

- *Developer Experience team (DX) must offer at least one LLM-backed developer productivity tool.* This tool should enhance the experience, speed, or quality of writing software in TypeScript. This tool should help us develop our thinking for next year, such that we have conviction increasing (or decreasing!) our investment. This tool should be available to all engineers. Adopting one tool is the required baseline; if DX identifies further interesting tools, e.g., GitHub Copilot, they are empowered to bring the request to the *Engineering Exec* team for review. Review will focus on balancing our rate of learning, vendor cost, and data security. We've modeled options for measuring LLMs' impact on developer experience.

  Vendor approvals to be reviewed in the `#cto` internal chat channel.

- *Internal Tools team (INT) must offer at least one LLM-backed ad hoc prompting tool.* This tool should support arbitrary non-engineering use cases for LLMs, such as text extraction, rewriting notes, and so on. It must be usable with customer data while also honoring our existing data-processing commitments. This tool should be available to all employees.

  Vendor approvals to be reviewed in `#coo`.

- *Refresh policy in six months.* Our primary goal is to quickly learn about this unfamiliar domain where we have limited internal expertise, then review whether we should increase our investment afterward.

  Flag questions and suggestions in the `#cto` internal chat channel.

DIAGNOSE

Here's a summary of the challenges we face in adopting LLMs at Theoretical Ride Sharing:

- There are, at minimum, *three distinct needs* that folks internally are asking us to solve (either separately or with a shared solution):
  - *Productivity tools for non-engineers,* e.g., ad hoc document rewriting, document summarization
  - *Productivity tools for engineers,* e.g., advanced autocomplete tooling like GitHub Copilot
  - *Product extensions,* e.g., high-quality document extraction in driver onboarding workflows
- Of the above, *we see product extensions as potential strategic differentiation,* and the other two as workflow optimizations that improve our productivity but don't necessarily differentiate us from the broader industry. Some of the opportunities for strategic differentiation we see are:
  - *Reactivating the departed and suspended drivers* is our largest lever to increasing active drivers, as explored in our model of the driver lifecycle in Figure 17-4.
  - *Faster driver onboarding* with less human involvement will not increase active drivers, but we see a clear opportunity for LLMs to reduce operating costs, which may be worthwhile even if it doesn't address the core problem of active drivers.
  - *Improved customer support* by increasing the response speed and quality of our responses to customer inquiries.
- *We currently have limited experience or expertise in using LLMs in the company and in the industry.* Prolific thought leadership to the contrary, there are very few companies or products using LLMs in scaled, differentiated ways. That's currently true for us as well.
- *We want to develop our expertise without making an irreversible commitment.* We think that our internal expertise is a limiter for effective problem selection and utilization of LLMs, and that developing our expertise will help us become more effective in iterative future decisions on this topic. Conversely, we believe that making a major investment now, prior to developing our in-house expertise, would be relatively high risk and low

reward given that no other industry players appear to have identified a meaningful advantage at this point.

- *Switching across foundational models and foundational model providers is cheap.* This is true both economically (low financial commitment) and from an integration cost perspective (APIs and usage are largely consistent across providers).
- *Foundational models and providers are evolving rapidly, and it's unclear how the space will evolve.* It's likely that current foundational model providers will train one or two additional generations of foundational models with larger datasets, but at some point they will become cost prohibitive to train (e.g., the next major versions of OpenAI or Anthropic models seem likely to cost $500m+ to train). Differentiation might move into developer-experience at that point. Open source models like LLaMa might become significantly cost-advantaged. Or something else entirely. The future is wide open.

  We've built a Wardley map to understand the possible evolution of the foundational model ecosystem (Document 17-3).
- *Training a foundational model is prohibitively expensive for our needs.* We've raised $400m, and training a competitive foundational model would cost somewhere between $3m to $100m to match the general models provided by Anthropic or OpenAI.

EXPLORE

LLMs operate on top of a foundational model. Training these foundational models is exceptionally expensive, and growing more expensive over time as competition for more sophisticated models accelerates. Meta allegedly spent $20–30 million training LLaMa 2 (*https://oreil.ly/RXIJn*), up from about $3 million in training costs for LLaMa 1. OpenAI's GPT-4 allegedly cost $100 million to train (*https://oreil.ly/Xog4g*). With some nuance related to the quality of corpus and its relevance to the task at hand, larger models outperform smaller models (*https://oreil.ly/o4BWg*), so there's not much incentive to train a smaller foundational model unless you have a large, unique dataset to train against, and even in that case you might be better off fine-tuning or using in-context learning (ICL).

Anthropic charges (*https://oreil.ly/Cr2cP*) between $0.25 and $15 per million tokens of input, and a bit more for output tokens. OpenAI charges (*https://oreil.ly/_lkgN*) between $0.50 and $60 per million tokens of input, and a bit more for output tokens. The average English word is about 1.3 tokens, which means you can do a significant amount of LLM work while spending less than most venture-funded startups spend on snacks.

There's significant debate on whether LLMs have reached a point where their performance improvements will slow (*https://oreil.ly/ncMVD*). Much like the ongoing debate around whether Moore's law (*https://oreil.ly/GVBdK*) has died, it's unclear how much LLM performance will improve going forward. From a cost to train perspective, it's unlikely that companies can continue to improve foundational models merely by spending more money on compute. Few companies can tolerate a $1B training cost, and fewer will tolerate a $10B training cost, but it's hard to imagine a world where any companies are building $100B models. However, algorithmic improvements and investment in datasets may well drive improvements without driving up compute costs. The only high-confidence prediction you can make in this space is that it's likely model improvement will double one or two more times over the next three years, after which it *might* continue doubling at that rate or it *might* plateau at that level of performance: either outcome is plausible.

For some decisions, there's a strategic imperative to get it right from the beginning. For example, migrating from AWS to Azure is very expensive due to the degree of customization and lock-in. However, LLMs don't appear to be in this category. Talking with industry peers, the majority of companies are experimenting with a variety of models from Anthropic, OpenAI, and elsewhere (e.g., Mistral (*https://mistral.ai*)). Behaviors do vary across models, but it's also true that the behavior of existing models varies over time (e.g., GPT-3.5 allegedly got "lazier" over time (*https://oreil.ly/yCFDy*)), which means the overhead of dealing with model differences is unavoidable even if you only adopt one. Vendor lock-in for models is low from a technical perspective. However, regulatory requirements—like updating data processing agreements—introduce some friction when switching providers.

Although there's an ongoing investment boom in AI, most scaled technology companies are still looking for ways to leverage these capabilities beyond the obvious, widespread practices like adopting GitHub Copilot (*https://oreil.ly/M51X_*). For example, Stripe is investing heavily in LLMs for internal productivity (*https://oreil.ly/yUOu1*), including presumably relying on them to perform some internal tasks that would have previously been performed by an employee, such as verifying a company's website matches details the company supplied in their onboarding application, but it's less clear that they have yet found an approach to meaningfully shift their product, or their product's user experience, using LLMs.

Looking at ride-sharing companies more specifically, there don't appear to be any breakout industry-specific approaches either. Uber is similarly adopting LLMs for internal productivity, and some operational efficiency improvements as documented in their August 2023 post describing their internal developer and operations productivity investments using LLMs (*https://oreil.ly/TyjtP*) and their May 2024 post describing those efforts in more detail (*https://oreil.ly/zTErq*).

Document 17-2: Modeling LLMs' Impact on the Developer Experience

LEARNINGS

This model's insights can be summarized in three charts. First, the baseline chart (Figure 17-1), which shows an eventual equilibrium between errors discovered in production and tickets that we've closed by shipping to production. This equilibrium is visible because tickets continue to get opened, but the total number of closed tickets stops increasing.

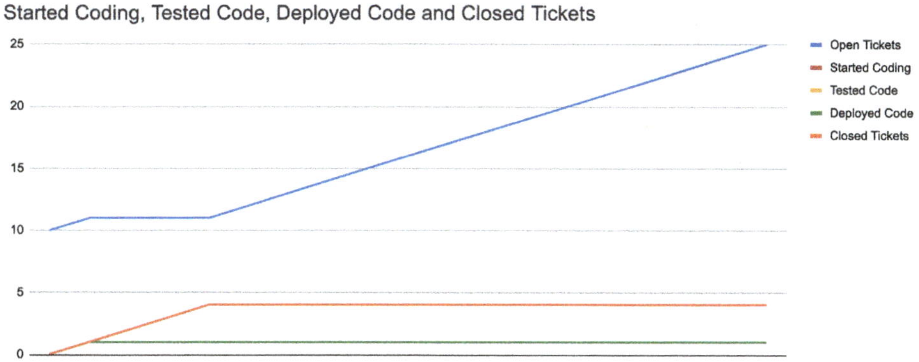

Figure 17-1. Baseline chart where number of closed tickets quickly stops increasing

Second, we show that we can shift that equilibrium by reducing the error rate in production. Specifically, the first chart models 25% of closed tickets in production experiencing an error, whereas the second chart (Figure 17-2) models only a 10% error rate. The equilibrium returns, but at a higher value of shipped tickets.

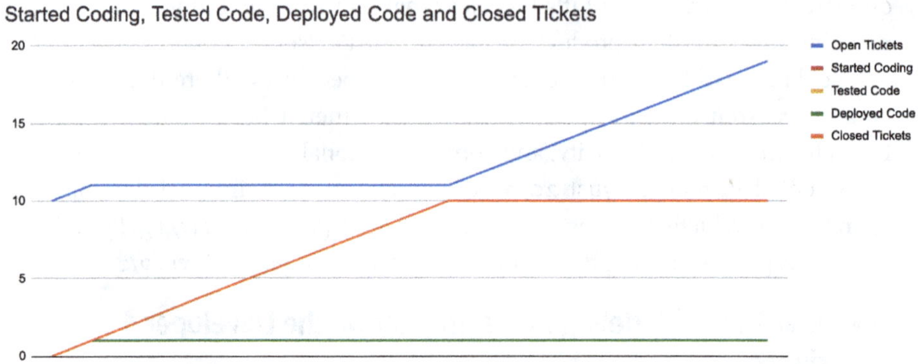

Figure 17-2. Reduced error rates delay, but don't prevent, reaching equilibrium of closed tickets

Finally, we can see that even tripling the rate that we start and test tickets doesn't meaningfully change the total number of completed tickets, as modeled in this third chart (Figure 17-3).

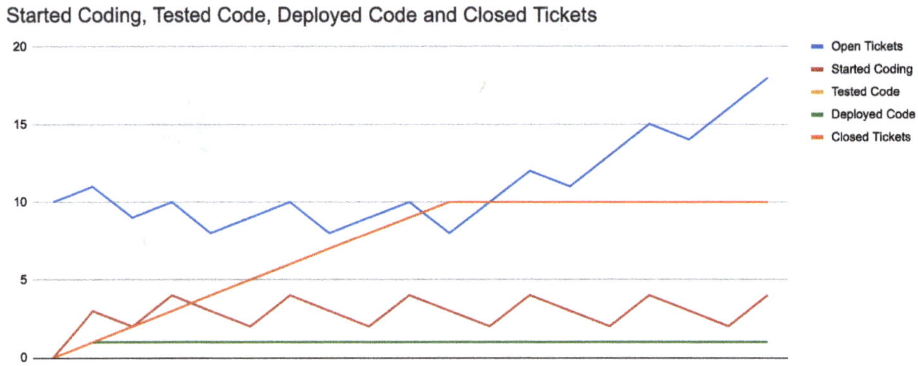

Figure 17-3. Starting or testing tickets faster creates noise but not progress

The constraint on this system is errors discovered in production, and any technique that changes something else doesn't make much of an impact. Of course, this is just *a model*, not reality. There are many nuances that models miss, but this helps us focus on what probably matters the most, and in particular highlights that any approach that increases development velocity while also increasing production error rate is likely net-negative.

With that summary out of the way, now we can get into developing the model itself.

SKETCH

Modeling in a spreadsheet is labor intensive, so we want to iterate as much as possible in the sketching phase, before we move to the spreadsheet. In this case, we're working with Excalidraw (*https://excalidraw.com*).

I sketched five stocks, shown in Figure 17-4, to represent a developer's workflow:

1. `Open Tickets` are tickets opened for an engineer to work on.
2. `Started Coding` is tickets that an engineer is working on.
3. `Tested Code` is tickets that have been tested.
4. `Deployed Code` is tickets that have been deployed.
5. `Closed Tickets` are tickets that are closed after reaching production.

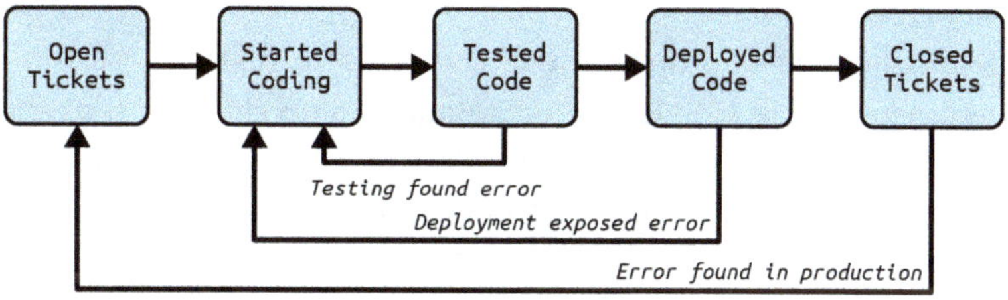

Figure 17-4. Five stages of development, with errors causing backward movement

There are four flows representing tickets progressing through this development process from left to right. Additionally, there are three exception flows that move from right to left:

1. `Testing found error` represents a ticket where testing finds an error, moving the ticket backward to `Started Coding`.
2. `Deployment exposed error` represents a ticket encountering an error during deployment, where it's moved backward to `Started Coding`.
3. `Error found in production` represents a ticket encountering a production error, which causes it to move all the way back to the beginning as a new ticket.

One of your first concerns seeing this model might be that it's embarrassingly simple. To be honest, that was my reaction when I first looked at it, too.

However, it's important to recognize that feeling and then dig into whether it matters.

This model is quite simple, but in the next section we'll find that it reveals several counterintuitive insights into the problem that will help us avoid erroneously viewing the tooling as a failure if time spent testing increases. The value of a model is in refining our thinking, and simple models are usually more effective at refining thinking across a group than complex models, simply because complex models are fairly difficult to align a group around.

REASON

As we start to look at this sketch, the first question to ask is how might LLM-based tooling show an improvement? The most obvious options are:

1. Increasing the rate at which tasks flow from `Started Coding` to `Tested Code`. Presumably these tools might reduce the amount of time spent on implementation.
2. Increasing the rate that `Tested Code` follows `Testing found error` to return to `Started Coding` because more comprehensive tests are more likely to detect errors. This is probably the first interesting learning from this model: if the adopted tool works well, it's likely that we'll spend *more* time in the testing loop, with a long-term payoff of spending less time solving problems in production where it's more expensive. This means that slower testing might be a successful outcome rather than a failure as it might first appear.

   A skeptic of these tools might argue the opposite, that LLM-based tooling will cause more issues to be identified "late" after deployment rather than early in the testing phase. In either case, we now have a clear goal to measure to evaluate the effectiveness of the tool: reducing the `Error found in production` flow. We also know *not* to focus on the `Testing found error` flow, which should probably increase.
3. Finally, we can also zoom out and measure the overall time from `Started Coding` to `Closed Tickets` for tasks that don't experience the `Error found in production` flow for at least the first 90 days after being completed.

These observations capture what I find remarkable about systems modeling: even a very simple model can expose counterintuitive insights. In particular, the sort of insights that build conviction to push back on places where intuition might lead you astray.

MODEL

For this model, we'll be modeling it directly in a spreadsheet, specifically Google Sheets. The completed spreadsheet model is available here (*https://oreil.ly/wtPfu*). As discussed in Chapter 14, spreadsheet modeling is brittle, slow, and hard to iterate on. I generally recommend that folks attempt to model something in a spreadsheet to get an intuitive sense of the math happening in their models, but I would almost always choose any tool other than a spreadsheet for a complex model.

This example is fairly tedious to follow, and you're entirely excused if you decide to pull open the sheet itself, look around a bit, and then skip the remainder of this section. If you are hanging around, it's time to get started.

The spreadsheet we're creating has three important worksheets:

- *Model* represents the model itself.
- *Charts* holds charts of the model.
- *Config* holds configuration values separately from the model to ease exercising the model after we've built it.

Going to the model worksheet, we want to start out by initializing each of the columns to the starting value, as shown in Figure 17-5.

1	Open Tickets	Started Coding	Tested Code	Deployed Code	Closed Tickets
2	10	0	0	0	0

Figure 17-5. Initial values of a systems model

While we'll use formulae for subsequent rows, the first row should contain literal values. I often start with a positive value in the first column and zeros in the other columns, but that isn't required. You can start with whatever starting values are more useful for studying the model that you're building.

With the initial values set, we're now going to implement the model in two passes. First, we'll model the left-to-right flows, which represent the standard development process. Second, we'll model the right-to-left flows, which represent exceptions in the process.

Modeling left-to-right

We'll start by modeling the interaction between the first two nodes: `Open Tickets` and `Started Coding`. We want to have open tickets increased over time at a fixed rate, so let's add a value in the config worksheet for `TicketOpenRate`, starting with 1.

Moving to the second stock, we want to start work on open tickets as long as we have at most `MaxConcurrentCodingNum` open tickets. If we have more than `MaxConcurrentCodingNum` tickets that we're working on, then we don't start working on any new tickets. To do this, we actually need to create an intermediate value (represented using an italics column name) to determine how many should be created by checking if the current number in started tickets is at maximum (another value in the config sheet) or if we should increment that by one.

That looks like:

```
// Config!$B$3 is max started tickets
// Config!$B$2 is rate to increment started tickets
// $ before a row or column, e.g., $B$3 means that the row or column
//   always stays the same -- not incrementing -- even when filled
//   to other cells
= IF(C2 >= Config!$B$3, 0, Config!$B$2)
```

This also means that our first column, `Open Tickets`, is decremented by the number of tickets that we've started coding:

```
// This is the definition of `Open Tickets`
=A2 + Config!$B$1 - B2
```

This leaves us with the values shown in Figure 17-6.

1	Open Tickets	*StartCodingMore?*	Started Coding	Tested Code	Deployed Code	Closed Tickets
2	10	0	0	0	0	0
3	11	1	1			
4	12	1	2			
5	13	1	3			
6	14	0	3			
7	15	0	3			
8	16	0	3			
9	17	0	3			
10	18	0	3			
11	19	0	3			
12	20	0	3			
13	21	0	3			
14	22	0	3			
15	23	0	3			
16	24	0	3			
17	25	0	3			
18	26	0	3			
19	27	0	3			
20	28	0	3			
21						

Figure 17-6. `Open Tickets`, `StartCodingMore?`, and `Started Coding` columns in spreadsheet model

Now we want to determine the number of tickets being tested at each step in the model. To do this, we create a calculation column, `NumToTest?`, which is defined as:

```
// Config$B$4 is the rate we can start testing tickets
// Note that we can only start testing tickets if there are tickets
// in `Started Coding` that we're able to start testing
=MIN(Config!$B$4, C3)
```

We then add that value to the previous number of tickets being tested:

```
// E2 is prior size of the Tested Code stock
// D3 is the value of `NumToTest?`
// F2 is the number of tested tickets to deploy
=E2 + D3 - F2
```

The result is shown in Figure 17-7.

1	Open Tickets	Started Coding	*NumToTest?*	Tested Code	Deployed Code	Closed Tickets
2	10	0	0	0	0	0
3	11	1	1	1		
4	11	1	1	2		
5	11	1	1	3		
6	11	1	1	4		
7	11	1	1	5		
8	11	1	1	6		
9	11	1	1	7		
10	11	1	1	8		
11	11	1	1	9		
12	11	1	1	10		
13	11	1	1	11		
14	11	1	1	12		
15	11	1	1	13		
16	11	1	1	14		
17	11	1	1	15		
18	11	1	1	16		
19	11	1	1	17		
20	11	1	1	18		

Figure 17-7. Spreadsheet showing three columns of systems modeling: `Started Coding`, `NumToTest?`, and `Tested Code`

Moving on to deploying code, let's keep things simple and start out by assuming that every tested change is going to get deployed. That means the calculation for `NumToDeploy?` is quite simple:

```
// E3 is the number of tested changes
=E3
```

Then the value for the `Deployed Code` stock is simple as well:

```
// G2 is the prior size of Deployed Code
// F3 is NumToDeploy?
// H2 is the number of deployed changes in prior round
=G2+F3-H2
```

The result is shown in Figure 17-8.

Open Tickets	Started Coding	Tested Code	NumToDeploy?	Deployed Code	NumToClose?	Closed Tickets
10	0	0	0	0	0	0
11	1	1	1	1		
11	1	1	1	2		
11	1	1	1	3		
11	1	1	1	4		
11	1	1	1	5		
11	1	1	1	6		
11	1	1	1	7		
11	1	1	1	8		
11	1	1	1	9		
11	1	1	1	10		
11	1	1	1	11		
11	1	1	1	12		
11	1	1	1	13		
11	1	1	1	14		
11	1	1	1	15		
11	1	1	1	16		
11	1	1	1	17		
11	1	1	1	18		

Figure 17-8. `NumToDeploy?` and `Deployed Code` columns in spreadsheet model

Now we're on to the final stock. We add the `NumToClose?` calculation, which assumes that all deployed changes are now closed:

```
// G3 is the number of deployed changes
=G3
```

This makes the calculation for the `Closed Tickets` stock:

```
// I2 is the prior value of Closed Tickets
// H3 is the NumToClose?
=I2 + H3
```

With that, we've now modeled the entire left-to-right flow, as shown in Figure 17-9.

1	Open Tickets	Started Coding	Tested Code	Deployed Code	NumToClose?	Closed Tickets
2	10	0	0	0	0	0
3	11	1	1	1	1	1
4	11	1	1	1	1	2
5	11	1	1	1	1	3
6	11	1	1	1	1	4
7	11	1	1	1	1	5
8	11	1	1	1	1	6
9	11	1	1	1	1	7
10	11	1	1	1	1	8
11	11	1	1	1	1	9
12	11	1	1	1	1	10
13	11	1	1	1	1	11
14	11	1	1	1	1	12
15	11	1	1	1	1	13
16	11	1	1	1	1	14
17	11	1	1	1	1	15
18	11	1	1	1	1	16
19	11	1	1	1	1	17
20	11	1	1	1	1	18

Figure 17-9. Entirety of left-to-right flows in spreadsheet model

The left-to-right flows are simple, with a few constrained flows and a few very scalable flows, but overall we see things progressing through the pipeline evenly. All that is about to change!

Modeling right-to-left

We've now finished modeling the happy path from left to right. Next we need to model all the exception paths where things flow right to left. For example, an issue found in production would cause a flow from `Closed Tickets` back to `Open Tickets`. This tends to be where models get interesting.

There are three right-to-left flows that we need to model:

1. `Closed Tickets` to `Open Tickets` represents a bug discovered in production.
2. `Deployed Code` to `Started Coding` represents a bug discovered during deployment.
3. `Tested Code` to `Started Coding` represents a bug discovered in testing.

To start, we're going to add configurations defining the rates of those flows (Figure 17-10). These are going to be percentage flows, with a certain percentage of the target stock triggering the error condition rather than proceeding. For example, perhaps 25% of the `Closed Tickets` are discovered to have a bug each round.

	A	B	C	D	E
1	TicketOpenRate	1			
2	StartCodingRate	1			
3	MaxConcurrentCodingNum	3			
4	TicketTestRate	1			
5	ErrorsInProd	0.25			
6	ErrorsInDeploy	0.25			
7	ErrorsInTest	0.25			

Figure 17-10. Introducing three additional values in model configuration

These are fine starter values, and we'll experiment with how adjusting them changes the model in the *Exercise* section next.

Now we'll start by modeling errors discovered in production, by adding a column to model the flow from `Closed Tickets` to `Open Tickets`, the `ErrorsFoundInProd?` column:

```
// I3 is the number of Closed Tickets
// Config!$B$5 is the rate of errors
=FLOOR(I3 * Config!$B$5)
```

Note the usage of `FLOOR` to avoid moving partial tickets. Feel free to skip that entirely if you're comfortable with the concept of fractional tickets, fractional deploys, and so on. This is an aesthetic consideration, and generally only impacts your model if you choose overly small starting values.

This means that our calculation for `Closed Tickets` needs to be updated as well to reduce by the prior row's result for `ErrorsFoundInProd?`:

```
// I2 is the prior value of ClosedTickets
// H3 is the current value of NumToClose?
// J2 is the prior value of ErrorsFoundInProd?
=I2 + H3 - J2
```

We're not quite done, because we *also* need to add the prior row's value of `ErrorsInProd?` into `Open Tickets`; this represents the errors' flow from closed to open tickets. Based on this change, the calculation for `Open Tickets` becomes:

```
// A2 is the prior value of Open Tickets
// Config!$B$1 is the base rate of ticket opening
// B2 is prior row's StartCodingMore?
```

```
// J2 is prior row's ErrorsFoundInProd?
=A2 + Config!$B$1 - B2 + J2
```

Now we have the full errors in production flow represented in our model (Figure 17-11).

	A	B	C	E	G	I	J
1	**Open Tickets**	*StartCodingMore?*	**Started Coding**	**Tested Code**	**Deployed Code**	**Closed Tickets**	*ErrorsFoundInProd?*
2	10	0	0	0	0	0	0
3	11	1	1	1	1	1	0
4	11	1	1	1	1	2	0
5	11	1	1	1	1	3	0
6	11	1	1	1	1	4	1
7	12	1	1	1	1	4	1
8	13	1	1	1	1	4	1
9	14	1	1	1	1	4	1
10	15	1	1	1	1	4	1
11	16	1	1	1	1	4	1
12	17	1	1	1	1	4	1
13	18	1	1	1	1	4	1
14	19	1	1	1	1	4	1
15	20	1	1	1	1	4	1
16	21	1	1	1	1	4	1
17	22	1	1	1	1	4	1
18	23	1	1	1	1	4	1
19	24	1	1	1	1	4	1
20	25	1	1	1	1	4	1

Figure 17-11. Modeling `ErrorsFoundInProd?` in spreadsheet model

Next, it's time to add the `Deployed Code` to `Started Coding` flow. Start by adding the `ErrorsFoundInProd?` calculation:

```
// G3 is deployed code
// Config!$B$6 is deployed error rate
=FLOOR(G3 * Config!$B$6)
```

Then we need to update the calculation for `Deployed Code` to decrease by the calculated value in `ErrorsFoundInProd?`:

```
// G2 is the prior value of Deployed Code
// F3 is NumToDeploy?
// H2 is prior row's NumToClose?
// I2 is ErrorsFoundInDeploy?
=G2 + F3 - H2 - I2
```

Finally, we need to increase the size of `Started Coding` by the same value, representing the flow of errors discovered in deployment:

```
// C2 is the prior value of Started Coding
// B3 is StartCodingMore?
// D2 is prior value of NumToTest?
// I2 is prior value of ErrorsFoundInDeploy?
=C2 + B3 - D2 + I2
```

We now have the working flow representing errors in production (Figure 17-12).

	A	C	E	G	H	I	J
1	Open Tickets	Started Coding	Tested Code	Deployed Code	*NumToClose?*	*ErrorsFoundInDeploy?*	Closed Tickets
2	10	0	0	0	0	0	0
3	11	1	1	1	1	0	1
4	11	1	1	1	1	0	2
5	11	1	1	1	1	0	3
6	11	1	1	1	1	0	4
7	12	1	1	1	1	0	4
8	13	1	1	1	1	0	4
9	14	1	1	1	1	0	4
10	15	1	1	1	1	0	4
11	16	1	1	1	1	0	4
12	17	1	1	1	1	0	4
13	18	1	1	1	1	0	4
14	19	1	1	1	1	0	4
15	20	1	1	1	1	0	4
16	21	1	1	1	1	0	4
17	22	1	1	1	1	0	4
18	23	1	1	1	1	0	4
19	24	1	1	1	1	0	4
20	25	1	1	1	1	0	4

Figure 17-12. `DeployedCode`, `NumToClose?`, and `ErrorsFoundInDeploy?` columns in spreadsheet model

Finally, we can add the `Tested Code` to `Started Coding` flow. This is pretty much the same as the prior flow we added, starting with adding an `ErrorsFoundInTest?` calculation:

```
// E3 is tested code
// Config!$B$7 is the testing error rate
=FLOOR(E3 * Config!$B$7)
```

Then we update `Tested Code` to reduce by this value:

```
// E2 is prior value of Tested Code
// D3 is NumToTest?
// G2 is prior value of NumToDeploy?
// F2 is prior value of ErrorsFoundInTest?
=E2 + D3 - G2 - F2
```

And update `Started Coding` to increase by this value:

```
// C2 is prior value of Started Coding
// B3 is StartCodingMore?
// D2 is prior value of NumToTest?
// J2 is prior value of ErrorsFoundInDeploy?
// F2 is prior value of ErrorsFoundInTest?
= C2 + B3 - D2 + J2 + F2
```

Now this last flow is instrumented (Figure 17-13).

	A	B	C	D	E	F	H	K
1	Open Tickets	StartCodingMore?	Started Coding	NumToTest?	Tested Code	ErrorsFoundInTest?	Deployed Code	Closed Tickets
2	10	0	0	0	0	0	0	0
3	11	1	1	1	1	0	1	1
4	11	1	1	1	1	0	1	2
5	11	1	1	1	1	0	1	3
6	11	1	1	1	1	0	1	4
7	12	1	1	1	1	0	1	4
8	13	1	1	1	1	0	1	4
9	14	1	1	1	1	0	1	4
10	15	1	1	1	1	0	1	4
11	16	1	1	1	1	0	1	4
12	17	1	1	1	1	0	1	4
13	18	1	1	1	1	0	1	4
14	19	1	1	1	1	0	1	4
15	20	1	1	1	1	0	1	4
16	21	1	1	1	1	0	1	4
17	22	1	1	1	1	0	1	4
18	23	1	1	1	1	0	1	4
19	24	1	1	1	1	0	1	4
20	25	1	1	1	1	0	1	4

Figure 17-13. Modeling `ErrorsFoundInTest?` in spreadsheet model

With that, we now have a complete model that we can start exercising! This exercise demonstrated that it's *quite possible* to represent a meaningful model in a spreadsheet, but also the challenges of doing so.

While developing this model, a number of errors became evident. Some of them I was able to fix relatively easily, and even more I left unfixed because fixing them makes the model *even harder* to reason about. This is a good example of why I encourage developing one or two models in a spreadsheet, but I ultimately don't believe it's the right mechanism to work in for most people: even very smart people make errors in their spreadsheets, and catching those errors is exceptionally challenging.

EXERCISE

Now that we're done building this model, we can finally start the fun part: exercising it. We'll start by creating a simple bar chart showing the size of each stock at each step. We are going to expressly *not* show the intermediate calculation columns such as `NumToTest?`, because those are implementation details rather than being particularly interesting.

Before we start tweaking the values, let's look at the baseline chart in Figure 17-14.

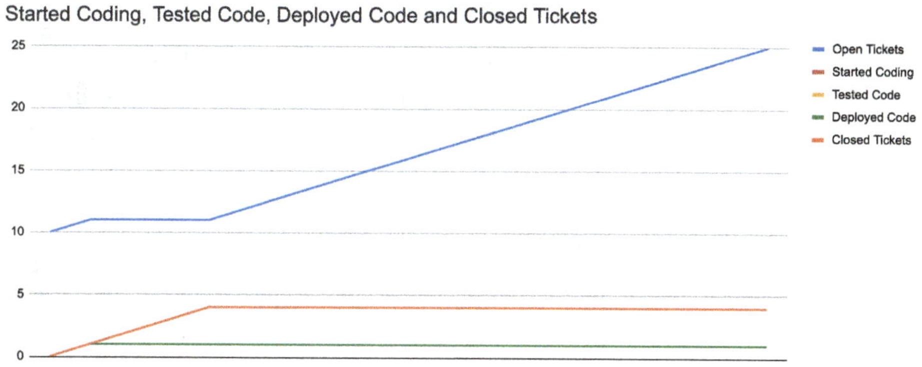

Figure 17-14. Baseline chart where number of closed tickets quickly stops increasing

The most interesting thing to notice is that our current model doesn't actually increase the number of closed tickets over time. We actually just get further and further behind over time, which isn't too exciting.

So let's start modeling the first way that LLMs might help, reducing the error rate in production. Let's shift `ErrorsInProd` from 0.25 down to 0.1 and see how that impacts the chart (Figure 17-15).

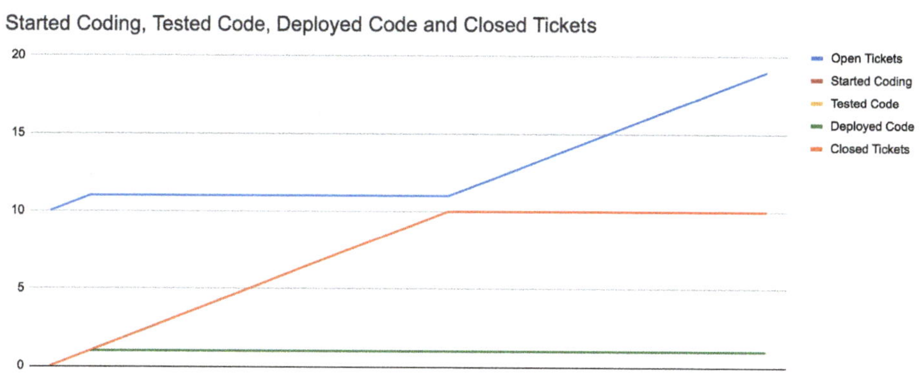

Figure 17-15. Reducing error rates delays, but doesn't prevent, reaching equilibrium of closed tickets

We can see that this allows us to make more progress on closing tickets, although at some point equilibrium is established between closed tickets and the error rate in production, preventing further progress. This does validate that reducing error rate in production matters. It also suggests that as long as error rate is a function of everything we've previously shipped, we are eventually in trouble.

Next, let's experiment with the idea that LLMs allow us to test more quickly, tripling `TicketTestRate` from 1 to 3. It turns out, increasing the testing rate doesn't change anything at all, because the current constraint is in starting tickets (Figure 17-16).

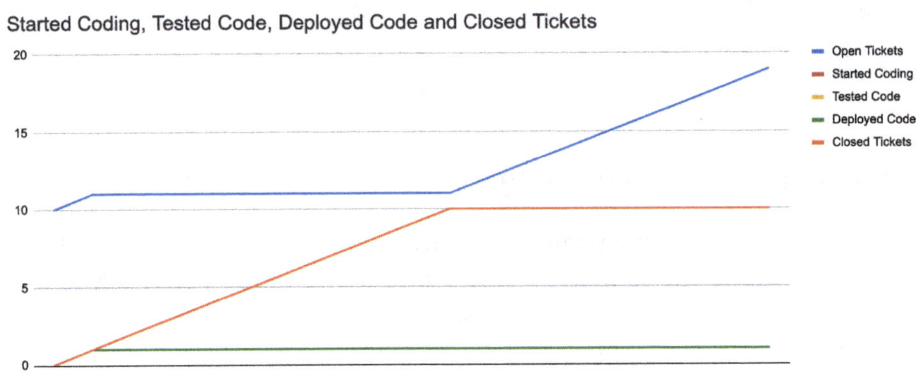

Figure 17-16. Changing testing rate doesn't change the model's behavior

So, let's test that. Maybe LLMs make us faster in starting tickets because *overall* speed of development goes down. Let's model that by increasing `StartCodingRate` from 1 to 3 as well (Figure 17-17).

This is a fascinating result, because tripling development and testing velocity has changed how much work we start, but ultimately the real constraint in our system is the error discovery rate in production.

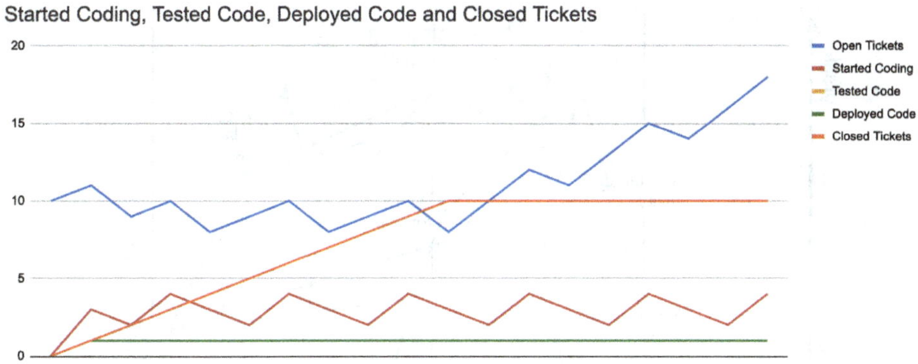

Figure 17-17. Starting or testing tickets faster creates noise but not progress

By exercising this model, we find an interesting result. To the extent that our error rate is a function of the volume of things we've shipped in production, shipping faster doesn't increase our velocity at all. The only meaningful way to increase productivity in this model is to reduce the error rate in production.

Models are imperfect representations of reality, but this one gives us a clear sense of what matters the most: if we want to increase our velocity, we have to reduce the rate that we discover errors in production. That might be reducing the error rate as implied in this model, or it might be ideas that exist outside of this model. For example, the model doesn't represent this well, but perhaps we'd be better off iterating more on fewer things to avoid this scenario. If we make multiple changes to one area, it still just represents one implemented feature, not many implemented features, and the overall error rate wouldn't increase.

Document 17-3: Wardley Mapping the LLM Ecosystem

HOW THINGS WORK TODAY

If retrieval-augmented generation (RAG) was the trending LLM pattern of 2023, and you could reasonably argue that agents—or agentic workflows—are the pattern of 2024, then it's hard to guess what the patterns of tomorrow will be, but it's likely that there are more, new patterns coming our way. LLMs are a proven platform today, and now are being applied widely to discover new patterns (Figure 17-18). It's a safe bet that validating these patterns will continue to drive product companies to support additional infrastructure components (e.g., search indexes to support RAG).

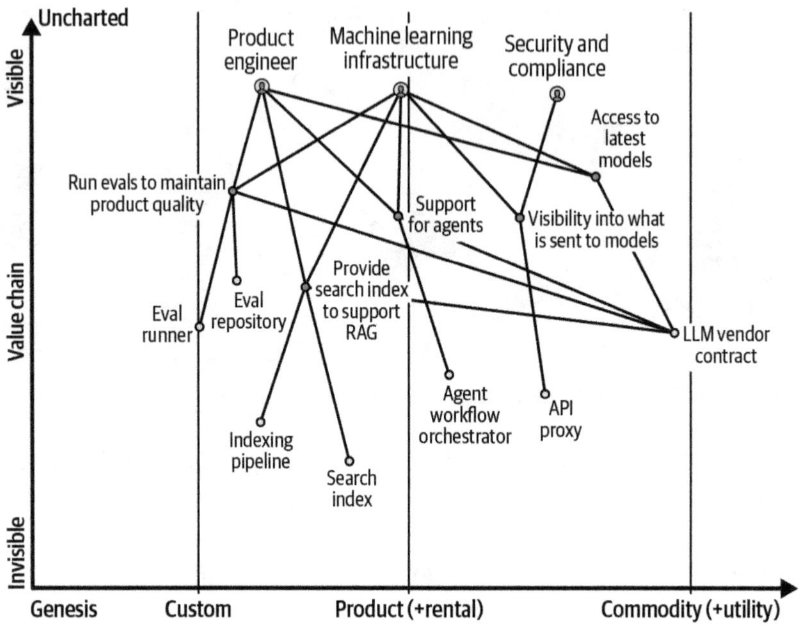

Figure 17-18. Current state of LLM ecosystem

This proliferation of patterns has created a significant cost for these product companies, a problem that market forces are likely to address as offerings evolve.

TRANSITION TO FUTURE STATE

Looking at the evolution of the LLM ecosystem, there are two questions that I believe will define the evolution of the space:

1. Will LLM framework platforms for agents, RAG, and so on remain bundled with model providers such as OpenAI and Anthropic? Or will they, instead, split with models and platforms being offered separately?
2. Which elements of LLM frameworks will be productizable in the short term? For example, running evals seems like a straightforward opportunity for bundling, as would providing *some* degree of agent support. Conversely, bundling RAG might seem straightforward but most production use cases would require real-time updates, incurring the full complexity of operating scaled search clusters.

Depending on the answers to those questions, you might draw a very different map (Figure 17-19). This map answers the first question by imagining that

LLM platforms will decouple from model providers, while also allowing you to license with that platform for model access rather than needing to individually negotiate with each model provider. It answers the second question by imagining that most non-RAG functionality will move into a bundled platform provider. Given the richness of investment in the current space, it seems safe to believe that every plausible combination will exist to some degree until the ecosystem eventually stabilizes in one dominant configuration.

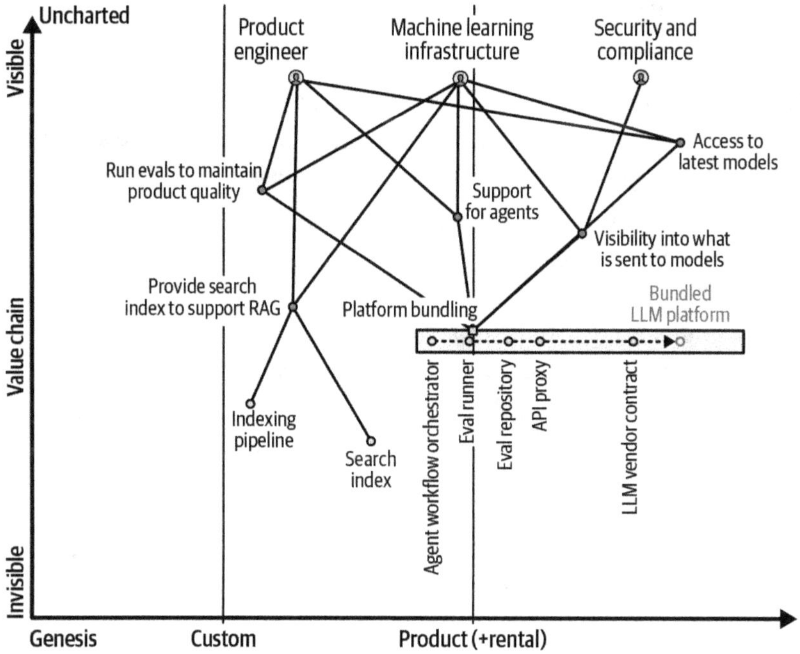

Figure 17-19. Pipeline of LLM platform bundling

The key drivers of this configuration are that the LLM ecosystem is investing in new patterns every year, and companies are spinning up haphazard internal solutions to validate those patterns, but ultimately few product companies are able to effectively fund these sorts of internal solutions in the long run.

If this map is correct, then it means eventual headwinds faced by both model providers (who are inherently limited to providing their own subset of models) as well as narrow LLM platform providers (who can only service a subset of LLM patterns). The likely best bet for a product company in this future is to adopt the broadest LLM pattern platforms today, and to explicitly decouple pattern platform from model provider.

USER AND VALUE CHAINS

The LLM landscape is evolving rapidly, with some techniques getting introduced and reaching widespread adoption within a single calendar year. Sometimes those widely adopted techniques are *actually* being adopted, and other times it's closer to "conference-talk-driven development" where folks with broad platforms inflate the maturity of industry adoption.

The three primary users attempting to navigate that dynamism are:

1. Product Engineers are looking for faster, easier solutions to deploying LLMs across the many, evolving parameters: new models, support for agents, solutions to offload the search dimensions of RAG, and so on.
2. The Machine Learning Infrastructure team is responsible for the effective usage of the mechanisms, and steering product developers toward effective adoption of these tools. They are also, in tandem with other infrastructure engineering teams, responsible for supporting common elements for LLM solutions, such as search indexes to power RAG implementations.
3. Security and Compliance—how to ensure models are hosted safely and securely, and that we're only sending approved information? How do we stay in alignment with rapidly evolving AI risks and requirements?

To keep the map focused on evolution rather than organizational dynamics, I've consolidated a number of teams in slightly artificial ways, and omitted a few teams that are certainly worth considering. Finance needs to understand the cost and volume of LLM usage. Security and Compliance are really different teams, with both overlapping and distinct requirements between them. Machine Learning Infrastructure could be split into two distinct teams with somewhat conflicting perspectives on who should own things like search infrastructure.

Depending on what *you* want to learn from the map, you might prefer to combine, split, and introduce a different set of combinations than I've selected here.

Document 17-4: Modeling Driver Onboarding

LEARNINGS

An obvious assumption is that making driver onboarding faster would increase the long-term number of drivers in a market. However, this model (Figure 17-20) shows that even doubling the rate at which we qualify applicant drivers as eligible has little impact on active drivers over time.

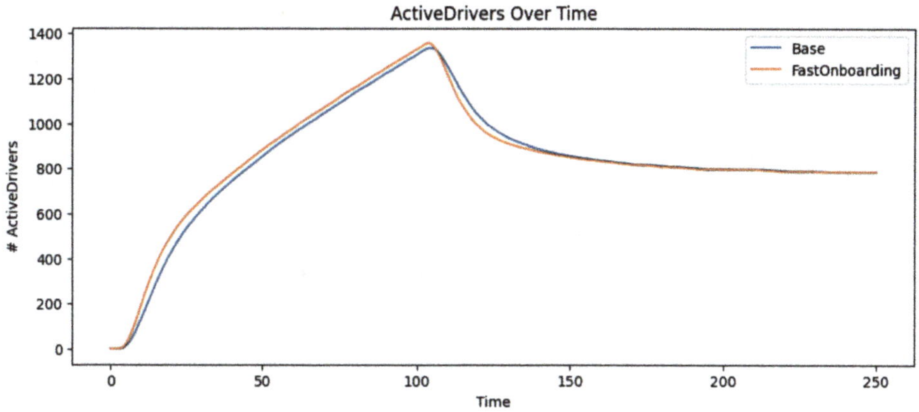

Figure 17-20. Speeding up onboarding doesn't impact active drivers in the long term

Conversely, it's clear that efforts to reengage departed drivers have a significant impact on active drivers. We believe that there are potential LLM applications that could encourage departed drivers to return to active driving; for example, mapping their rationale for departing against our recent product changes and driver retention promotions could generate high-quality, personalized emails (Figure 17-21).

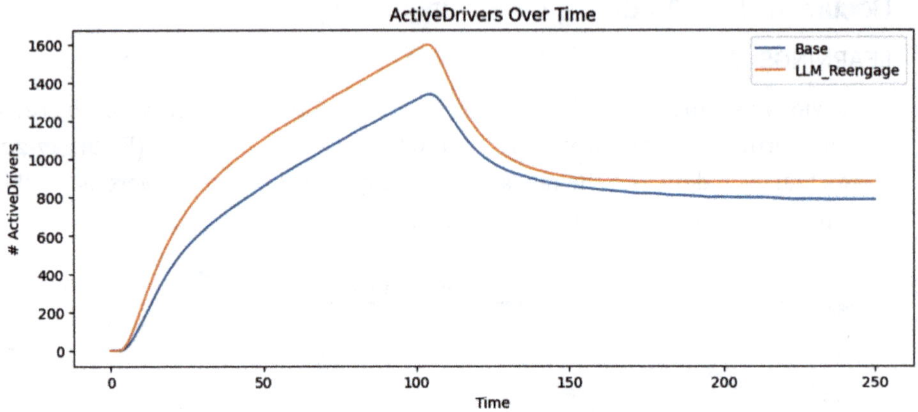

Figure 17-21. Improving driver reengagement does increase active drivers

Finally, the model shows (Figure 17-22) that increasing reactivation of either departed or suspended drivers is significantly less impactful than increasing both. If either rate is low, we lose an increasingly large number of drivers over time.

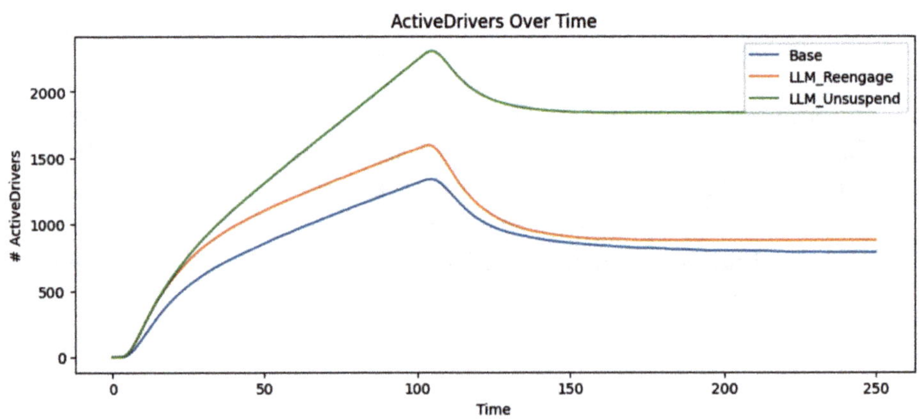

Figure 17-22. Increasing the reactivation rate of suspended drivers has the highest impact

The only meaningful opportunities for us to increase active drivers with LLMs are improving those two reactivation rates.

SKETCH

The first step in modeling a system is sketching it (using Excalidraw (*https://excalidraw.com*)). Here we're developing a model for onboarding and retaining drivers for a ride-sharing application in one city (Figure 17-23).

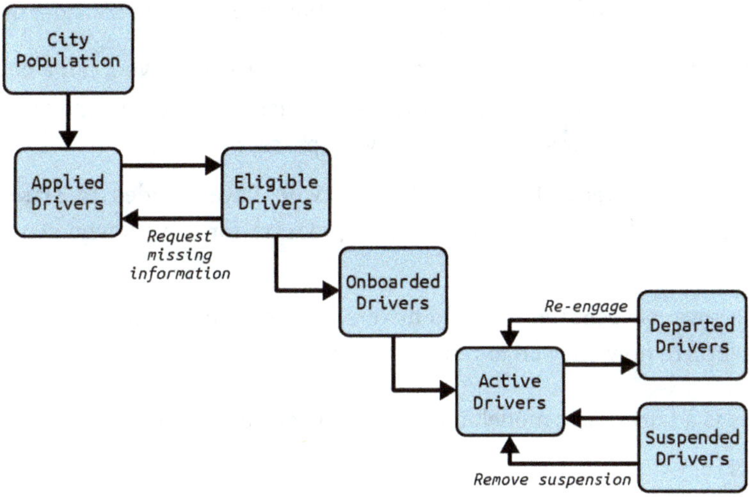

Figure 17-23. Sketch of onboarding drivers onto a ride-sharing application

The stocks are:

1. `City Population` is the total population of a city.
2. `Applied Drivers` are the number of people who've applied to be drivers.
3. `Eligible Drivers` are the number of applied drivers who meet eligibility criteria (e.g., provided a current driver's license, etc.).
4. `Onboarded Drivers` are eligible drivers who have successfully gone through an onboarding program.
5. `Active Drivers` are onboarded drivers who are actually performing trips on a weekly basis.
6. `Departed Drivers` were active drivers, but voluntarily stopped performing trips (e.g., took a different job).
7. `Suspended Drivers` were active drivers, but involuntarily stopped performing trips (i.e., are no longer allowed to drive on the platform).

Looking at the left-to-right flows, there is a flow from each of those stocks to the following stock in the pipeline. These are all simple one-to-one flows, with the exception of those coming from `Active Drivers`, which leads to two distinct stocks: `Departed Drivers` and `Suspended Drivers`. These represent voluntary and involuntary departures.

There are a handful of right-to-left, exception path flows to consider as well:

1. `Request missing information` represents a driver who can't be moved from `Applied Drivers` to `Eligible Drivers` because their provided information proved insufficient in a review process.
2. `Re-engage` tracks `Departed Drivers` who have decided to start driving again, perhaps because of a bonus program for drivers who start driving again.
3. `Remove suspension` refers to drivers who were involuntarily removed, but who are now allowed to return to driving.

This is a fairly basic model, but let's see what we can learn from it.

REASON

Now that we've sketched the system, we can start thinking about which flows are going to have the largest impact, and where an LLM might increase those flows. Some observations from reasoning about it:

- If a city's population is infinite, then what really matters in this model is how many new drivers we can encourage to join the system. On the other hand, if a city's population is finite, then onboarding new drivers will be essential in the early stages of coming online in any particular city, but long term, reengaging departed drivers is probably at least as important.
- LLM tooling could speed up validating eligible drivers. If we speed that process up enough, we could greatly reduce the rate of the `Request missing information` flow by identifying missing information in real-time rather than requiring a human to review the information later.
- We could potentially develop LLM tooling to craft personalized messaging to departed drivers that explains which of our changes since their departure might be most relevant to their reasons for stopping. This could increase the rate of the `Re-engage` flow.

- While we likely wouldn't want an LLM approving the removal of suspensions, we could have it look at requests to be revalidated and identify promising requests to focus human attention on those with the highest potential for approval.
- We could build LLM-powered tooling that helps a city resident decide whether they should apply to become a driver by answering questions they might have.

As we exercise the model later, we know that our assumptions about whether this city has already exhausted potential drivers will quickly steer us toward a specific subset of these potential options. If all potential drivers are already tapped, only work to reactivate prior drivers will matter. If there are more potential drivers, then activating them will likely be a better focus.

MODEL

For this model, we'll be using the `lethain/systems` (*https://github.com/lethain/systems*) library that I wrote. For a more detailed introduction, I recommend working through the tutorial in the repository (*https://github.com/lethain/systems/blob/master/README.md*), but I'll introduce the basics here as well. While systems is far from a perfect tool, as you experiment with different modeling techniques like spreadsheet-based modeling and SageModeler (*https://oreil.ly/9c2Gt*), I think this approach's emphasis on rapid development and reproducible, sharable models is somewhat unique.

If you want to see the finished model, you can find the model and visualizations in the JupyterHub notebook in `lethain/eng-strategy-models` (*https://github.com/lethain/eng-strategy-models/blob/main/DriverOnboarding.ipynb*). Here we'll work through the steps behind implementing that model.

We'll start by creating a stock for the city's population, with an initial size of 10,000:

```
# City population is 10,000
CityPop(10000)
```

Next, we want to initialize the `Applied Drivers` stock, and specify a constant rate of 100 people in the city applying to become drivers each round. This will only happen until the 10,000 potential drivers in the city are exhausted, at which point there will be no one left to apply:

```
# 100 folks apply to become drivers per round
# the @ 100 format is called a "rate" flow
CityPop > AppliedDrivers @ 100
```

Now we want to initialize the `Eligible Drivers` stock, and specify that 25% of the folks in `Applied Drivers` will advance to become eligible each round.

Before, we used `@ 100` to specify a fixed rate. Here we're using `@ Leak(0.25)` to specify the idea of 25% of the folks in `Applied Drivers` advancing into `Eligible Drivers`:

```
# 25% of applied drivers become eligible each round
AppliedDrivers > EligibleDrivers @ Leak(0.25)
```

You could write this as `@ 0.25`, but you'd actually get different behavior. That's because `@ 0.25` is actually shorthand for `@ Conversion(0.25)`, which is similar to a leak but destroys the unconverted portion.

Using an example to show the difference, let's imagine that we have 100 applied drivers and 100 eligible drivers, and then see the consequences of applying a leak versus a conversion:

- `Leak(0.25)` would end with 75 applied drivers and 125 eligible drivers.
- `Conversion(0.25)` would end with 0 applied drivers and 125 eligible drivers.

Depending on what you are modeling, you might need leaks, conversions, or both.

Moving on, next we model our first right-to-left flow. Specifically, the `Request missing information` flow, where some eligible drivers end up not being eligible because they need to provide more information:

```
# This is "Request missing information", with 10%
# of folks moving backward each round
EligibleDrivers > AppliedDrivers @ Leak(0.1)
```

Note that the syntax for left-to-right and right-to-left flows is identical, without making a distinction.

Now, 25% of `Eligible Drivers` become `Onboarded Drivers` each round:

```
# 25% of eligible drivers onboard each round
EligibleDrivers > OnboardedDrivers @ Leak(0.25)
```

Then 50% of `Onboarded Drivers` become `Active Drivers`, actually providing rides:

```
# 50% of onboarded drivers become active
OnboardedDrivers > ActiveDrivers @ Leak(0.50)
```

The `Active Drivers` stock is drained by two flows: drivers who voluntarily depart become `Departed Drivers`, and drivers who are suspended become `Suspended Drivers`. Both flows take 10% of active drivers each round:

```
# 10% of active drivers depart voluntarily and involuntarily
ActiveDrivers > DepartedDrivers @ Leak(0.10)
ActiveDrivers > SuspendedDrivers @ Leak(0.10)
```

Finally, we also see 5% of `Departed Drivers` returning to driving each round. Similarly, we unsuspend 1% of `Suspended Drivers`:

```
# 5% of DepartedDrivers become active
DepartedDrivers > ActiveDrivers @ Leak(0.05)
# 1% of SuspendedDrivers are reactivated
SuspendedDrivers > ActiveDrivers @ Leak(0.01)
```

We already sketched this model out earlier, but it's worth noting that systems will allow you to export models via Graphviz (*https://graphviz.org*). These diagrams are generally harder to read than a custom-drawn one, but it's certainly possible to use this toolchain to combine sketching and modeling into a single step (Figure 17-24).

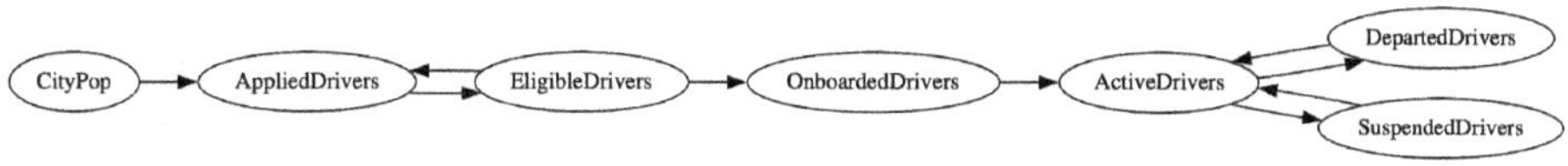

Figure 17-24. Graphviz representation of systems model

Now that we have the model, we get to exercise it to learn its secrets.

EXERCISE

Our base model acquires initial drivers quickly, then slows as the city population is exhausted (Figure 17-25).

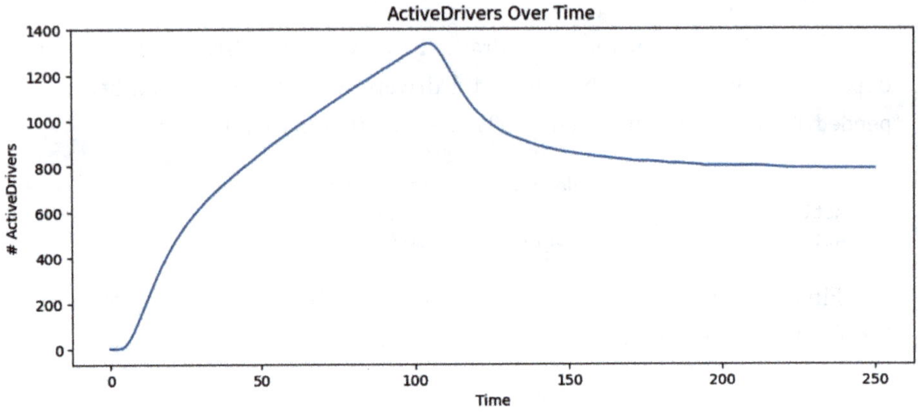

Figure 17-25. Base onboarding model stabilizing around 800 active drivers

Now let's imagine that our LLM-powered tool can speed up eligible drivers, doubling the speed that we move applied drivers to eligible drivers. Instead of 25% of applied drivers becoming eligible each round, we'll instead see 50%.

```
# old
AppliedDrivers > EligibleDrivers @ Leak(0.25)
# new
AppliedDrivers > EligibleDrivers @ Leak(0.50)
```

Unfortunately, we can see that even doubling the speed at which we're onboarding drivers to be eligible has a minimal impact (Figure 17-26).

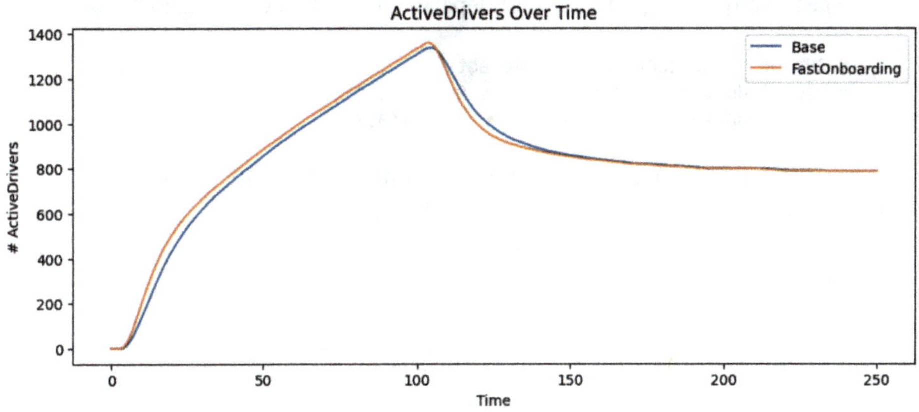

Figure 17-26. Speeding up onboarding doesn't impact active drivers in the long term

To finish testing this hypothesis, we can eliminate the `Request missing information` flow entirely and see if this changes things meaningfully, commenting out that line (Figure 17-27).

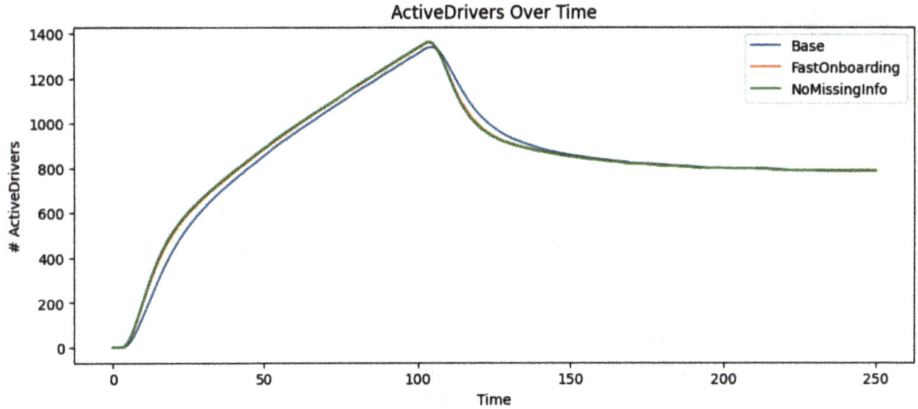

Figure 17-27. Eliminating `Request missing information` error doesn't impact active drivers in the long term

Unfortunately, even eliminating the missing-information error rate has little impact on the number of active drivers. So, it seems like the opportunity for our LLM solutions to increase active drivers is going to need to focus on reactivating existing drivers.

Specifically, let's go from 5% of departed drivers reactivating to 20%:

```
# 20% of DepartedDrivers become active
# DepartedDrivers > ActiveDrivers @ Leak(0.05)
# DepartedDrivers > ActiveDrivers @ Leak(0.2)
```

For the first time, we're seeing a significant shift in impact. We reach a much higher percentage of drivers at peak, and even after we exhaust all drivers in a city, the total number of active drivers reaches a higher equilibrium (Figure 17-28).

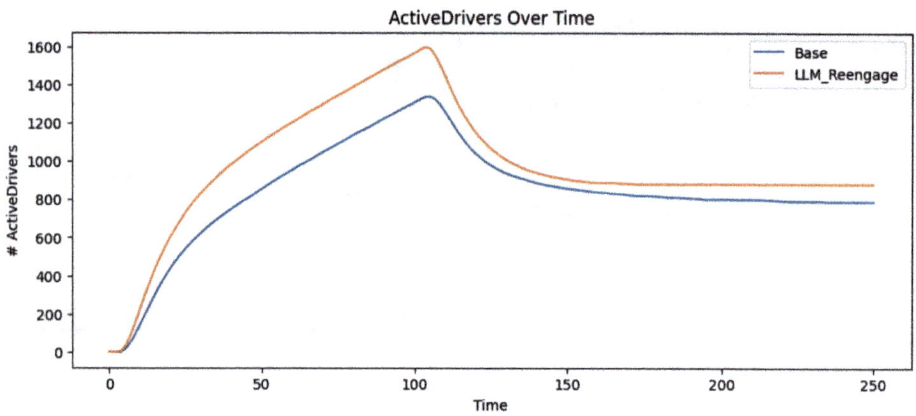

Figure 17-28. Improving driver reengagement does increase active drivers

Presumably, increasing the rate that we reactivate suspended drivers from 1% to 2.5% would have a similar, meaningful but smaller impact on active drivers over time. So let's model that change:

```
# 2.5% of SuspendedDrivers are reactivated
#SuspendedDrivers > ActiveDrivers @ Leak(0.01)
SuspendedDrivers > ActiveDrivers @ Leak(0.025)
```

However, surprisingly, the impact of increasing the reactivation rate of suspended drivers is actually much higher than reengaging departed drivers (Figure 17-29).

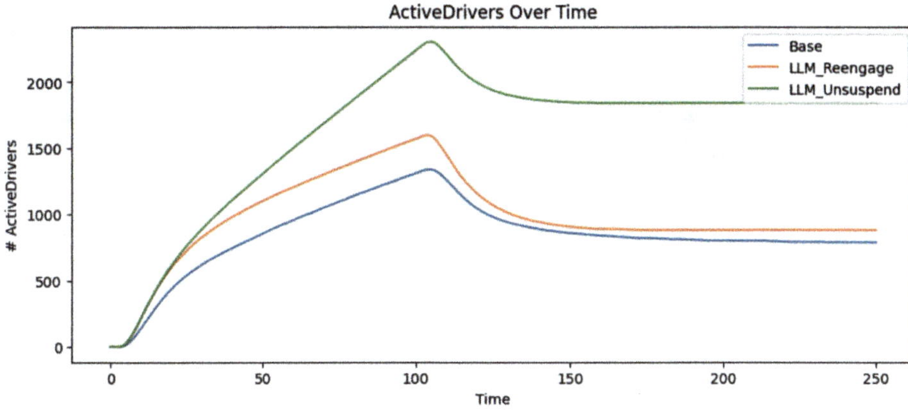

Figure 17-29. Increasing the reactivation rate of suspended drivers has the highest impact

This is an interesting and somewhat counterintuitive result. Increasing the rate for both suspended and departed rates is more impactful than increasing either, because ultimately there's a growing population of drivers in the slower deflating stock. This means, surprisingly, that a tool that helps us quickly determine which drivers could be unsuspended might matter more than the small size of the flow indicates.

At this point, we've probably found the primary story that this model wants to tell us: we should focus efforts on reactivating departed and suspended drivers. Changes elsewhere might reduce operational costs of our business, but they won't solve the problem of increasing active drivers.

Summary

When these strategies were written in 2024, dreams of LLM adoption were everywhere, but there was no certainty about how LLMs would actually evolve over time. Similarly, there were extremely few teams or leaders with meaningful experience adopting these technologies, but a great deal of pressure from the industry to incorporate them as quickly and broadly as possible.

These documents show how strategy, particularly the refinement techniques, can support leaders in finding a reasonable path forward despite the impossible combination of urgency and uncertainty.

18

Private Equity Ownership Strategy

This chapter's documents take on the role of an engineering organization attempting to navigate new ownership by a private equity group. It's an increasingly frequent scenario: after many years of learning to operate under the direction of its original founders, and the brief excitement of going public, now there's a short runway to change operating models.

Let's call this company Fungible Ecommerce Company. It's a platform for supporting online commerce, and Document 18-1 is its Engineering leadership team's attempt to think through their options while waiting for the new ownership to provide concrete guideposts.

One of the trademarks of private equity ownership is the expectation that either the company maintains its current margin and grows revenue at 25% to 30%, or grows more slowly and increases its free cash flow year over year. In many organizations, engineering costs have a major impact on free cash flow. There are many costs to reduce—cloud hosting and such—but inevitably, part of the discussion is addressing engineering headcount costs directly.

One of the largest contributors to engineering headcount costs is an organization's seniority mix: more senior engineers are paid quite a bit more than earlier career engineers. Document 18-2 models how various policies impact an organization's seniority mix.

Reading These Documents

The documents in this chapter are combinations of real documents addressing several similar circumstances across multiple companies. They are:

Document 18-1: Navigating Private Equity Ownership
: This document summarizes the Engineering organization's strategy for working with new Private Equity ownership.

Document 18-2: Engineering Organization Seniority-Mix Model
: This system model explores how different cost-management strategies will impact the Engineering organization's cost structure over time.

If you're reading these documents with the goal of applying the strategies they put forward, start at the top and read to the end. If, on the other hand, your main goal is to understand the thinking behind them, read the sections in reverse order, starting with *Explore*, then *Diagnose*, and so on. For more on this structure, see Chapter 11.

As with the other chapters in Part IV, this chapter reproduces a set of documents, provides context and commentary in footnotes, and concludes by drawing out some key takeaways. The full model and visualizations for each iteration in Document 18-2 are available on GitHub (*https://github.com/lethain/eng-strategy-models/blob/main/BackfillPolicy.ipynb*).

Document 18-1: Navigating Private Equity Ownership

POLICY

Our policy for managing our new ownership structure is:[1]

- We believe our new ownership will provide a specific target for Research and Development (R&D) operating expenses during the upcoming financial year planning. We will revise these policies again once we have explicit targets, and will delay planning around reductions until we have those numbers to avoid running two overlapping processes.

  That said, looking at our R&D investment relative to comparably growing peer sets, we believe that we'll get pressure to moderately reduce our spend. *We aim to accomplish that reduction through a series of policies and*

1 Relative to the default structure, this document has been refactored in two ways to improve readability: first, *Operation* has been folded into *Policy*; second, *Refine* has been embedded in *Diagnose*.

one-off infrastructure projects, without requiring a major reduction in headcount spend.

- *We will move to an "N-1" backfill policy,* where departures are backfilled with a less senior level. We will also institute a strict maximum of one Principal Engineer per business unit, with any exceptions approved in writing by the CTO—this applies for both promotions and external hires. These policies are effective immediately, and are based on our model of engineering-org seniority mix (Document 18-2).

  We commit to this policy of reducing headcount costs by approximately 5% YoY every year for the foreseeable future.

- We evaluated a number of potential changes to our geographical hiring strategy, but we believe that staffing engineers with cross-functional partners (Product, Marketing, Sales, and so on) is a priority. We have not been able to reach an agreement cross-functionally, and as such *we are not changing our geographical hiring strategy at this time.*

  If we can agree on a policy here, we could accomplish a 10%–20% reduction in cost over two to three years, but the details matter a great deal, so we cannot commit to a specific outcome until we get more cross-functional alignment.

- Our infrastructure spend has grown significantly more slowly than revenue for the past two years, meaning that we've successfully implemented our infrastructure spend strategy of growing infrastructure costs more slowly than revenue (*https://oreil.ly/wZBpX*). *We will continue our current infrastructure efficiency strategy,* and believe there are relatively few high-impact efficiency opportunities at this point.

  We commit to growing infrastructure spend at no more than 5% YoY, significantly lower than our projected revenue increase of 25% YoY.

- There are two narrow infrastructure spend opportunities, both related to the integration of prior acquisitions into our shared infrastructure and away from one-off approaches. *We will prioritize the post-acquisition integration work next quarter,* with the goal of fully standardizing all infrastructure across the company into the stack maintained by our centralized Infrastructure Engineering team.

  We commit to a one-time reduction in infrastructure of 3% YoY.

- We believe there are significant opportunities to reduce R&D maintenance investments, but we don't have conviction about which particular efforts we should prioritize. *We will kick off a working group to identify the features with the highest support load.*

DIAGNOSE

We've diagnosed Fungible Ecommerce Company's current state as:

- Fungible Ecommerce Company's revenue has grown 20%–25% YoY for the past two years, and our target for next year is 25% YoY revenue growth. While this is not a guarantee—we grew slower than 25% last year—it's a defensible goal that we have a good chance of achieving.
- Our Engineering headcount costs have grown by 15% YoY this year, and 18% YoY the prior year. Headcount grew 7% and 9% respectively, with the difference between headcount and headcount costs explained by salary band adjustments (4%), a focus on hiring senior roles (3%), and increased hiring in higher cost geographic regions (1%).
- Based on general practice, it seems likely that our new Private Equity ownership will expect us to reduce R&D headcount costs through a reduction. However, without concrete details, we cannot yet make structured decisions. Our strategy will depend significantly on the scale of any proposed reductions.
- Infrastructure engineering spend (including vendors) has grown by 4%–5% YoY for the past three years. We made a significant push on reducing costs three years ago, and have grown slower than revenue since then.

  There are few remaining opportunities to significantly reduce infrastructure costs, but we've made several acquisitions since our prior infrastructure consolidation that represent significant potential savings: roughly one-time 1.5% YoY reductions for each of the two largest opportunities.
- A significant portion of our current R&D spend goes into maintaining our existing functionality, particularly functionality related to earlier geo-expansion efforts that only apply narrowly to some small markets. We suspect there's an opportunity to reduce maintenance overhead here.

However, we lack believable metrics on both (1) time spent maintaining the software and (2) time that would be saved by these cleanup efforts. As a result, it's hard to pitch projects of this sort as revenue saving with much conviction.

EXPLORE

Financial markets evaluate companies in comparison to their peers. This is most obvious in public markets, where there's significant information transparency about business performance, and sufficient liquidity to allow markets to revalue companies in something approaching real-time. While private equity firms generally take controlling interest of private businesses, or with the intent of taking the business private if it happens to be public, they value businesses in the same way.

In this exploration, we're going to dig into two particular questions. First, we're going to dig into a dataset on the performance of public technology companies, and then second, we're going to look into the concrete example of Zendesk, who were taken private in 2022 (*https://oreil.ly/IKRd-*) after being bought by two private equity firms.

Comparable companies

Exploring the benchmarking question first, most investors evaluate engineering within the context of the overall Research and Development (R&D) investment. They generally judge that spend by constructing a scatterplot of R&D spend versus year-over-year revenue growth for a cohort of similar companies. Perfectly similar companies don't exist, so this cohort is generally constructed from companies in similar industries, with similar revenue, and operating in the same regions.

We have reached out to our investors to see if they can provide the internal datasets they use for this analysis, but in the meantime we've developed a directionally useful dataset using the 2023 R&D Investment Scoreboard (*https://oreil.ly/PnYSK*), with some rough cutting of the data (*https://oreil.ly/df4TP*) to remove outliers, as shown in Figure 18-1. (If we repeat this process, we will use the SEC's EDGAR database (*https://oreil.ly/z7UpB*) to pull a more specifically helpful dataset, but this has been a useful starting point.)

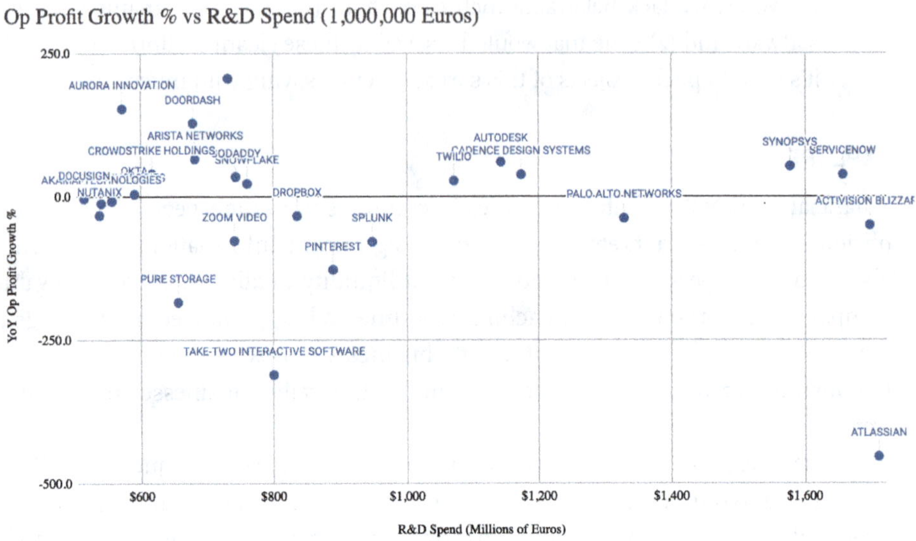

Figure 18-1. R&D investment versus operating profit growth at public companies

This isn't a perfect dataset (we prefer revenue growth over growth in operating profit), but it's the best option within the dataset that we were able to quickly pull down. Nonetheless, there's a clear strong performer quadrant in the top-left that we can plot ourselves into to understand our general performance, which is discussed further in the preceding *Diagnose* section.

Zendesk

The second topic of exploration we dug into is understanding the general sequence of steps taken by private equity ownership after acquiring a company. For an example with available public documentation, we focused on the purchase of Zendesk in 2022 (*https://oreil.ly/IKRd-*).

To start, we pulled Zendesk's final 10-Q before going private (*https://oreil.ly/PmEPZ*) (Figure 18-2).

	Three Months Ended June 30,		Six Months Ended June 30,	
	2022	2021	2022	2021
Revenue	$ 407,208	$ 318,216	$ 795,535	$ 616,264
Cost of revenue (1)	82,790	66,743	158,468	127,637
Gross profit	324,418	251,473	637,067	488,627
Operating expenses (1):				
Research and development	110,539	82,826	218,616	156,609
Sales and marketing	209,160	165,250	410,820	322,768
General and administrative	97,210	45,818	160,748	88,951
Total operating expenses	416,909	293,894	790,184	568,328
Operating loss	(92,491)	(42,421)	(153,117)	(79,701)

Figure 18-2. Zendesk's P&L from their 2022 10-Q

Taking those values, we can reformat them into a chart (Figure 18-3) focusing on the year-over-year changes in the six-month period ending in 2022 versus the same period in 2021.

	2021	2022	YoY
Revenue	616264	795535	29.09%
R&D Expenses	156609	218616	39.59%
S&M Expenses	322768	410820	27.28%
G&A Expenses	88951	160748	80.72%

Figure 18-3. Zendesk's P&L from their 2022 10-Q, reformatted to show year-over-year changes

The changes are a bit concerning. Sales and Marketing (S&M) costs have grown more slowly than revenue, which is positive, but Research and Development (R&D) expenses have grown about 50% faster than revenue, and General and Administration (G&A) charges have grown more than twice as quickly as revenue.

From those growth rates, we would assume that the new ownership might push to aggressively reduce spend in those two areas, which is indeed what history suggests happened, with a November 2022 reduction (*https://oreil.ly/VTStf*), followed some months later by a May 2023 reduction (*https://oreil.ly/D76_1*). It's hard to get precise data here, but it's our impression that these reductions focused on areas where expenses were growing quickly, with particular focus on G&A functions.

Document 18-2: Engineering Organization Seniority-Mix Model

LEARNINGS

An organization without a "backfill at N-1" hiring policy, e.g., an organization that hires a Software Engineer (SWE) 2 to replace a departed SWE2, will have an increasingly top-heavy organization over time (Figure 18-4).

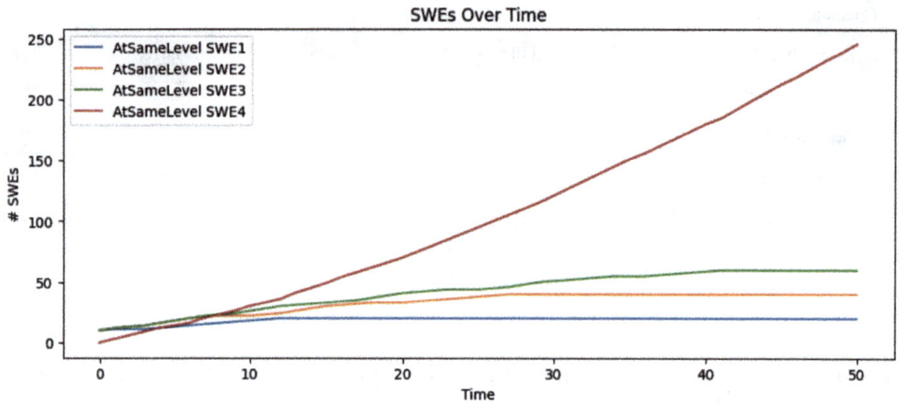

Figure 18-4. Ratio of engineers at most senior level becomes increasingly heavy over time

However, even introducing the "backfill at N-1" hiring policy is insufficient, as our representation at senior levels will become far too high, even if we stop hiring externally into our most senior levels (Figure 18-5).

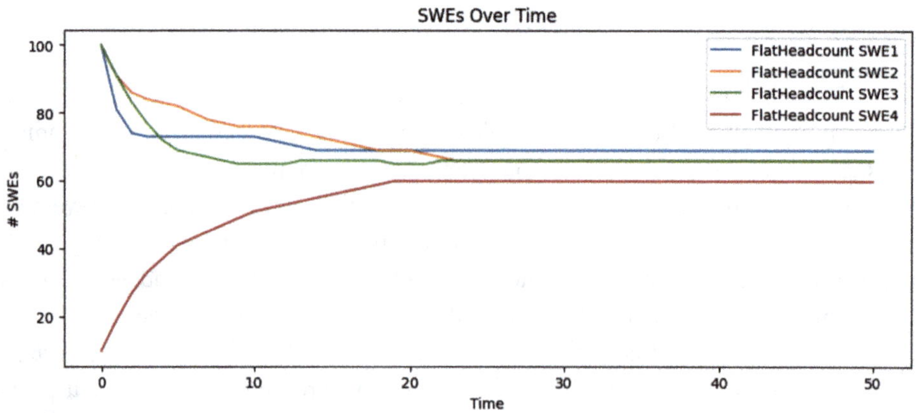

Figure 18-5. Implementing an N-1 backfill policy prevents unbounded increase of rate of most senior engineers

To fully accomplish our goal of a healthy seniority mix, we must stop hiring at the most senior levels, implement a "backfill at N-1" policy, and cap the maximum number of individuals at the most senior level (Figure 18-6).

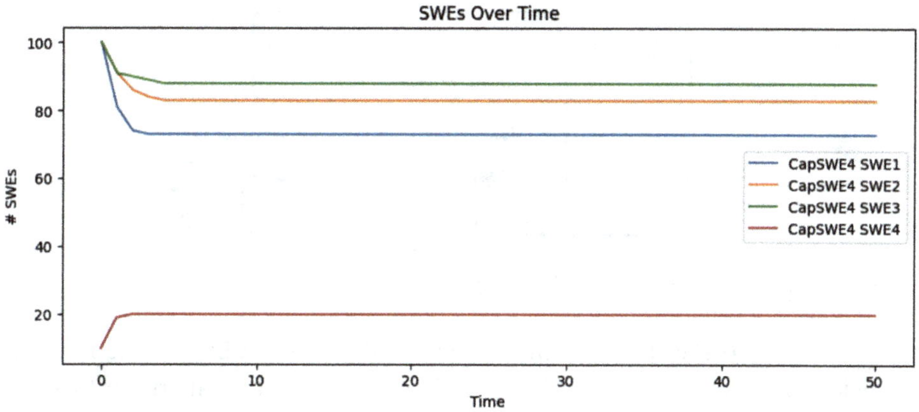

Figure 18-6. N-1 backfill policy and capping number of engineers at most senior level

Any collection of lower-powered policies simply will not impact the model's outcome.

SKETCH

We'll start by sketching this system in Excalidraw (*https://excalidraw.com*). It's always fine to use whatever tool you prefer, but simpler sketching tools generally help you focus on iterating the stocks and flows—without getting distracted by tuning settings—much like a designer starting with messy wireframes rather than pixel-perfect designs.

We'll start with sketching the most junior level: SWE1 (Figure 18-7).

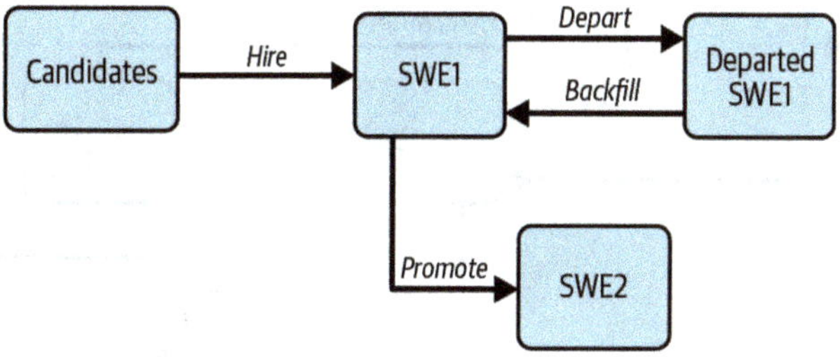

Figure 18-7. Hiring, departures, and promotions for SWE1 engineers

We hire external candidates to become SWE1s. We have some get promoted to SWE2, some depart, and we then backfill those departures with new SWE1s (Figure 18-8).

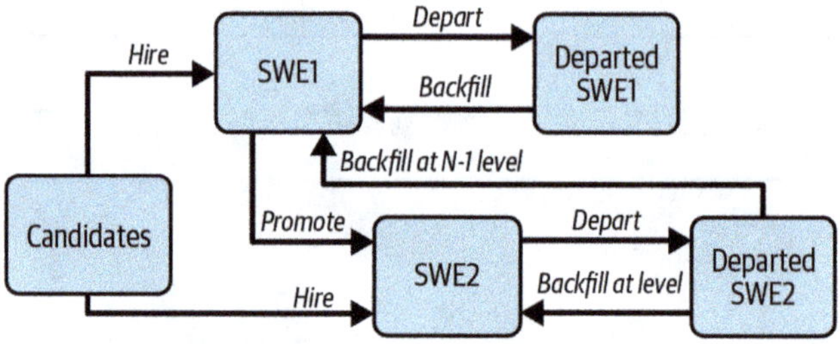

Figure 18-8. Hiring and promotion lifecycle for SWE1 and SWE2

As we start sketching the full stocks and flows for SWE2, we also introduce the idea of backfilling at the prior level. As we replicate this pattern for two more career levels—SWE3 and SWE4—we get the complete model (Figure 18-9).

The final level, SWE4, is simplified relative to the prior levels, as it's no longer possible to get promoted to a further level. We could go further than this, but the model will simply get increasingly burdensome to work with, so let's stop with four levels.

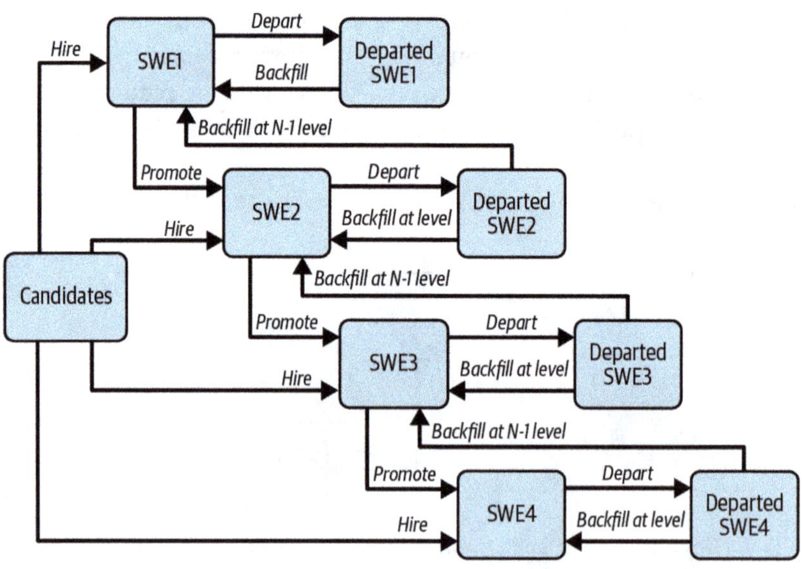

Figure 18-9. Hiring and promotion lifecycle for four levels of career ladder

REASON

When reviewing the sketched system, a few interesting conclusions emerge:

- If promotion rates at any level exceed the rate of hiring at that level plus rate of N-1 backfill at that level, then the proportion of engineers at that level will grow over time
- If you are not hiring much, then this problem simplifies to promotion rate versus departure rate. A company that does little hiring and has high retention cannot afford to promote frequently. Promotion into senior roles will become financially restrained, even if the policy is explained by some other mechanism.
- Many companies use the "career level" policy (*https://lethain.com/career-levels-and-more*) as the mechanism to identify a level where promotions *generally* stop happening. The rationale is often not explicitly described, but we can conclude it's likely a financial constraint that typically incentivizes this policy.

With those starter insights, now we can get into modeling the details.

MODEL AND EXERCISE

We're going to build this model using `lethain/systems` (*https://github.com/lethain/systems*). The first version will be relatively simple, albeit with a number of stocks given the size of the model, and then we'll layer on a number of additional features as we iteratively test out a number of different scenarios.

I've chosen to combine the *Model* and *Exercise* steps to showcase how each version of the model can inspire new learnings that prompt new questions that require a new model to answer.

If you'd rather view the full model and visualizations, each iteration is available on GitHub (*https://github.com/lethain/eng-strategy-models/blob/main/BackfillPolicy.ipynb*).

Backfill-at-level

The first policy we're going to explore is backfilling a departure at the same level. For example, if an SWE2 departs, then you go ahead and backfill them at SWE2. This intuitively makes sense, because you needed an SWE2 before to perform the work, so why would you hire someone less senior?

There are two new systems concepts introduced in this model:

1. For easier iteration, we're going to use the systems modeling concept of an "information link," which is basically using a stock as a variable to define a flow. Specifically, we'll create a stock named `HiringRate` with a size of two. Then we'll use that stock's size to define hiring flows at each career level. In programming terms, you can think of this as defining a reusable variable, but you can use any stock's size to define flows.
2. There are effectively an infinite number of potential candidates for your company, so we're going to use an infinite stock, represented by initializing a new stock surrounded by `[` and `]`. Specifically, in this case this is `[Candidates]`; if we wanted a fixed-size stock with 100 people in it, we could have initialized it as `Candidates(100)`. Depending on what you're modeling, both options are useful.

With those in mind, our initial model is defined as:

```
HiringRate(2)

[Candidates] > SWE1(10) @ HiringRate
SWE1 > DepartedSWE1 @ Leak(0.1)
DepartedSWE1 > SWE1 @ Leak(0.5)

Candidates > SWE2(10) @ HiringRate
SWE1 > SWE2 @ Leak(0.1)
SWE2 > DepartedSWE2 @ Leak(0.1)
DepartedSWE2 > SWE2 @ Leak(0.5)

Candidates > SWE3(10) @ HiringRate
SWE2 > SWE3 @ Leak(0.1)
SWE3 > DepartedSWE3 @ Leak(0.1)
DepartedSWE3 > SWE3 @ Leak(0.5)

Candidates > SWE4(0)  @ HiringRate
SWE3 > SWE4 @ Leak(0.1)
SWE4 > DepartedSWE4 @ Leak(0.1)
DepartedSWE4 > SWE4 @ Leak(0.5)
```

To confirm that we've done something reasonable, we can model this using Graphviz (Figure 18-10).

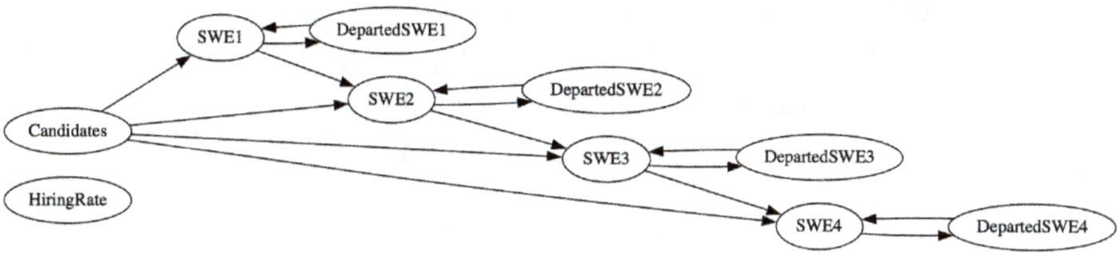

Figure 18-10. Graphviz representation of systems model

That looks like the same model we sketched before, without the downlevel backfill flows that we haven't yet added to the model, so we're in a good spot.

With that confirmed, let's inspect the four distinct flows happening for the SWE2 stock. In order they are:

1. External candidates being hired at the SWE2 level, at the fixed `HiringRate` defined here as two hires per round.
2. SWE1s being promoted to SWE2 at a 10% rate. This is a leak because someone being promoted to SWE2 doesn't mean the other SWE1s disappear.
3. SWE2s who are leaving the company at a 10% rate.
4. Backfill hires of departed SWE2s, who are rehired at the same level.

Running that model, we can see how the populations of the various levels grow over time (Figure 18-11).

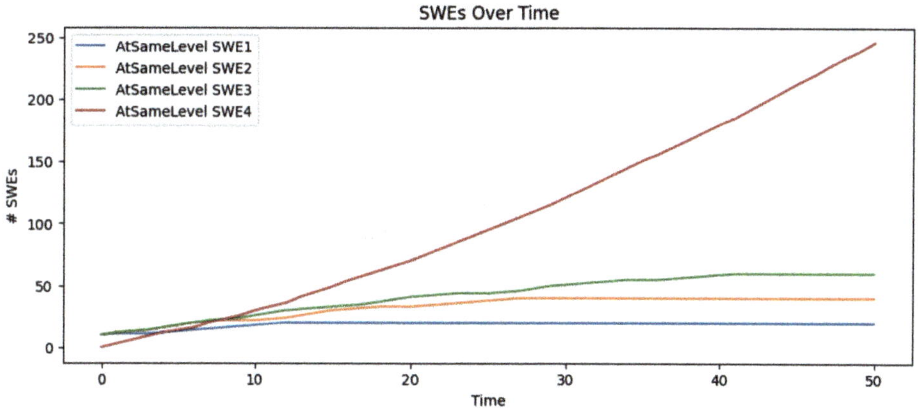

Figure 18-11. Ratio of engineers at most senior level becomes increasingly heavy over time

We can tell that this backfill-at-level policy is pretty inefficient, because our organization just becomes more and more top-heavy with SWE4s over time. Something needs to change.

Backfill at N-1

To reduce the number of SWE4s in our company, let's update the model to backfill all hires at the level below the departed employee. For example, a departing SWE2 would cause hiring an SWE1. This specifically means replacing all these lines:

```
DepartedSWE2 > SWE2 @ Leak(0.5)
```

To instead hire into the prior level:

```
DepartedSWE2 > SWE1 @ Leak(0.5)
```

The one exception is that SWE1s are still backfilled as SWE1s: as it's the most junior level, there's no lower level to backfill into.

Running this updated model, we get a better-looking organization (Figure 18-12).

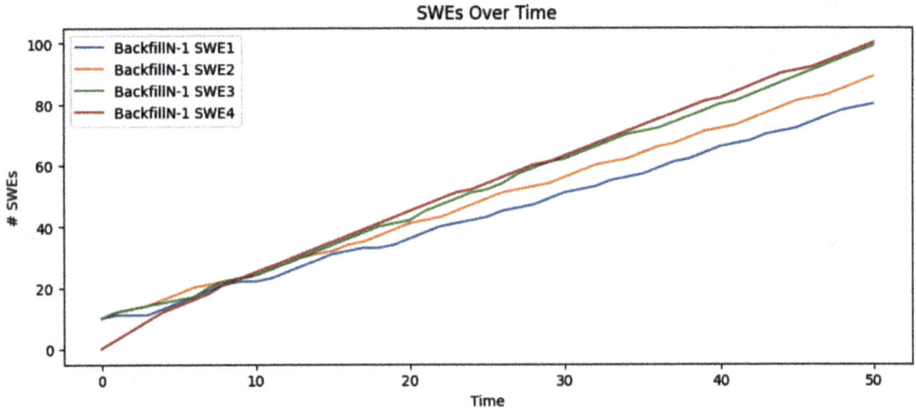

Figure 18-12. N-1 backfill policy without overall hiring cap

We're still top-heavy, but we've turned an exponential growth problem into a linear growth problem, so that's an improvement. However, this is still a very expensive engineering organization to run, and certainly *not* an organization that's reducing costs.

No hiring

One reason our model shows so many SWE4s is that we're hiring at an even rate across all levels, which isn't particularly realistic. Also, it's unlikely that we're growing headcount at all to the extent that we're aiming to reduce our engineering costs over time.

We can model this by setting a `HiringRate` of zero, and then setting more representative initial values for each cohort of engineers (note that I'm only showing the changed lines; check GitHub (*https://github.com/lethain/eng-strategy-models/blob/main/BackfillPolicy.ipynb*) for the full model):

```
HiringRate(0)

[Candidates] > SWE1(100) @ HiringRate
Candidates > SWE2(100) @ HiringRate
Candidates > SWE3(100) @ HiringRate
Candidates > SWE4(10)  @ HiringRate
```

Now we're starting out with 100 SWE1s, SWE2s, and SWE3s. We have a smaller cohort of SWE4s, with just 10 initially. Running the model gives us an updated perspective (Figure 18-13).

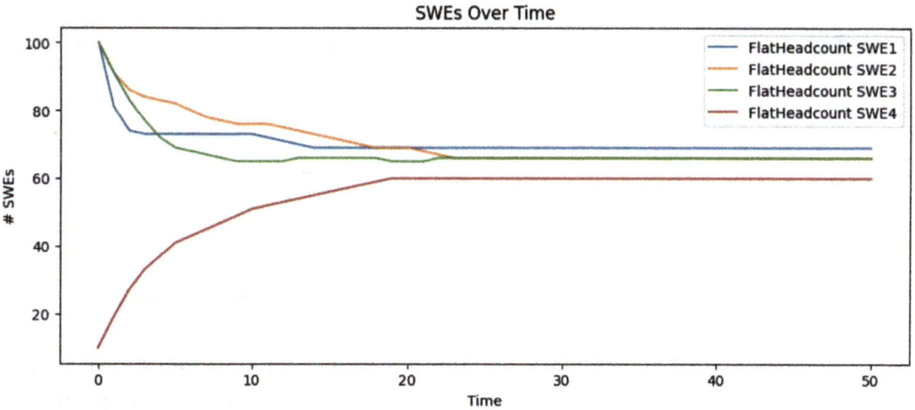

Figure 18-13. Implementing an N-1 backfill policy prevents unbounded increase of rate of most senior engineers

We can see that eliminating hiring *improves* the ratio of SWE4s to the other levels, but it's still just too high. We're ending up with roughly 1.25 SWE1s for each SWE4, when the ratio should be closer to five to one.

Capped size of SWE4s

Finally, we're going to introduce a stock with a maximum size. No matter what flows *want* to accomplish, they cannot grow a flow over that maximum. In this case, we're defining `SWE4` as a stock with an initial size of 10 and a maximum size of 20:

```
SWE4(10, 20)
Candidates > SWE4  @ HiringRate
```

This could also be combined into a one-liner, although it's potentially easy to miss in that case:

```
Candidates > SWE4(10, 20)  @ HiringRate
```

With that one change, we're getting close to an engineering organization that works how we want (Figure 18-14).

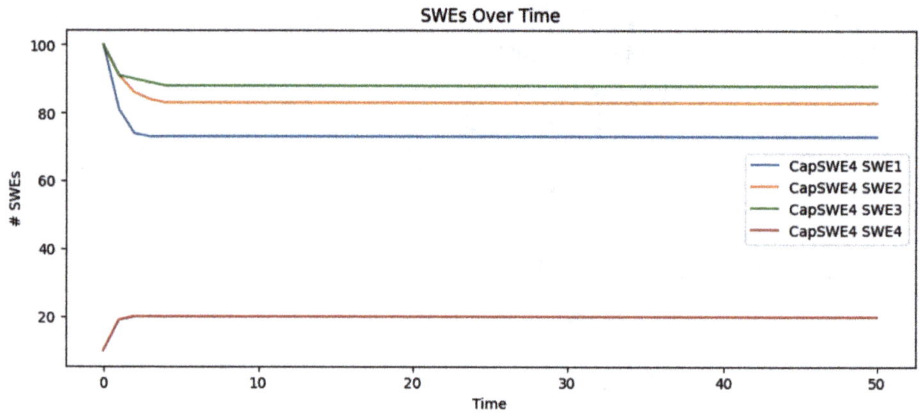

Figure 18-14. N-1 backfill policy and capping number of engineers at the most senior level

The ratio of SWE4s to other functions is right, although we can see that the backpressure means that we have a surplus of SWE3s in this organization. You could imagine other policy work that might improve that as well, e.g., presumably more SWE3s depart than SWE2s, because the SWE3s see their ability to be promoted is capped by the departure rate of existing SWE4s. However, I think we've already learned quite a bit from this model, so I'm going to end modeling here.

Summary

One of the recurring themes in interesting strategy documents is finding a way to make progress despite imperfect information, and that theme certainly shows up in these documents. Work is usually easy when you have clear, stable plans and goals, but those rarely exist. This strategy accepts the absence of a clear goal and instead focuses on using the available time to validate options for moving forward. Sometimes the only path forward is preparation, and then all you can do is prepare.

Customer Data Access Strategy

At some point in a startup's lifecycle, its leaders decide that they need to be ready to go public in 18 months, and a flurry of IPO-readiness activity kicks off. This strategy focuses on a company working on IPO readiness that has identified a gap in internal controls for managing user data access. The company *wants* to meaningfully improve its security posture around user data access, but it has had a number of failed security initiatives over the years.

Most of those initiatives failed because they significantly degraded internal workflows for teams like customer support, reverting and subverting the initial progress over time and eventually resulting in little long-term effect. This strategy represents the Chief Information Security Officer's (CISO's) attempt to acknowledge and overcome those historical challenges while meeting the company's IPO readiness obligations and—most importantly—doing right by its users.

Reading This Document

This chapter contains just one document, Document 19-1: How Should We Control Access to User Data?, from 2022. Security topics are always sensitive, and as such this document is not from any given company, but is rather the amalgamation of experiences at several distinct companies.

If you're reading this document with the goal of applying the strategies it puts forward, start at the top and read to the end. If, on the other hand, your main goal is to understand the thinking behind it, read the sections in reverse order, starting with *Explore*, then *Diagnose*, and so on. Chapter 11 explains this approach to separating reading from thinking and details the general structure of strategy documents. My commentary appears in the footnotes.

Document 19-1: How Should We Control Access to User Data?

POLICY AND OPERATIONS

Our new policies, and the mechanisms to operate them, are:[1]

- *Controls for accessing user data must be significantly stronger prior to our IPO.* Senior leadership, legal, compliance, and security have decided that we are not comfortable accepting the status quo of our user data access controls as a public company. We must meaningfully improve the quality of resource-level access controls (e.g., how we determine which rows, rather than tables, a user has permission to access) as part of our pre-IPO readiness efforts.

  Our Security team is accountable for the exact mechanisms and approach to addressing this risk.

- *We will continue to prioritize a hybrid solution to resource-access controls.* This has been our approach thus far, and the fastest available option.

- *Directly expose the log of our resource-level accesses to our users.* We will build toward a user-accessible log of all company accesses of user data, and ensure we are comfortable explaining each and every access. In addition, this means that each rationale for access must be comprehensible and reasonable from a user perspective.

  This is important because it aligns our approach with our users' perspectives. They will be able to evaluate how we access their data, and make decisions about continuing to use our product based on whether they agree with our use.

- *Good security discussions don't frame decisions as a compromise between security and usability.* We will pursue multi-dimensional tradeoffs (*https://lethain.com/multi-dimensional-tradeoffs*) to simultaneously improve security and efficiency. Whenever we frame a discussion as trading off between security and utility, it's a sign that we are having the wrong discussion, and that we should rethink our approach.

1 Relative to the default structure, this document has been refactored in two ways to improve readability: first, *Operation* has been folded into *Policy*; second, *Refine* has been embedded in *Diagnose*.

We will prioritize mechanisms that can both automatically authorize *and* document the rationale for access to customer data. The most obvious example of this is automatically granting access to a customer support agent for users who have an open support ticket assigned to that agent (and removing that access when that ticket is reassigned or resolved).

- *Measure progress on percentage of customer data access requests justified by a user-comprehensible, automated rationale.* This will anchor our approach on simultaneously improving the security of user data and the usability of our colleagues' internal tools. If we only expand requirements for accessing customer data, we won't view this as progress because it's not automated (and consequently is likely to encourage workarounds as teams try to solve problems quickly). Similarly, if we only improve usability, charts won't represent this as progress because we won't have increased the number of supported requests.

  As part of this effort, we will create a private channel where the security and compliance team has visibility into all manual rationales for user data access, and will notify the manager of anyone who repeatedly uses a manual justification for accessing user data.

- *Expire unused roles to move toward the principle of least privilege.* Today we have a number of roles granted in our role-based access control (RBAC) system to users who do not use the granted permissions. To address that issue, we will automatically remove roles from colleagues after 90 days of not using the role's permissions.

  Engineers in an active on-call rotation are the exception to this automated permission pruning.

- *Weekly reviews until we see progress; monthly access reviews in perpetuity.* Starting now, there will be a weekly sync between the Security Engineering team, teams working on customer data access initiatives, and the CISO. This meeting will focus on rapid iteration and problem solving.

  This is explicitly a forum for ongoing strategy testing, with the CISO serving as the meeting's sponsor, and the Principal Security Engineer serving as the meeting's guide. It will continue until we have clarity on the path to 100% coverage of user-comprehensible, automated rationales for access to customer data.

Separately, we are also starting a monthly review of sampled accesses to customer data to ensure the proper usage and function of the rationale-creation mechanisms we build. This meeting's goal is to review access rationales for quality and appropriateness, both by reviewing sampled rationales in the short term, and identifying more automated mechanisms for identifying high-risk accesses to review in the future.

- *Exceptions must be granted in writing by the CISO.* While our overarching Engineering Strategy states that we follow an advisory architecture process as described in *Facilitating Software Architecture* (*https://oreil.ly/ZzxGp*) (Andrew Harmel-Law, O'Reilly, 2024), the customer data access policy is an exception and must be explicitly approved, with documentation, by the CISO. Start that process in the `#ciso` channel.

DIAGNOSE

We have a strong baseline of RBAC and audit logging. However, we have limited mechanisms for ensuring assigned roles follow the principle of least privilege (*https://oreil.ly/u_SsK*). This is particularly true in cases where individuals change teams or roles over the course of their tenure at the company: some individuals have collected numerous unused roles over five-plus years at the company.

Similarly, our audit logs are durable and pervasive, but we have limited proactive mechanisms for identifying anomalous usage. Instead they are typically used to understand what occurred after an incident is identified by other mechanisms.

For resource-level access controls, we rely on a hybrid approach between a third-party platform for incoming user requests, and approval mechanisms within our own product. Providing a rationale for access across these two systems requires manual work, and those rationales are later manually reviewed for appropriateness in a batch fashion.

There are two major ongoing problems with our current approach to resource-level access controls. First, the teams making requests view them as a burdensome obligation without much benefit to them or on behalf of the user. Second, because the rationale review steps are manual, there is no verifiable evidence of the quality of the review.

We've found no evidence of misuse of user data. When colleagues do access user data, we have uniformly and consistently found that there is a clear and reasonable rationale for that access. For example, a ticket in the user support system where the user has raised an issue.

However, the quality of our documented rationales is consistently low because it depends on busy people manually copying over significant information many times a day. Because the rationales are of low quality, the verification of these rationales is somewhat arbitrary. From a literal compliance perspective, we do provide rationales and auditing of these rationales, but it's unclear if the majority of these audits increase the security of our users' data.

Historically, we've made significant security investments that caused temporary spikes in our security posture. However, looking at those initiatives a year later, in many cases we see a pattern of increased scrutiny followed by a gradual repeal or avoidance of the new mechanisms.

We have found that most of them involved increased friction for essential work performed by other internal teams. In the natural order of performing work, those teams would subtly subvert the improvements because they interfered with their immediate goals (e.g., supporting customer requests).

As such, we have high conviction from our track record that our historical approach can create optical wins internally. We have limited conviction that it can create long-term improvements outside of significant, unlikely internal changes (e.g., colleagues are markedly less busy a year from now than they are today). It seems likely we need a new approach to meaningfully shift our stance on these kinds of problems.

EXPLORE

Our experience is that best practices around managing internal access to user data are widely available through our networks, and otherwise hard to find. The exact rationale for this is hard to determine, but it seems possible that it's a topic that folks are generally uncomfortable discussing in public on account of potential future liability and compliance issues.

In our exploration, we found two standardized dimensions (role-based access controls, audit logs) and one highly divergent dimension (resource-specific access controls):

- *Role-based access controls* (RBAC) are a highly standardized approach at this point. The core premise is that users are mapped to one or more roles, and each role is granted a certain set of permissions. For example, a role representing the customer support agent might be granted permission to deactivate an account, whereas a role representing the sales engineer might be able to configure a new account.

- *Audit logs* are similarly standardized. All access and mutation of resources should be tied in a durable log to the human who performed the action. These logs should be accumulated in a centralized, queryable solution.

  One of the core challenges is determining how to utilize these logs proactively to detect issues rather than reactively when an issue has already been flagged.
- *Resource-level access controls* are significantly less standardized than RBAC or audit logs. We found three distinct patterns adopted by companies, with little consistency across companies on which pattern is adopted.

Those three patterns for resource-level access control were:

1. *Third-party enrichment* where access to resources is managed in a third-party system such as Zendesk. This requires enriching objects within those systems with data and metadata from the product(s) where those objects live. It also requires implementing actions on the platform, such as archiving or configuration, allowing them to live entirely in that platform's permission structure.

   The downside of this approach is tight coupling with the platform vendor, any limitations inherent to that platform, and the overhead of maintaining engineering teams familiar with both your internal technology stack and the platform vendor's technology stack.
2. *First-party tool implementation* where all activity, including creation and management of user issues, is managed within the core product itself. This pattern is most common in earlier-stage companies or companies whose customer support leadership "grew up" within the organization without much exposure to the approach taken by peer companies.

   The advantage of this approach is that there is a single, tightly integrated and infinitely extensible platform for managing interactions. The downside is that you have to build and maintain all of that work internally rather than pushing it to a vendor that ought to be able to invest more heavily into their tooling.
3. *Hybrid solutions* where a third-party platform is used for most actions and is also used to permit resource-level access within the first-party system. For example, you might be able to access a user's data only while there is

an open ticket created by that user, and assigned to you, in the third-party platform.

The advantage of this approach is that it allows the support of complex workflows that don't fit within the platform's limitations, and allows you to avoid complex coupling between your product and the vendor platform.

Generally, our experience is that all companies implement RBAC, audit logs, and one of the resource-level access control mechanisms. Most companies pursue either third-party enrichment with a sizable, long-standing team owning the platform implementation, or rely on a hybrid solution where they are able to avoid creating a longstanding dedicated team by lumping that work into existing teams.

Summary

There are two dimensions of this strategy document that I find particularly interesting. First, it's a concrete example of using strategy testing led by an executive to work through misalignment across teams. This is the most effective mechanism I've found for working through persistent organizational friction. Second, it shows how policy can be used to explicitly constrain a team into alignment. With this strategy, the Security team's prior behaviors were effectively outlawed, creating a path to a more effective mode of working.

Service Architecture Strategy

Since the first introduction of microservices in 2005 (*https://oreil.ly/NeJrn*), the debate between adopting a microservices architecture, a monolithic service architecture, or a hybrid between the two has become one of the least reversible decisions that most engineering organizations make. Even migrating to a different database technology is *generally* a less expensive change than moving from monolith to microservices or from microservices to monolith.

The industry has in many ways gone full circle on that debate. While most hyperscalers in the 2010s took part in multiyear monolith-to-microservices migrations, Kelsey Hightower's iconic 2017 tweet (*https://oreil.ly/gBz_o*) predicted that "Monolithic applications will be back in style after people discover the drawbacks of distributed monolithic applications."

Even as popular sentiment has generally turned away from microservices, many engineering organizations have a bit of both, often the remnants of one or more earlier but incomplete migration efforts. This service architecture strategy looks at a fictional organization stuck with a bit of both approaches and looking to determine its path forward. Let's call it Theoretical Compliance Company.

Reading This Document

This chapter contains just one document, Document 20-1: Should We Decompose Our Monolith?, written in 2022.

If you're reading this document with the goal of applying the strategies it puts forward, start at the top and read to the end. If, on the other hand, your main goal is to understand the thinking behind it, read the sections in reverse order, starting with *Explore*, then *Diagnose*, and so on. Chapter 11 explains this approach to separating reading from thinking and details the general structure of strategy documents. My commentary appears in the footnotes.

Document 20-1: Should We Decompose Our Monolith?

POLICY

Our policy for service architecture is documented here.[1] All exceptions to this policy must escalate *to* a local Staff-plus engineer for their approval, and then escalate *with* that Staff-plus engineer to the CTO. If you have questions about the policies, ask in `#eng-strategy`.

Our policy is:

- *Business units should always operate in their own code repository and monolith.* They should not provision many different services. They should rarely work in other business units' monoliths. There will be nuanced cases; in these cases, prefer decisions that move us closer to this policy.
- *New integrations across business unit monoliths should be done using gRPC.* The emphasis here is on *new* integrations; it's desirable but not urgent to migrate existing integrations that use other implementations (HTTP/JSON, etc.).

  When the decision is subtle (e.g., changes to an existing endpoint), optimize for business velocity rather than technical purity. When the decision is far from subtle (e.g., brand new endpoint), comply with the policy.
- *Except for new business unit monoliths, we don't allow new services.* You should work within the most appropriate business unit monolith or within the existing infrastructure repositories. Provisioning a new service, unless it corresponds with a new business unit, always requires approval from the CTO in `#eng-strategy`.

  That approval generally will *not* be granted, unless the new service requires significantly different nonfunctional requirements than an existing monolith. For example, if it requires significantly higher compliance review prior to changes such as our existing payments service, or if it requires radically higher requests per second, and so on.

---

1 Relative to the default structure, this document has been refactored in two ways to improve readability: first, *Operation* has been folded into *Policy*; second, *Refine* has been embedded in *Diagnose*.

- *Merge existing services into business unit monoliths where you can.* We believe that each choice to move existing services back into a monolith should be made "in the details" rather than from a top-down strategy perspective. Consequently, we generally encourage teams to wind down their existing services outside of their business unit's monolith, but defer to teams to make the right decision for their local context.

DIAGNOSE

Theoretical Compliance Company has a complex history with decomposing our monolith. We are also increasing our number of business units, while limiting our investment into our core business unit. These are complex times, with a lot of constraints to juggle. To improve readability, we've split the diagnosis into two sections: "business constraints" and "engineering constraints."

Our business constraints are:

- We sell business-to-business compliance solutions to other companies on an annual subscription. There is one major, established business line, and two smaller partially validated business lines that are intended to attach to the established business line to increase average contract value.
- There are 2,000 people at the company. About 500 of those are in the engineering organization. Within that 500, about 150 work on the broadest definition of "infrastructure engineering," things like developer tools, compute and orchestration, networking, security engineering, and so on.
- The business is profitable, but revenue growth has been 10%–20% YoY, creating persistent pressure on spend from our board, based on mild underperformance relative to public market comparables. *Unless we can increase YoY growth by 5%–10%, they expect us to improve free cash flow by 5%–10% each year,* which jeopardizes our ability to maintain long-term infrastructure investments.
- Growth in the primary business line is shrinking. The company's strategy includes spinning up more adjacent business units to increase average contract value with new products. We need to fund these business units without increasing our overall budget, which means budget for the new business units must be pulled away from either our core business or our platform teams.

In addition to needing to fund our new business units, *there's ongoing pressure to make our core business more efficient*, which means either accelerating growth or reducing investment. It's challenging to accelerate growth while reducing investment, which suggests that most improvement will come from reducing our investment.

- Our methodology to allocate platform costs against business units does so proportionately to the revenue created by each business unit. *Our core business generates the majority of our revenue, which means it is accountable for the majority of our platform costs*, even if those costs are motivated by new business lines.

  This means that, even as the burden placed on platform teams increases due to spinning up multiple business units, there's significant financial pressure to reduce our platform spend because it's primarily represented as a cost to the core business whose efficiency we have to improve. This means we have little tolerance for anything that increases infrastructure overhead.

Our engineering constraints are:

- Our infrastructure engineering team is 150 engineers supporting 350 product engineers, and it's certain *that infrastructure will not grow significantly in the foreseeable future*.
- We spun up two new business units in the past six months, and *plan to spin up an additional two new business units in the next year*. Each business unit is led by a general manager, with engineering and product within that business unit principally accountable to that general manager. Our CTO and CPO still set practice standards, but it's situationally specific whether these practice standards or direction from the general manager is the last word on any given debate.

  For example, one business unit has been unwilling to support an on-call rotation for their product, because their general manager insists it is a wasteful practice. Consequently, that team often doesn't respond to pages, even when their service is responsible for impacting the stability of shared functionality.
- We have conviction that, in general, *it's more overhead for infrastructure to support more services*. We also found that in our organization, the rate

of service ownership changing due to team reorganizations counteracts much of the initial productivity gains from leaving the monolith.

- There is some tension between the two preceding observations: it's generally more overhead to have more services, but it's *even more* overhead to have irresponsible business units breaking a shared monolithic service. For example, we can much more easily rate-limit usage from a misbehaving service than fix a misbehaving codepath within a shared service.
- We also have a payments service that moves money from customers to us. *Our compliance and security requirements for changes to this service are significantly higher* than for the majority of our software, because the blast radius is essentially infinite.
- Our primary programming language is Ruby, which generally relies on blocking IO, and service-oriented architectures generally spend more time on blocking IO than monoliths. Similarly, Ruby is *relatively* inefficient at serializing and deserializing JSON payloads, which our service architecture requires as part of cross-service communication.
- We've previously attempted to decompose, and have *a number of lingering partial migrations that don't align cleanly with our current business unit ownership structure*. The number of these new services continues to grow over time, creating more burden on both infrastructure today and product teams in the future as they try to maintain these services through various team reorganizations.

EXPLORE

In the late 2010s, most large or scaling companies adopted services to some extent. Few adopted microservices, with the majority of adopters opting for a service-oriented architecture (*https://oreil.ly/KFm9z*) instead. Kelsey Hightower's iconic tweet on the perils of distributed monoliths (*https://oreil.ly/gBz_0*) in 2017 captured the beginning of a reversal, with more companies recognizing the burden of operating service-oriented architectures.

In addition to the wider recognition of those burdens, many of the cloud infrastructure challenges that originally motivated service architectures began to mellow. Most infrastructure engineers today *only* know how to operate with cloud-native patterns, rather than starting from machine-oriented approaches. Standard database technologies like PostgreSQL have significantly improved capabilities. Cloud providers have fast local caches for quickly retrieving verified upstream packages. The supply and cost of cloud compute are affordable. Slow programming languages are faster than they were a decade ago. Untyped languages have reasonable incremental paths to typed codebases.

As a result of this shift, if you look at a new, emerging company, it's particularly likely to have a monolith in one backend and one frontend programming language. However, if you look at a five-plus-year-old company, you might find almost anything. One particularly common case is a monolith with most functionality, and an inconsistent constellation of team-scoped macroservices scattered across the organization.

The shift away from a zero interest-rate policy (*https://oreil.ly/zGGUp*) has also impacted trends, as service-oriented architectures tend to require more infrastructure to operate efficiently, such as service meshes, service provisioning and deprovisioning, etc. Properly tuned, service-oriented architectures ought to be cost competitive, and potentially superior in complex workloads, but it's hard to maintain the required investment in infrastructure teams when in a cost-cutting environment. This has encouraged new companies to restrict themselves to monolithic approaches, and pushed existing companies to *attempt* to reverse their efforts to decompose their prior monoliths, with mixed results.

Summary

While the details matter a great deal when it comes to identifying an effective strategy, this document shows how the broad strokes of many strategies can be ported across companies. I could have written most of this about Stripe, Calm, or even Carta. The details, however, would have been quite different in every case. If I had exactly copied the approach from any one of those companies to another, it would have gone quite poorly, whereas copying the general strokes worked quite well.

Product Engineering Strategy

In my career, the majority of the strategy work I've done has been in nonexecutive roles, things like Uber's service migration (Document 16-1). Joining Calm was my first executive role, where I was able to not only propose but also mandate strategy.

Like almost all startups, the engineering team was scattered when I joined. Was our most important work creating more scalable infrastructure? Was our greatest risk the failure to adopt leading programming languages? How could we rescue the stuck service decomposition initiative?

These strategies are where the Calm engineering team and I aligned after numerous rounds of iteration, debate, and inevitably some disagreement. As strategies, they're both basic and also unambiguous about our values, and I believe it's a reasonably good starting point for any low scalability-complexity consumer product (*https://lethain.com/quality*).

Reading These Documents

The documents in this chapter are rewritten from memory to capture the strategies we pursued during my time at Calm. They are:

Document 21-1: "We're a Product Engineering Company!": Engineering Strategy at Calm

This document outlines Calm's strategy for focusing on product engineering work, explicitly not focusing on infrastructure-style foundational work, and the rationale behind that approach.

Document 21-2: How to Resource Engineering-Driven Projects at Calm

This document summarizes Calm's approach to investing in Engineering priorities when the prior prevailing belief within Engineering was that the company was not willing to make such investments.

If you're reading these documents with the goal of applying the strategies they put forward, start at the top and read to the end. If, on the other hand, your main goal is to understand the thinking behind them, read the sections in reverse order, starting with *Explore*, then *Diagnose*, and so on. Chapter 11 explains this approach to separating reading from thinking and details the general structure of strategy documents. Read on for the documents themselves.

Document 21-1: "We're a Product Engineering Company!": Engineering Strategy at Calm

POLICY AND OPERATION

Our new policies, and the mechanisms to operate them, are:

- *We are a product engineering company.* Users write in every day to tell us that our product has changed their lives for the better. Our technical infrastructure doesn't get many user letters—and this is unlikely to change going forward as our infrastructure is relatively low-scale and low-complexity. Rather than attempting to change that, we want to devote the absolute maximum possible attention to product engineering.
- *We exclusively adopt new technologies to create valuable product capabilities.* We believe our technology stack as it exists today can solve the majority of our current and future product roadmaps. In the rare case where we adopt a new technology, we do so because a product capability is inherently impossible without adopting a new technology.

  We do not adopt new technologies for other reasons. For example, we would not adopt a new technology because someone is interested in learning about it. Nor would we adopt a technology because it is 30% *better suited* to a task.

- *We write all code in the monolith.* It has been ambiguous if new code (especially new application code) should be written in our JavaScript monolith, or if all new code *must* be written in a new service outside of the monolith. This is no longer ambiguous: all new code must be written in the monolith.

  In the rare case that there is a functional requirement that makes writing in the monolith implausible, then you should request an exception as described below.

- *Exceptions are granted by the CTO, and must be in writing.* The above policies are deliberately restrictive. Sometimes they may be wrong, and we will make exceptions to them. However, each exception should be deliberate and grounded in concrete problems we are aligned both on solving and how we solve them. If we all scatter toward our preferred solution, then we'll create negative leverage for Calm rather than serving as the engine that advances our product.

  All exceptions must be written. If they are not written, then you should operate as if it has not been granted. Our goal is to avoid ambiguity around whether an exception has, or has not, been approved. If there's no written record that the CTO approved it, then it's not approved.

Proving the point about exceptions, there are two confirmed exceptions to the above strategy:

1. *We are incrementally migrating to TypeScript.* We have found that static typing can prevent a number of our user-facing bugs. TypeScript provides a clean, incremental migration path for our JavaScript codebase, and we aim to migrate the entirety over the next six months.

   Our Web engineering team is leading this migration.

2. *We are evaluating Postgres Aurora as our primary database.* Many of our recent production incidents are caused by index scans for tables with high write velocity such as tracking customer logins. We believe Aurora will perform better under these workloads.

   Our Infrastructure engineering team is leading this initiative.

DIAGNOSE

The current state of our engineering organization:

- *Our product is not limited by missing infrastructure capabilities.* Reviewing our roadmap, there's nothing that we are trying to build today or over the next year that is constrained by our technical infrastructure.
- *Our uptime, stability, and latency are OK but not great.* We have semi-frequent stability and latency issues in our application, all of which are caused by one of two issues. First, deploying new code with a missing index because it performed well enough in a test environment. Second, writes to a small number of extremely large, skinny tables have become expensive in combination with scans over those tables' indexes.
- *Our infrastructure team is split between supporting monolith and service workflows.* One way to measure technical debt is to understand how much time the team is spending maintaining the current infrastructure. Today, that is meaningful but not overwhelming work for our team of three infrastructure engineers supporting 30 product engineers.

  However, we *are* finding infrastructure engineers increasingly pulled into debugging incidents for components moved out of the central monolith into our service architecture. This is partially due to increased inherent complexity, but it's more due to exposing lack of monitoring and ambiguous accountability in services' production incidents.
- *Our product and executive stakeholders experience us as competing factions.* Engineering exists to build and operate software in the company. Part of that is being easy to work with. We should not necessarily support every ask from Product if we believe they are misaligned with Engineering's goals (e.g., maintaining security), but this should generally provide a consistent perspective across our team.

  Today, our stakeholders believe they will get radically different answers to basic questions of capabilities and approach depending on who they ask. If they try to get a group of engineers to agree on an approach, they often find that we derail into debate about the approach rather than articulating a clear point of view that allows the conversation to move forward.
- *We're spending an outsized amount of time debating technology adoptions and rewrites.* Most of our disagreements stem from adopting new technologies or rewriting existing components into new technology stacks. For example,

can we extend this feature or do we have to migrate it to a service before extending it? Can we add this to our database or should we move it into a new Redis cache instead? Is JavaScript a sufficient programming language, or do we need to rewrite this functionality in Go?

This is particularly relevant to next steps around the ongoing services migration, which has been in-flight for over a year, but is yet to move any core production code.

- *We are spending more time on infrastructure and platform work than product work.* This is the combination of all the above issues, from the stability issues we are encountering in our database design, to the lack of engineering alignment on execution. This places us at odds with stakeholders' expectations that we are predominantly focused on new product development.

EXPLORE

Calm is a mobile application that guides users to build and maintain either a meditation or sleep habit. Recommendations and guidance across content are individual to the user, but the content is shared across all customers and is amenable to caching on a content delivery network (CDN). As long as the CDN is available, the mobile application can operate despite the inability to access servers (i.e., the application remains usable from a user's perspective, even if the non-CDN production infrastructure is unreachable).

In 2010, enabling a product of this complexity would have required significant bespoke infrastructure, along with likely maintaining a physical presence in a series of datacenters to run your software. In 2020, comparable applications are generally moving toward maintaining as little internal infrastructure as possible. This perspective is summarized effectively in Intercom's "Run Less Software" (*https://oreil.ly/X3693*) and Dan McKinley's "Choose Boring Technology" (*https://oreil.ly/P3TY9*).

New companies founded in this space view essentially all infrastructure as a commodity bought off your cloud provider. This even extends to areas of innovation, such as machine learning, where the training infrastructure is typically run on an offering like AWS Bedrock, and the model infrastructure is provided by Anthropic or OpenAI.

Document 21-2: How to Resource Engineering-Driven Projects at Calm

One of the recurring challenges in any organization is how to split your attention across long-term and short-term problems. Your software might be struggling to scale with ramping user load, while you also know that you have a series of meaningful security vulnerabilities that need to be closed sooner rather than later. How do you balance across them?

These sorts of balance questions occur at every level of an organization. A particularly frequent format is the debate between Product and Engineering about how much time goes toward developing new functionality versus improving what's already been implemented. In 2020, Calm was growing rapidly as we navigated the COVID-19 pandemic, and the team was struggling to make improvements, as they felt saturated by incoming new requests. This strategy for resourcing Engineering-driven projects was our attempt to solve that problem.

POLICY AND OPERATION

Our policies for resourcing Engineering-driven projects are:

- We will protect one Engineering-driven project per product engineering team, per quarter. These projects should represent a maximum of 20% of the team's bandwidth. Each project must advance a measurable metric, and execution must be designed to show progress on that metric within four weeks.
- These projects must adhere to Calm's existing Engineering strategies (see Document 21-1).
- We resource these projects first in the team's planning, rather than last. However, only concrete projects are resourced. If there are no concrete proposals, then the team won't have time budgeted for Engineering-driven work.
- The team's engineering manager is responsible for deciding on the project, ensuring the project is valuable, and pushing back on attempts to defund the project.
- Project selection does not require CTO approval, but you should escalate to the CTO if there's friction or disagreement.

- CTO will review Engineering-driven projects each quarter to summarize their impact and provide feedback to teams' engineering managers on project selection and execution. They will also review teams that did *not* perform a project to understand why not.

As we've communicated this strategy, we've frequently gotten conceptual alignment that this sounds reasonable, coupled with uncertainty about what sort of projects should actually be selected. At some level, this ambiguity is an acknowledgment that we believe teams will identify the best opportunities bottoms-up. However, we also wanted to give two concrete examples of projects we're greenlighting in the first batch:

- *Code-free media release*: Historically, we've needed to make a number of pull requests to add, organize, and release new pieces of media. This is high-urgency work, but Engineering doesn't exercise much judgment while doing it, and manual steps often create errors. We aim to track and eliminate these pull requests, while also increasing the number of releases that can be facilitated without scaling the content release team.
- *Machine learning content placement*: Developing new pieces of media is often a multi-week or -month process. After content is ready to release, there's generally a debate on where to place the content. This matters for the company, as this drives engagement with our users, but it matters even more to the content creator, who is generally evaluated in terms of their content's performance.

  This often leads to Product and Engineering getting caught up in debates about how to surface particular pieces of content. This project aims to improve user engagement by surfacing the best content for their interests, while also giving the Content team several explicit positions to highlight content without Product and Engineering involvement.

Although these projects are similar, it's not intended that *all* Engineering-driven projects are of this variety. Instead it's happenstance based on what the teams view as their biggest opportunities today.

DIAGNOSIS

Our assessment of the current situation at Calm is:

- We are spending a high percentage of our time on urgent but low engineering value tasks. Most significantly, about one-third of our time is going into launching, debugging, and changing content that we release into our product. Engineering is involved due to implementation limitations, not because our involvement adds inherent value. (We mostly just make releases slowly and inadvertently introduce bugs of our own.)
- We have a bunch of fairly clear ideas around improving the platform to empower the Content team to speed up releases, and to eliminate the Engineering involvement. However, we've struggled to find time to implement them, or to validate that these ideas will work.
- If we don't find a way to prioritize, and succeed at implementing, a project to reduce Engineering involvement in Content releases, we will struggle to support our goals to release more content and to develop more product functionality this year.
- Our Infrastructure team has been able to plan and make these kinds of investments stick. However, when we attempt these projects within our Product Engineering teams, things don't go that well. We are good at getting them onto the initial roadmap, but then they get deprioritized due to pressure to complete other projects.
- Our Engineering team of 20 engineers is not very fungible, largely due to specialization across roles like iOS, Android, Backend, Frontend, Infrastructure, and QA. We would like to staff these kinds of projects onto the Infrastructure team, but in practice that team does not have the product development experience to implement this kind of project.
- We've discussed spinning up a Platform team, or moving product engineers onto Infrastructure, but that would either (1) break our goal to maintain joint pairs between Product Managers and Engineering Managers, or (2) be indistinguishable from prioritizing within the existing team because it would still have the same Product Manager and Engineering Manager pair.
- Company planning is organic, occurring in many discussions and limited structured processes. If we make a decision to invest in one project, it's easy for that project to get deprioritized in a side discussion missing context on why the project is important.

These reprioritization discussions happen both in executive forums and in team-specific forums. There's imperfect awareness across these two sorts of forums.

EXPLORE

Prioritization is a deep topic with a wide variety of popular solutions (*https://oreil.ly/oDGK1*). For example, many software companies rely on "RICE" scoring, calculating priority as (Reach times Impact times Confidence) divided by Effort. At the other extreme are complex methodologies like the Scaled Agile Framework (*https://oreil.ly/aVK-W*).

In addition to generalized planning solutions, many companies carve out special mechanisms to solve for particular prioritization gaps. Google historically offered 20% time (*https://oreil.ly/BcyES*) to allow individuals to work on experimental projects that didn't align directly with top-down priorities. Stripe's Foundation Engineering organization developed the concept of Foundational Initiatives to prioritize cross-pillar projects with long-term implications; these projects otherwise struggled to get prioritized within the team-led planning process.

All these methods have clear examples of succeeding, and equally clear examples of struggling. Where these initiatives have succeeded, they had an engaged executive sponsoring the practice's rollout, including triaging escalations when the rollout inconvenienced supporters of the prior method. Where they lacked a sponsor, or were misaligned with the company's culture, these methods have consistently failed despite the fact that they've previously succeeded elsewhere.

Summary

A surprising number of executives start new roles by mandating a brand-new process or architecture. These Calm strategy documents capture a different approach that I've consistently found more effective: identifying approaches that are already working well within the company, and eliminating the less effective, competing approaches. At its best, selecting from existing, successful techniques means you can bypass strategy refinement entirely.

22

Developer, API, and Acquisition Strategy at Stripe

The hypergrowth companies of the 2010s adopted a number of techniques to balance the constraints of running a rapidly growing business without being overwhelmed by the technical complexity created by quick expansion. One common technique was decomposing their monoliths; another was acquiring existing companies with missing functionality. Both are conceptually simple, but they went wrong for many adopting companies.

This chapter focuses on Stripe's somewhat atypical approaches to three specific challenges that it encountered during that period: API deprecation, managing a large monolithic codebase, and integrating the Index acquisition. For example, Stripe did not decompose its monolithic Ruby codebase, sticking with a centralized codebase as it grew past three thousand engineers. Even in 2025, Stripe has relied on techniques such as creating the Sorbet static type checker rather than migrating to a statically typed language or decomposing into isolated codebases.

These documents are a particular testament to how much the details matter in strategy—I imagine these approaches would not consistently work if adopted elsewhere—and the value of enduring strategy. Almost all the impact of these strategies would have been undermined if they'd only lasted a year or two, but they've been remarkably effective over the course of a consistent decade of application.

Reading These Documents

The documents in this chapter are:

Document 22-1: How Should Stripe Deprecate APIs?
While Stripe is widely admired for things like its creation of the Sorbet typer project, I personally think that its most interesting strategy work is also among its most subtle: its willingness to significantly prioritize API stability. This strategy is almost invisible externally. Internally, discussions around it were frequent and detailed, but mostly confined to dedicated API design conversations. API stability isn't just a technical design quirk; it's a foundational decision in an API-driven business, and I believe it is one of the unsung heroes of Stripe's business success.

Document 22-2: A Systems Model of API Deprecation
While there was internal data to correlate deprecation with churn, we built this model to help us decide if we believed that correlation and causation were aligned in this case. You can find a full implementation of this model on GitHub (*https://github.com/lethain/eng-strategy-models/blob/main/APIDeprecationModel.ipynb*).

Document 22-3: Why Did Stripe Build Sorbet?
This strategy explains why Stripe chose to delay decomposition for so long, and how the Product Infrastructure team invested in developer productivity to deal with the challenges of a large Ruby codebase managed by a large software engineering team with low average tenure caused by rapid hiring.

Sorbet is a custom static and runtime type checker for Ruby that was initially designed and implemented by Stripe engineers on their Product Infrastructure team. Stripe's Product Infrastructure team had similar goals to other companies' Developer Experience or Developer Productivity teams, but it focused on preventing errors and improving productivity through changes in the internal architecture of the codebase itself, rather than relying solely on external tooling or processes.

I want to explicitly acknowledge that this strategy was spearheaded by Stripe's Product Infrastructure team, not by me. Although I ultimately became responsible for that team, I can't take credit for this strategy's thinking. Rather, I was initially skeptical, preferring an incremental migration to an existing strongly typed programming language, either Java for library coverage or Golang for Stripe's existing familiarity. Despite my initial doubts, the Sorbet project eventually won me over with its indisputable results.

Document 22-4: How to Integrate Stripe's Acquisition of Index?
Discussions around acquisitions often focus on technical diligence (*https://lethain.com/engineering-in-mergers-and-acquisition*) and deciding whether to make the acquisition. However, the integration that follows afterward can be even more complex. There are few irreversible trapdoor decisions in engineering, but decisions made early in an integration tend to be surprisingly durable.

This engineering strategy explores Stripe's approach to integrating its 2018 acquisition of Index (*https://oreil.ly/CsFGM*). While a business book would focus on the rationale for the acquisition itself, here that rationale is merely part of the diagnosis that defines the integration tradeoffs. The integration itself is the area of focus.

Like most acquisitions, the team responsible for the integration only learned about the project after the deal closed, which means early efforts are a scramble to apply strategy testing to distinguish between optimistic dates and technical realities.

To apply this strategy, start at the top with *Policy*. To understand the thinking behind this strategy, read sections in reverse order, starting with *Explore*.

More detail on this structure is in Chapter 11, as well as in "Making Engineering Strategies More Readable" (*https://lethain.com/readable-engineering-strategy-documents*).

Document 22-1: How Should Stripe Deprecate APIs?

POLICY AND OPERATION

Our policies for managing API changes are:

- *Design for long API lifetime.* APIs are not inherently durable. Instead we have to design thoughtfully to ensure they can support change. When designing a new API, build a test application that doesn't use this API, then migrate to the new API. Consider how integrations might evolve as applications change. Perform these migrations yourself to understand potential friction with your API. Then think about the future changes that *we* might want to implement on our end. How would those changes impact the API, and how would they impact the application you've developed?

At this point, take your API to API Review for initial approval as described below. Following that approval, identify a handful of early adopter companies who can place additional pressure on your API design, and test with them before releasing the final, stable API.

- *All new and modified APIs must be approved by API Review.* API changes may not be enabled for customers prior to API Review approval. Change requests should be sent to the `api-review` email group. For examples of prior reviews, search the `api-review` archive for prior requests and the feedback they received.

  All requests must include a written proposal. Most requests will be approved asynchronously by a member of API Review. Complex or controversial proposals will require live discussions to ensure API Review members have sufficient context before making a decision.

- *We never deprecate APIs without an unavoidable requirement to do so.* Even if it's technically expensive to maintain support, we incur that support cost. To be explicit, we define API deprecation as *any* change that would require customers to modify an existing integration.

  If such a change were to be approved as an exception to this policy, it must first be approved by API Review, followed by our CEO. One example where we granted an exception was the deprecation of TLS 1.2 support due to PCI compliance obligations.

- *When significant new functionality is required, we add a new API.* For example, we created `/v1/subscriptions` (*https://oreil.ly/loS_V*) to support those workflows rather than extending `/v1/charges` (*https://oreil.ly/Adl3W*) to add subscriptions support.[1]

- *We manage this policy's implied technical debt via an API translation layer.* We release changed APIs into versions, tracked in our API version changelog (*https://oreil.ly/LgiU9*). However, we only maintain one implementation internally, which is the implementation of the latest version of the API. On top of that implementation, a series of version transformations are maintained, which allow us to support prior versions without maintaining them

2 With the benefit of hindsight, a good example of this policy in action was the introduction of the Payment Intents API to maintain compliance with Europe's Strong Customer Authentication requirements (*https://oreil.ly/Z3jPY*). Even in that case the `charge` API continued to work as it did previously, albeit only for non–European Union payments.

directly. While this approach doesn't *eliminate* the overhead of supporting multiple API versions, it significantly reduces complexity by enabling us to maintain just a single, modern implementation internally.

All API modifications *must* also update the version transformation layers to allow the new version to coexist peacefully with prior versions.

- *In the future, SDKs may allow us to soften this policy.* While a significant number of our customers have direct integrations with our APIs, that number has dropped significantly over time. Instead, most new integrations are performed via one of our official API SDKs.

  We believe that in the future, it may be possible for us to make more backward-incompatible changes because we can absorb the complexity of migrations into the SDKs we provide. That is certainly *not* the case yet today.

DIAGNOSIS

Our diagnosis of the impact of API changes and deprecation on our business is:

- If you are a small startup composed of mostly engineers, integrating a new payments API seems easy. However, for a small business without dedicated engineers—or a larger enterprise involving numerous stakeholders—handling external API changes can be particularly challenging.

  Even if this is only marginally true, we've modeled the impact of minimizing API changes on long-term revenue growth (Document 22-2), and it has a significant impact, unlocking our ability to benefit from other churn reduction work.

- While we believe API instability directly creates churn, we also believe that API stability directly retains customers by increasing the migration overhead even if they wanted to change providers. Without an API change forcing them to change their integration, we believe that hypergrowth customers are particularly unlikely to change payments API providers absent a concrete motivation like an API change or a payment plan change.

- We are aware of relatively few companies that provide long-term API stability in general, and particularly few for complex, dynamic areas like payments APIs. We can't assume that companies that make API changes are ill-informed. Rather it appears that they experience a meaningful technical debt tradeoff between the API provider and API consumers, and aren't willing to consistently absorb that technical debt internally.

- Future compliance or security requirements—along the lines of our upgrade from TLS 1.2 to TLS 1.3 for PCI—may necessitate API changes. There may also be new tradeoffs exposed as we enter new markets with their own compliance regimes. However, we have limited ability to predict these changes at this point.

Document 22-2: A Systems Model of API Deprecation

LEARNINGS

In an initial model that has a 10% baseline for customer churn per round, reducing customers experiencing API deprecation from 50% to 10% per round only increases the steady state of integrated customers by about 5%, as shown in Figure 22-1.

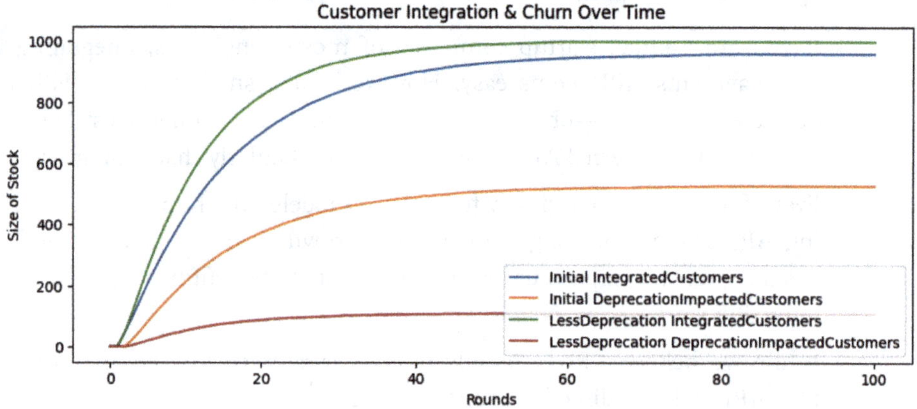

Figure 22-1. Impact of 10% and 50% API deprecation on integrated customers

However, if we eliminate the baseline for customer churn entirely (Figure 22-2), then we see a massive difference between a 10% and 50% rate of API deprecation.

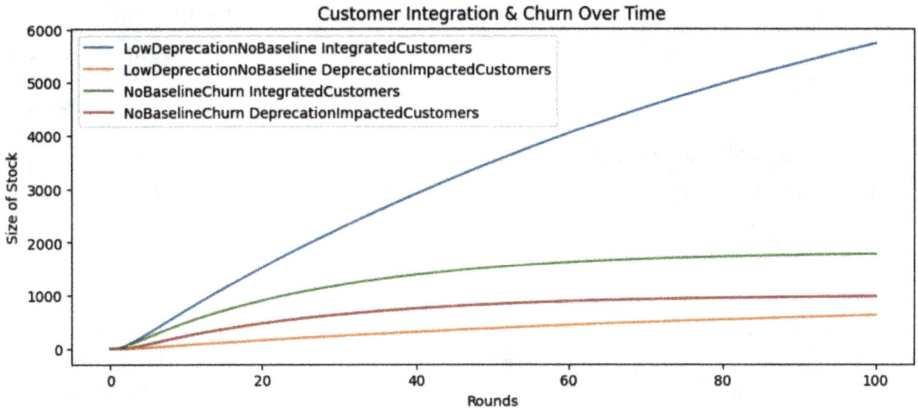

Figure 22-2. Impact of rates of API deprecation with zero baseline churn

The biggest takeaway from this model is that eliminating API-deprecation churn alone won't significantly increase the number of integrated customers. However, we also can't fully benefit from reducing baseline churn without simultaneously reducing API deprecations. Meaningfully increasing the number of integrated customers requires lowering both types of churn in tandem.

SKETCH

We'll start by sketching the model's happiest path: potential customers flowing into engaged customers and then becoming integrated customers (Figure 22-3). This represents a customer who decides to integrate with Stripe's APIs and successfully completes that integration process.

Figure 22-3. Happiest path for Stripe API integration

Business would be good if that were the entire problem space. Unfortunately, customers do occasionally churn. This churn is represented in two ways:

- `Baseline churn`, where integrated customers leave Stripe for any number of reasons, including things like dissolution of their company

- `Experience deprecation` followed by `Deprecation-influenced churn`, which represents the scenario where a customer decides to leave after an API they use is deprecated

There is also a `Reintegrated` flow, where a customer impacted by API deprecation can choose to update their integration to comply with the API changes.

Pulling things together, the final sketch (Figure 22-4) shows five stocks and six flows.

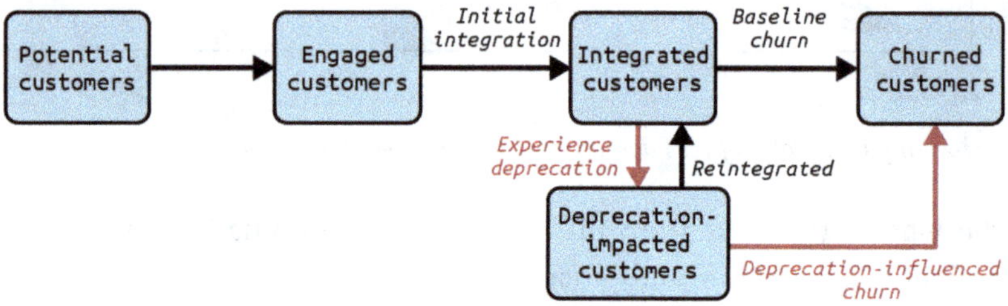

Figure 22-4. Final version of systems model for API deprecation

You could imagine modeling additional dynamics, such as recovery of churned customers, but it seems unlikely that this would significantly influence our understanding of how API deprecation impacts churn.

REASON

In terms of acquiring customers, the most important flows are customer acquisition and initial integration with the API. Optimizing those flows will increase the number of existing integrations.

The flows driving churn are baseline churn and the combination of API deprecation and deprecation-influenced churn. It's difficult to move baseline churn for a payments API, as many churning customers leave due to company dissolution. From a revenue-weighted perspective, baseline churn is largely driven by non-technical factors, primarily pricing. In either case, it's challenging to impact this flow without significantly lowering margin.

Engineering decisions, on the other hand, have a significant impact on both the number of API deprecations and on the ease of reintegration after a migration. Because the same work to support reintegration also supports the initial integration experience, that's a promising opportunity for investment.

MODEL

You can find the full implementation of this model on GitHub (*https://github.com/lethain/eng-strategy-models/blob/main/APIDeprecationModel.ipynb*) if you want to see the full model rather than these emphasized snippets.

Now that we have identified the most interesting avenues for experimentation, it's time to develop the model to evaluate which flows are most impactful.

Our initial model specification is:

```
# User Acquisition Flow
[PotentialCustomers] > EngagedCustomers @ 100
# Initial Integration Flow
EngagedCustomers > IntegratedCustomers @ Leak(0.5)
# Baseline Churn Flow
IntegratedCustomers > ChurnedCustomers @ Leak(0.1)
# Experience Deprecation Flow
IntegratedCustomers > DeprecationImpactedCustomers @ Leak(0.5)
# Reintegrated Flow
DeprecationImpactedCustomers > IntegratedCustomers @ Leak(0.9)
# Deprecation-Influenced Churn
DeprecationImpactedCustomers  > ChurnedCustomers @ Leak(0.1)
```

Whether these are *reasonable* values depends largely on how we think about the length of each round. If a round was a month, then assuming half of integrated customers would experience an API deprecation would be quite extreme. If we assume it was a year, then it would still be high, but there are certainly some API providers that routinely deprecate at that rate. (From my personal experience, I can say with confidence that Facebook's Ads API deprecated at least one important field on a quarterly basis in the 2012–2014 period.)

Admittedly, for a payments API this would be a high rate, and is intended primarily as a contrast with more reasonable values in the following *Exercise* section.

EXERCISE

Our goal with exercising this model is to understand how much API deprecation impacts customer churn. We'll start by charting the initial baseline (Figure 22-5), then move to compare it with a variety of scenarios until we build an intuition for how the lines move.

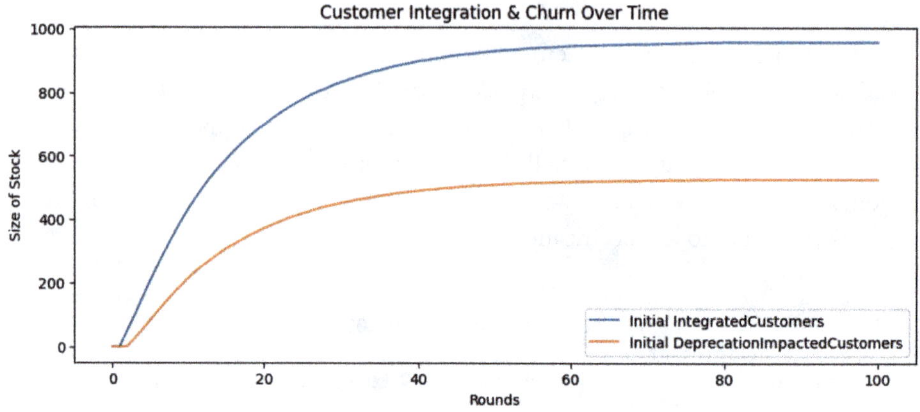

Figure 22-5. Initial model stabilizing integrated customers around 1,000 customers

The initial chart stabilizes in about 40 rounds, maintaining about 1,000 integrated customers and 400 customers dealing with deprecated APIs. Now let's change the `Experience deprecation` flow to impact significantly fewer customers:

```
# Initial setting with 50% experiencing deprecation per round
IntegratedCustomers > DeprecationImpactedCustomers @ Leak(0.5)

# Less deprecation, only 10% experiencing per round
IntegratedCustomers > DeprecationImpactedCustomers @ Leak(0.1)
```

After those changes, we can compare the two scenarios (Figure 22-6).

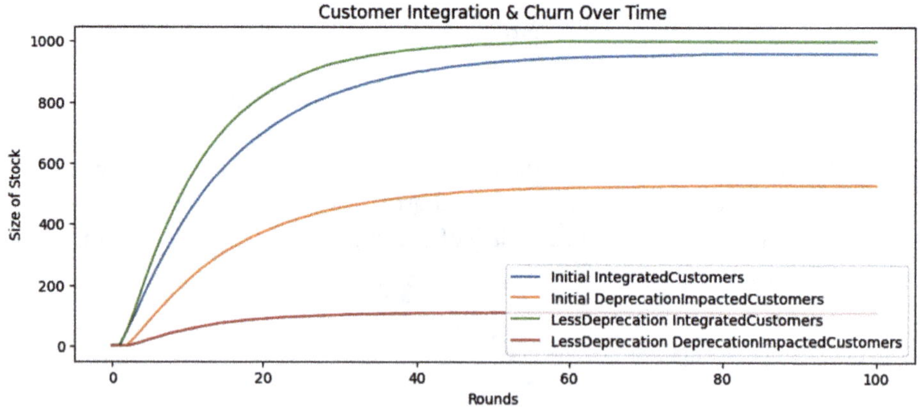

Figure 22-6. Impact of 10% and 50% API deprecation on integrated customers

Lowering the deprecation rate significantly reduces the number of companies dealing with deprecations at any given time, but it has a relatively small impact on increasing the steady state for integrated customers. This must mean that another flow is significantly impacting the size of the `Integrated customers` stock.

Since there's only one other flow impacting that stock, `Baseline churn`, that's the one to exercise next. Let's set the `Baseline churn` flow to zero to compare that with the initial model:

```
# Initial Baseline Churn Flow
IntegratedCustomers > ChurnedCustomers @ Leak(0.1)

# Zeroed out Baseline Churn Flow
IntegratedCustomers > ChurnedCustomers @ Leak(0.0)
```

These results make a compelling case that baseline churn is dominating the impact of deprecation. With no baseline churn, the number of integrated customers stabilizes at around 1,750, as opposed to around 1,000 for the initial model (Figure 22-7).

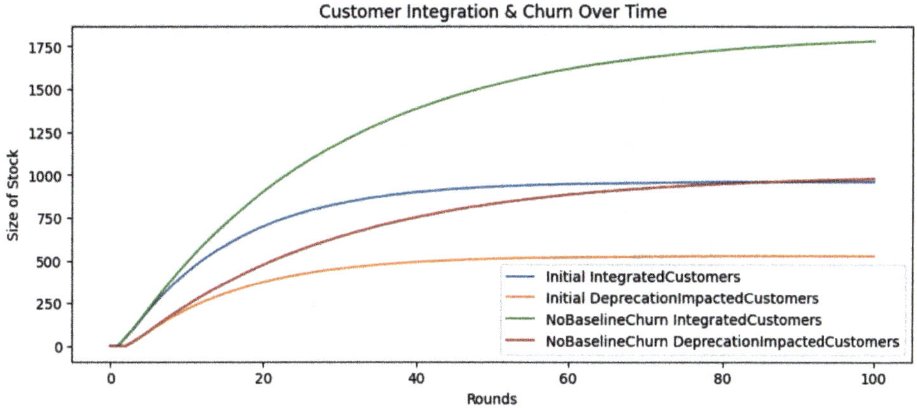

Figure 22-7. Impact of eliminating baseline churn from model

Next, let's compare two scenarios without baseline churn (Figure 22-8), where one has high API deprecation (50%) and the other has low API deprecation (10%).

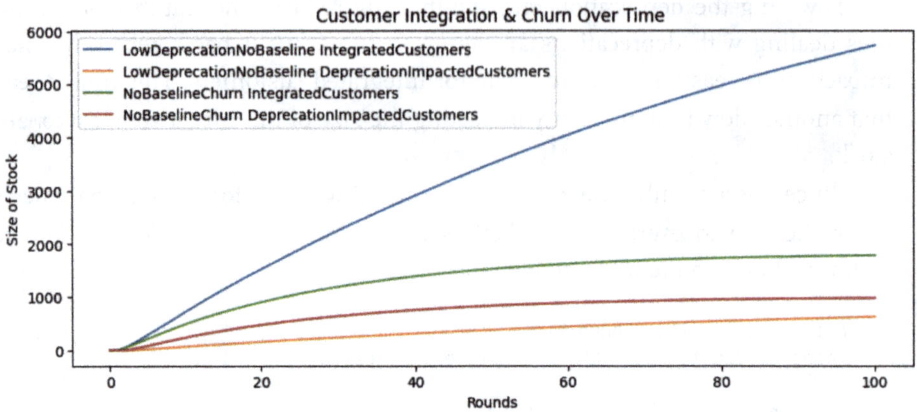

Figure 22-8. Impact of rates of API deprecation with zero baseline churn

In the case of two scenarios without baseline churn, we can see that having an API deprecation rate of 10% leads to about 6,000 integrated customers, as opposed to 1,750 for a 50% rate of API deprecation. More importantly, in the 10% scenario, the integrated customers line shows no sign of flattening and continues to grow over time rather than stabilizing.

The takeaway here is that significantly reducing either baseline churn or API deprecation magnifies the benefits of reducing the other. These results also reinforce the value of treating churn reduction as a system-level optimization, not merely a collection of discrete improvements.

Document 22-3: Why Did Stripe Build Sorbet?

POLICY AND OPERATION

The Product Infrastructure team is investing in Stripe's developer experience by doing the following.

Every six months, Product Infrastructure will select its three highest-priority areas to focus on, and invest a significant majority of its energy into those. We will provide minimal support for other areas.

We commit to refreshing our priorities every half after running the developer productivity survey. We will further share our results, and priorities, in each Quarterly Business Review.

Our three highest-priority areas for this half are:

1. Add static typing to the highest-value portions of our Ruby codebase, such that we can run the type checker locally and on the test machines to identify errors more quickly.
2. Support selective test execution such that engineers can quickly determine and run the most appropriate tests on their machine rather than delaying until tests run on the build server.
3. Instrument test failures such that we have better data to prioritize future efforts.

Static typing is not a typical solution to developer productivity, so it requires some explanation when we say this is our highest-priority area for investment. Doubly so when we acknowledge that it will take us 12–24 months of much of the team's time to get our type checker to an effective place.

Our type checker, which we plan to name Sorbet, will allow us to continue developing within our existing Ruby codebase. It will further allow our product engineers to remain focused on developing new functionality rather than migrating existing functionality to new services or programming languages. Instead, our Product Infrastructure team will centrally absorb both the development of the type checker and the initial rollout to our codebase.

It's possible for Product Infrastructure to take on both, despite its fixed size. We'll rely on a hybrid approach of deep-dives to add typing to particularly complex areas, and scripts to rewrite our code's Abstract Syntax Trees (AST) for less complex portions. In the relatively unlikely event that this approach fails, the cost to Stripe is of a small, known size: approximately six months of half the Product Infrastructure team, which is what we anticipate requiring to determine if this approach is viable.

Based on our knowledge of Facebook's Hack (*https://hacklang.org*) project, we believe we can build a static type checker that runs locally and is significantly faster than our test suite. It's hard to make a precise guess now, but we think it will take less than 30 seconds to type our entire codebase, despite it being quite large. This will allow for a highly productive local development experience, even if we are not able to speed up local testing. Even if we do speed up local testing, typing would help us eliminate one of the categories of errors that testing has been unable to eliminate, which is passing of unexpected types across code paths that have been tested for expected scenarios but not for entirely unexpected scenarios.

Once the type checker has been validated, we can incrementally prioritize adding typing to the highest-value places across the codebase. We do not need to wholly type our codebase before we can start getting meaningful value.

In support of these static-typing efforts, we will advocate for product engineers at Stripe to begin development using the Command Query Responsibility Segregation (CQRS) design pattern (*https://oreil.ly/Y_cgo*), which we believe will provide high-leverage interfaces for incrementally introducing static typing into our codebase.

Selective test execution will allow developers to quickly run appropriate tests locally. This will allow engineers to stay in a tight local development loop, speeding up development of high-quality code.

Given that our codebase is not currently statically typed, inferring which tests to run is rather challenging. With our very high test coverage, and the fact that all tests will still be run before deployment to the production environment, we believe that we can rely on statistically inferring which tests are likely to fail when a given file is modified.

Instrumenting test failures is our third, and lowest priority, project for this half. Our focus this half is purely on annotating errors for which we have high conviction about their source, whether infrastructure or test issues.

For escalations and issues, reach out in the `#product-infra` channel.

DIAGNOSE

In 2017, Stripe is a company of about 1,000 people, including 400 software engineers. We aim to grow our organization by about 70% year-over-year to meet increasing demand for a broader product portfolio and to scale our existing products and infrastructure to accommodate user growth. As our production stability has improved over the past several years, we have now turned our focus toward improving developer productivity.

Our current diagnosis of our developer productivity is as follows.

We primarily fund developer productivity for our Ruby-authoring software engineers via our Product Infrastructure team. The Ruby-focused portion of that team has about 10 engineers on it today and is unlikely to significantly grow in the future. (If we do expand, we are likely to staff non-Ruby ecosystems like Scala or Golang.)

We have two primary mechanisms for understanding our engineers' developer experience. The first is standard productivity metrics around deploy time, deploy stability, test coverage, test time, test flakiness, and so on. The second is a twice-a-year developer productivity survey.

Looking at our productivity metrics, our test coverage remains extremely high, with coverage above 99% of lines, and tests are quite slow to run locally. They run quickly in our infrastructure because they are multiplexed across a large fleet of test runners.

Tests have become slow enough to run locally that an increasing number of developers run an overly narrow subset of tests, or skip running tests entirely until after pushing their changes. They instead rely on our test servers to run against their pull request's branch, which works well enough, but significantly slows down developer iteration time because the merge, build, and test cycle takes 20 to 30 minutes to complete. By the time their build-test cycle completes, they've lost their focus and maybe take several hours to return to addressing the results.

There is significant disagreement about whether tests are becoming flakier due to test infrastructure issues, or due to quality issues of the tests themselves. At this point, there is no trustworthy dataset that allows us to distinguish between those two causes.

Feedback from the twice-a-year developer productivity survey supports the above diagnosis, and adds some additional nuance. Most concerning, although long-tenured Stripe engineers find themselves highly productive in our codebase, we increasingly hear in the survey that newly hired engineers with long tenures at other companies find themselves unproductive in our codebase. Specifically, they find it very difficult to determine how to safely make changes in our codebase.

Our product codebase is entirely implemented in a single Ruby monolith. There is one narrow exception, a Golang service handling payment tokenization, which we consider out of scope for two reasons. First, it is kept intentionally narrow in order to absorb our SOC1 compliance obligations. Second, developers in that environment have not raised concerns about their productivity.

Our data infrastructure is implemented in Scala. While these developers have concerns—primarily slow build times—they manage their build and deployment infrastructure independently, and the group remains relatively small.

Ruby is not a highly performant programming language, but we've found it sufficiently efficient for our needs. Similarly, other languages are more cost-efficient from a compute resources perspective, but a significant majority of our spend is on real-time storage and batch computation. For these reasons alone, we would not consider replacing Ruby as our core programming language.

Our Product Infrastructure team is about 10 engineers, supporting about 250 product engineers. We anticipate this group growing modestly over time, but certainly sublinearly to the overall growth of product engineers.

Developers working in Golang and Scala routinely ask for more centralized support, but it's challenging to prioritize those requests as we're forced to consider the return on improving the experience for 240 product engineers working in Ruby versus 10 in Golang or 40 data engineers in Scala.

If we introduced more programming languages, this prioritization problem would become increasingly difficult, and we are already failing to support additional languages.

Document 22-4: How to Integrate Stripe's Acquisition of Index?

POLICY AND OPERATION

We're starting with little shared context between the acquired and acquiring engineering teams, and we have a six-month timeline to launch a joint product. So our starting policy is a mix of a commitment to joint refinement and several provisional architectural policies:

- *Meet at least weekly until the initial release is complete.* The involved leadership from Stripe and Index will hold a weekly sync meeting to refine our approach until we fulfill our initial release timeline.

  This meeting is jointly owned by Stripe's Head of Traffic Engineering and Index's Head of Engineering.

- *Minimize changes to tokenization environment.* Because point-of-sale devices directly work with customer payment details, the API that directly supports the point-of-sale device must live within our secured environment where payment details are stored.

  However, any other functionality *must not* be added to our tokenization environment.

- *All other functionality must exist in standard environments:* Except for the minimum necessary functionality moving into the tokenization environment, everything else must be operated in our standard, non-tokenization environments. In particular, any software that requires frequent changes, or introduces complex external dependencies, should exist in the standard environments.

- *Defer making a decision regarding the introduction of Java to a later date.* The introduction of Java is incompatible with our existing engineering strategy, but at this point we've also been unable to align stakeholders on how to address this decision. Further, we see attempting to address this issue as a distraction from our timely goal of launching a joint product within six months.

  We will take up this discussion after launching the initial release.

- *Escalations come to paired leads.* Given our limited shared context across teams, all escalations must come to both Stripe's Head of Traffic Engineering and Index's Head of Engineering.
- *Security review of changes impacting tokenization environment.* We need to move quickly to launch the combined point-of-sale and payments product, but we *must not* cut corners on security to launch faster. Security must be included and explicitly sign off on any integration decisions that involve our tokenization environment.

DIAGNOSE

There are generally four categories of acquisitions: talent acquisitions to bring on a talented team, business acquisitions to buy a company's revenue and product, technology acquisitions to add a differentiated capability that would be challenging to develop internally, and time-to-market acquisitions where you could develop the capability internally but can develop it meaningfully faster by acquiring a company.

While most acquisitions have a flavor of several of these dimensions, this acquisition is primarily a time-to-market acquisition aimed at addressing these constraints:

- Several of our largest customers are pushing for us to provide a point-of-sale device integrated with our API-driven payments ecosystem. At least one has implied that we either provide this functionality on a committed timeline or they may churn to a competitor.
- We currently have no homegrown expertise in developing or integrating with hardware such as point-of-sale devices. Based on other zero-to-one efforts internally, we believe it would take about a year to hire the team and

develop and launch a minimum viable product for a point-of-sale device integrated into our platform.

- Where we've taken a horizontal approach to supporting web payments via an API, at least one of our competitors, Square, has taken a vertically integrated approach. While their API ecosystem is less developed than ours, they are a plausible destination for customers threatening to churn.
- We believe that at least one of our enterprise customers will churn if our best commitment is launching a point-of-sale solution 12 months from now.
- We've decided to acquire a small point-of-sale startup, which we will use to commit to a six-month timeframe for supporting an integrated point-of-sale device with our API ecosystem.
- We will need to rapidly integrate the acquired startup to meet this timeline. We only know a small number of details about what this will entail. We *do* know that point-of-sale devices directly operate on payment details (i.e., the point-of-sale device knows the credit card details of the card it reads).

  Our compliance obligations restrict such activity to our "tokenization environment," a highly secured and isolated environment with direct access to payment details. This environment converts payment details into a unique token that other environments can utilize to operate against payment details without the compliance overhead of having direct access to the underlying payment details.
- Going into this technical integration, we have few details about the acquired company's technology stack. We do know that they are primarily a Java shop running on AWS, whereas we are primarily a Ruby (with some Go) shop running on AWS.

EXPLORE

Prior to this acquisition, we have done several small acquisitions. None of those acquisitions had a meaningful product to integrate with ours, so we don't have much of an internal playbook in which to anchor our approach.

We do have limited experience in integrating technical acquisitions from prior companies we've worked in, along with talking to peers at other companies to mine their experience. Synthesizing those experiences, some recurring patterns are:

1. Usually, deal teams have made certain commitments, or the acquired team has understood certain commitments, that will be challenging to facilitate. This is doubly true when you are unaware of what those commitments might be.

   If folks seem to be behaving oddly, it might be one such misunderstanding, and it's worth engaging directly to debug the confusion.

2. There should be an executive sponsor for the acquisition, and the sponsor is typically the best person to ask about the company's intentions. If you can't find the executive sponsor, or they are not engaged, try to recruit a new executive sponsor rather than trying to make things work without one.

3. Close the culture gap quickly where there's little friction, and cautiously where there's little trust.

   We do need to bring the acquired company into our culture, but we have years to do that. The most successful stories of doing this leaned on a mix of moving folks into and out of the acquired team rather than applying force.

4. The long-term cost of supporting a new technology stack is high, and in conflict with our technology strategy of consolidating on as few programming languages as possible.

   This is not the place to be flexible, as each additional feature in the new stack will take you further from your desired outcome.

5. Finally, find a way to derisk key departures. Things can go wrong quickly. One of the easiest starting points is consolidating infrastructure immediately, even if the product or software takes longer.

Altogether, this was not the most reassuring exploration: it was a bit abstract, and much of our research returned strongly held, conflicting perspectives. Perhaps acquisitions, like starting a new company, are among those places where there's simply no right way to do it well.

Summary

Reiterating the chapter introduction, what I find most valuable about these documents is that they're a great example of not following the standard patterns of the time they were written. API deprecations were viewed as essential for maintaining developer velocity, but Stripe largely eschewed them. Decomposing monolithic codebases into isolated services and reusable libraries was viewed as a foundational strategy for both reliability and developer velocity, but Stripe didn't do it. Integrating acquisitions is always tricky, especially when there's a tight timeline to bring the product to market, but Stripe found a path forward.

One way to frame the successes here is around thinking from first principles, and I think that's a useful framing. However, I think an even more useful framing is that the extremely detail oriented, enduring first-principles thinking was the deciding factor between these strategies' success and failure.

PART | V

Going Forward

At this point, you've read this book's thesis on strategy, and worked through all the concrete strategies it has to offer. What's left is answering the two most important questions. First, how do you evaluate whether a strategy is any good? Second, how do you personally continue to improve at strategy? After you've finished reading those, it's time to set this book down and get to the more interesting work: doing engineering strategy of your own.

23

Is This Strategy Any Good?

You've read a lot of strategy at this point in the book. You can judge a strategy's format and its construction: both are useful things. However, format is a *predictor* of quality, not quality itself. So how should you assess whether a particular strategy is any good?

Uber's service migration strategy (Document 16-1) unblocked the entire organization, allowing it to make rapid progress. It also led to a sprawling architecture problem down the line. Was it a great strategy or a terrible one? Reasonable people will disagree, but it's worthwhile to develop a point of view on why you should prefer one interpretation or the other.

This chapter will focus on:

- Common techniques for evaluating strategies
- A rubric for evaluating strategies in phases
- Why ending a strategy is often a sign of a good strategist
- The problem with evaluating other companies' strategies
- Why you can learn just as much from bad strategies as from good ones

Time to refine your judgment about strategy quality.

How Are Strategies Evaluated Across the Industry?

Before suggesting my own rubric, I want to explore some of the software industry's methods for evaluating strategies in practice. I don't particularly agree with these approaches—I think each misses at least one important nuance—but understanding their flaws is a foundation to build on.

Grading strategy on its outputs is by far the most prevalent approach, and it does make sense that a strategy's results are more important than anything else. However, as appealing as it is, this line of thinking can go awry. When massive companies like Google do things like move to service architectures, other companies copy them because, if it worked for Google, it'll likely work for them, right? As discussed in Chapter 20, however, it did not work particularly well for most adopters.

The challenge with looking *only* at outputs is that it doesn't let you distinguish between how much better your results are *because* of your strategy, and the expected outcome if you *hadn't* used the strategy. For example, acquiring Index allowed Stripe to build a point-of-sale business line (see Chapter 22), but Stripe was also on track to build that business internally. Looking *only* at outputs can't help distinguish whether it would have been better to build the business via acquisition or internally. But one of those paths must have been the better strategy.

Similarly, there are also strategies that succeed, but at unreasonably high costs. Stripe's API deprecation strategy (Document 22-2) is a good example of a strategy that was *extremely* well worth the cost for the company's first decade, but eventually became too expensive to maintain as the evolving regulatory environment created more overhead. Fortunately, Stripe modified its strategy to allow some deprecations, but if the company had attempted to maintain its original strategy, it would likely have failed due to its accumulating costs.

Confronting these problems with judging strategies on their outputs, it's compelling to switch to the opposite lens and evaluate strategies purely on their inputs. As long as the sum of the strategy's parts makes sense, it's a good strategy, even if it doesn't accomplish its goals. This approach is appealing because it appears to focus *purely* on how much better your results are because of your strategy.

Unfortunately, I find this view similarly deficient. For example, the strategy in Document 17-1 offers a cautious approach to adopting LLMs. However, if that company loses significant revenue because its competitors better incorporate LLMs, I would argue that this strategy isn't a great one, even if it's rooted in a proper diagnosis and effective policies. Doing good strategy requires reconciling the theoretical with the practical, so inputs alone aren't enough to evaluate strategy work. If a strategy is conceptually sound but struggling to make an impact, then its authors should continue to refine it. If its authors take a single pass and ignore subsequent information that it's not working, then it's a failed strategy, regardless of how thoughtful the first pass was.

While these mechanisms are incomplete, they're still instructive. Incorporating bits of each gets us surprisingly close to a rubric that avoids these particular downfalls.

A Rubric for Evaluating Strategy

The lightweight rubric I've found effective for evaluating strategy, which attempts to balance the strengths and flaws of the previous section's ideas, consists of three questions:

Speed: How quickly can the strategy be refined?

If a strategy starts out bad but improves quickly, that's a better strategy than a mostly right strategy that never evolves. Strategy thrives when its practitioners understand it is a living endeavor.

Assign 3 points for a strategy that facilitates daily or weekly iteration, 2 points for monthly iteration, 1 point for quarterly iteration, and 0 points for anything that requires longer periods of time.

Cost: How expensive will it be to refine the strategy, especially in terms of cross-team impact?

Just as culture eats strategy for breakfast, good policy loses to poor operational mechanisms every time. Especially early on, good strategy should be validated cheaply. Expensive strategies are often discarded before they can be validated, let alone improved.

Assign 3 points for a strategy that can be implemented by a cross-team working group or within a single team, 2 points for small cross-team dependencies, 1 point for large cross-team dependencies with flexible timing, and 0 points for anything with large cross-team dependencies with rigid timing.

Impact: How well does the current iteration of the strategy solve its diagnosis?

Ultimately, strategy does have to address the diagnosis it starts from. Even if you're learning quickly and at a low cost, at some point you do have to actually make changes. Strategy must eventually be graded on its impact.

Assign 3 points for a strategy that directly solves the full problem at hand, 2 points for a strategy that solves the most difficult or essential portion, 1 point for a strategy that solves a simple portion, and 0 points otherwise.

Add those points up. They will range from 0 to 9. Any strategy with a score of 6 or higher is a high-quality strategy that I'd encourage pursuing. Lower scores should trigger some strong introspection on whether this is an effective path forward.

With this rubric in hand, we can finally assess Uber's service migration strategy. That strategy is evaluated as follows:

Speed: 3 points
: The approach supported daily iteration by starting with structured requests that provided an interface we could rapidly iterate behind.

Cost: 2 points
: The platform and integration could mostly be implemented by a single team. Migrating an existing service did require coordination with existing teams, but on a flexible schedule.

Impact: 2 points
: Supporting the high volume of requests for new services created the most pressing problem, incrementally freeing up time to work on moving the biggest existing services.

That gives the strategy a total score of 7, which is quite good.

However, that high score raises an interesting question. While the Uber service migration strategy worked exceptionally well initially, it also created a great deal of long-term problems as the number of services grew. Does that mean it really wasn't a good strategy after all? The idea that strategies can start out good but degrade over time brings me to the final component of the strategy quality rubric: the recognition that strategy exists across multiple phases. Each phase is defined by new information—whether or not this information is known by the strategy's authors—that renders the diagnosis incomplete.

Think of the Uber strategy as existing across two phases. Phase 1 used service provisioning to address developer productivity challenges in the monolith; Phase 2 engaged with the consequences of a sprawling service architecture. Evaluating this second phase, where the service provisioning platform was wholly adopted and engineers needed to build complex systems on top of it, might generate a very different evaluation from the rubric:

Speed: 1 point

Changes within a given service happen on a daily basis, but changes across services are quite challenging and can take quarters to accomplish.

Cost: 1 point

Any significant service architecture change requires coordination across numerous teams, sometimes many dozens of teams, even for a relatively straightforward change.

Impact: 2 points

The service provisioning problem is wholly solved, but operating those provisioned services is challenging at scale.

In this second phase, our judgment of 7 has degraded down to 4. The high rating in the first phase is still appropriate, but the second phase's challenges are real as well. Very effective strategies are particularly prone to difficult phases after their initial rollout, because it's impossible to foresee and prevent every possible challenge ahead of time. The bad news is that strategy work never ends. That's the good news, too.

Does Stopping a Strategy Mean It's a Bad Strategy?

Now that we have a rubric, we can use it to evaluate an important question: does giving up on a strategy mean that the strategy is a bad one?

The vocabulary of strategy phases helps us here, and I think it's uncontroversial to say that your prior diagnosis might evolve in ways that make it appropriate to abandon a strategy. For example, Digg owned its own servers in 2010, but would certainly *not* have bought its own servers if it had started 10 years later. Circumstances change.

Sometimes aborting a strategy in its first phase is actually a good sign. That's generally true when the rate of learning is outpaced by the cost of learning. I recently sponsored a developer-productivity strategy that had some impact, but less than we'd intended. We adopted a few of the smaller pieces, and then returned to exploring a lower-altitude strategy owned by the teams, rather than the high-altitude strategy that I owned as an executive.

Essentially, all strategies are competing with strategies at other altitudes, so I think giving up on strategies, especially high-altitude strategies, is almost always a good idea. The opportunity cost of high-altitude strategy is high, so I recommend explicitly giving ownership back to lower-altitude strategy unless there's a proven, highly impactful strategy to push above it.

The Unpierceable Veil

Working within our industry, engineers are often called upon to evaluate strategies from afar. As other companies rolled out LLMs in their products or microservices for their architectures, our companies pushed us on why we weren't making these changes as well. The exploration step of strategy helps determine where another company's strategy might be useful for you, but even that doesn't really help you evaluate after the fact whether its strategy or strategists were effective.

There are simply too many dimensions of the rubric that you cannot evaluate from the outside. For example, how many phases did your competitors go through before they arrived at the idea that became the external representation of the strategy? How much did those early stages cost to implement? Is the *real* mastery in the operational mechanisms that are never reported on outside the organization? Is the blog post they wrote about their magical transformation real, or just something they put together to attract potential hires?

It's generally impossible to evaluate strategies happening in other companies accurately or with much conviction. Even if you want to, the missing context is an impenetrable veil. That's not to say that you shouldn't try to evaluate your competitors' strategies; that's something that you'll be forced to do in your own strategy work. Instead, it's a reminder not to invest too much confidence in those appraisals: you're guaranteed to be missing something.

Learning from Failed Strategies

Although I believe it's valuable to judge the quality of strategies, I want to caution you against concluding that you can't learn from poor strategies. As long as you are aware of its quality, I believe you can learn just as much from a strategy's failure as from its success.

Even failed strategies have early phases that work extremely well. Also, strategies tend to fail for interesting reasons. I learned just as much from Stripe's failed rollout of Agile, which struggled due to missing operational mechanisms, as I did from Calm's successful transition to focusing primarily on product engineering. Without a clear point of view on which of these worked, you'd be at risk of learning the wrong lessons—but with forewarning, you don't run that risk.

Once you've determined that a strategy has been unsuccessful, it's particularly valuable to determine at which phase and where in the strategy steps things went wrong. Was it a lack of operational mechanisms? Was the policy itself a poor match for the diagnosis? Was the diagnosis willfully ignorant of a problem, like a truculent executive? Answering these questions will teach you more about strategy than only studying successful strategies, because you'll develop an intuition for which parts truly matter.

Summary

Finishing this chapter, you now have a structured rubric for evaluating a strategy, moving beyond "good strategy" and "bad strategy" to a nuanced assessment. This assessment is not just useful for grading strategy, but also makes it possible to specifically improve your strategy work.

Maybe your approach is sound, but your operational mechanisms are too costly for the rate of learning they facilitate. Maybe you've treated strategy as a single-iteration exercise, rather than recognizing that even excellent strategy goes stale over time. Keep those ideas in mind as we head into the next chapter, on how you personally can get better at strategy work.

24

How to Get Better at Strategy

One of the most memorable quotes in Arthur Miller's 1949 play *Death of a Salesman* is Uncle Ben's description of his path to wealth: "When I was seventeen, I walked into the jungle, and when I was twenty-one I walked out. And by God I was rich."

I wish I could describe the path to learning engineering strategy in similar terms, but by all accounts it's a much slower path. Two decades in, I am still learning more from each project I work on. This book has aimed to accelerate your learning path, but my experience is that there's still a great deal left to learn, despite what this book has hoped to accomplish.

You are already familiar with my general suggestions on creating strategy, so this chapter provides focused advice on creating your own strategy to get better at strategy. It covers:

- Where to find strategies you can learn from
- How to diagnose the strategies you've found to ensure you learn the right lessons
- How to perform and practice strategy within your organization, whether or not you have organizational authority
- Operational mechanisms to hold yourself accountable for developing a strategy practice

With that preamble, let's write this book's final strategy: your personal strategy for developing your strategy practice.

Exploring Strategy Creation

Ideally, you could begin improving your engineering strategy skills by reading publicly available examples to learn from others' experience. Unfortunately, there simply aren't many easily available. The three most useful places to look are:

- Public resources on engineering strategy, such as companies' engineering blogs
- Private and undocumented strategies available through your professional network
- Learning communities that you build with others, including ongoing learning circles

Each of these is explored in its own section that follows.

PUBLIC RESOURCES

This book's Appendix collects a number of public engineering strategy resources, including some blog posts that are adjacent to this topic. You can go a long way by searching and prompting your way into these resources, including the LLM companion created for this book!

As you read public strategies, it's important to recognize that they are often misleading, as discussed in Chapter 23. Everyone writing in public has an agenda, and that agenda often means that they'll omit important details to make themselves, or their company, come off well. Make sure you read between the lines rather than taking things too literally.

PRIVATE RESOURCES

Ironically, I've found it much easier to find privately held strategy resources. While private recollections are still prone to inaccuracies, the incentives to massage the truth are less pronounced in private.

Strategies are often oral histories, and they are shared freely among peers within and across companies. As you build your professional network, you can usually get access to a company's engineering strategy on any topic by just asking.

There are brief exceptions: even a close peer won't share a sensitive strategy before its existence becomes externally obvious, but they'll be glad to after it does. People tend to overestimate how much information companies can keep private anyway. Even reading recent job postings can expose a surprising amount about a company.

While surprisingly few organizations formally collect their strategies into a repository, their tenured members tend to collect stories informally. These folks are the company's *strategy archaeologists*, and you can learn a great deal by consulting them.

You can also become a strategy archaeologist yourself, whether or not you're a tenured member of your company. You can learn a tremendous amount by starting to build your own strategy repository. As you start collecting strategies, you'll interest others in contributing theirs as well.

Over time, you can foster a culture of documentation where one didn't exist before. Even better, building that culture doesn't require any explicit authority—just an ongoing show of excitement.

There are other sources as well, like attending the "hallway track" at conferences or organizing dinners where people share stories with a commitment to privacy.

WORKING IN COMMUNITY

My final suggestion for seeing how others work on strategy is to form a learning circle (*https://lethain.com/rough-notes-learning-circles*). I did this when I first moved into an executive role (*https://lethain.com/crowdsourcing-cto-vpe-learning-circles*), and I've now been running it for more than five years. What's surprised me the most is how much I've learned from it.

There are a few reasons why ongoing learning circles are exceptional for sharing strategy:

- Bidirectional discussion allows so much more learning and understanding than unidirectional forms of communication, like conference talks and documents.
- Groups allow you to learn from others' experiences and questions, rather than having to guide all of the learning yourself.
- Continuity allows you to see the strategy at its inception, during the rollout, and after it's been in practice for some time.
- Trust is built slowly, and you'll only get the full details about a problem when you've already successfully held trust about smaller things. An ongoing group makes this sort of sharing feasible, whereas a transient group does not.

Although putting one of these communities together requires commitment, they are the best mechanism I've found.

Many people get stuck on how they can get invited to an existing learning circle, but that's almost always the wrong question to ask. If you want to join a learning circle, make one. That's how I got invited to mine.

Diagnosing Your Prior and Current Strategy Work

Collecting strategies to learn from is a valuable part of improving, but it's only the first step. You also have to determine what to take away from each strategy. For example, you have to determine whether Calm's approach to resourcing Engineering-driven projects (Document 21-2) is something to copy or to avoid.

I recommend applying the strategy rubric from Chapter 23 to each of the strategies you've collected. Even by splitting a strategy into its various phases, you'll learn a lot. Applying the rubric to each phase will teach you more. Each time you do this to another strategy, you'll get a bit faster at applying the rubric, and you'll start to see interesting, recurring patterns.

As you split a strategy into phases, apply the evaluation rubric, and dig in, here are a handful of questions to ask:

- How long did it take to determine that this strategy's initial phase could be improved? How high was the cost to fund that initial phase's discovery?
- Why did the strategy reach its final stage and get repealed or replaced? How long did it take to get there?
- If you had to pick only one, did this strategy fail in its approach to exploration, diagnosis, policy, or operations?
- To what extent did this strategy outlive the tenure of its primary author? Did it get repealed quickly after their departure, did it endure, or was it perhaps replaced during their tenure?
- Would you generally repeat this strategy, or would you strive to avoid repeating it? If you did repeat it, what conditions seem necessary to make it succeed?
- How might you apply this strategy to your current opportunities and challenges?

It's not necessary to work through all of these questions for every strategy you're learning from. Pick the two that seem most interesting for a given strategy.

Policy for Improving at Strategy

For improving your strategic abilities at a high level, there are two key policies to consider. The first is implementing strategy, and the second is practicing implementing strategy. As for more detailed options, here are some worth considering:

- If your company's existing strategies are not working, debug one and work to fix it. If you lack the authority to work at the company scope, decrease altitude until you find an altitude you can work at. Perhaps setting Engineering organizational strategies is beyond your circumstances, but strategy for your team is entirely accessible.
- If your company has no documented strategies, document one to make it debuggable. Again, if operating at a high altitude isn't attainable for some reason, operate at a lower altitude that is within reach.
- If your company or team has an effective strategy with low adoption, see if you can iterate on operational mechanisms to increase adoption. Many such mechanisms require no authority at all, such as low-noise nudges or the model-document-share approach (*https://lethain.com/model-document-share*).
- If existing strategies are effective and have high adoption, see if you can build excitement for a new strategy. Start by asking which problems Staff-plus engineers and senior managers believe are important. Once you find one, you have a valuable strategy vein to start mining.
- If you don't feel comfortable sharing your work internally within the company, try sharing your proposals with just a few trusted peers, perhaps within a learning circle that you create or join. You can even go further to only share proposals with trusted *external* peers.

Trying all of these at once would be overwhelming, so I recommend picking one in any given phase. If you can't gain traction, try another approach until something works. It's particularly important to recognize in your diagnosis where things are not working. Perhaps you simply don't have the sponsorship you need to enforce strategy, so you need to switch toward suggesting strategies instead. Once you acknowledge this, you'll find something that works.

WHAT IF YOU'RE NOT ALLOWED TO DO STRATEGY?

If you're looking to find a reason why you can't do strategy in your current environment, you'll always unearth one, as you saw in Chapter 3. Don't believe the hype: you can always do strategy work.

If you believe your current role prevents you from engaging in strategy work, I've found two useful approaches. First, lower your altitude: there's always a scale where you can perform strategy, even if it's just your team or even just yourself. Only you can forbid yourself from developing personal strategies.

Second, *practice* strategy work rather than performing it. Organizations can only absorb so much strategy development at a given time, so sometimes they won't be open to you doing more. Only you can stop yourself from practicing.

Operating Your Strategy Improvement Policies

As the refrain goes, even the best policies don't accomplish much if they aren't paired with operational mechanisms to ensure the policies actually happen and, if they don't, to debug why. It's tempting to overlook operations in discussing personal habits, but that would be a mistake. Our habits profoundly impact us in the long term, yet they're easiest to neglect because others rarely inquire about them.

Some mechanisms I recommend:

- Clearly track the strategies you've implemented, refined, documented, or read. Maintain a document, spreadsheet, or folder that makes it easy to monitor your progress.
- Review your tracked strategies every quarter: are you working on the expected number and in the expected way? If not, why not? Ideally, review them in community with a peer or a learning circle. It's too easy to deceive yourself, but much harder to trick someone else.
- If your periodic review shows that you're simply not doing the work you expected to do, sit down for an hour with someone that you trust—ideally someone equally or more experienced than you—and debug what's going wrong. Commit to doing this *before* your next periodic review.

Tracking your personal habits can feel odd, but it's worthwhile. I've been setting and tracking personal goals for some time now—for example, as discussed in my 2024 year in review (*https://lethain.com/2024-in-review*)—and have benefited greatly from it.

TOO BUSY FOR STRATEGY

Many companies convince themselves that they're in too much of a rush to make good decisions. I've certainly gotten stuck in this view at times myself, although at this point in my career I recognize that I have the tools to create time for strategy and an obligation to do strategy rather than inflicting poor decisions on the organizations I work in. Here's my advice for creating time:

- If you're not tracking how often you're creating strategies, start there.
- If you haven't worked on a single strategy in the past six months, then start with one.
- If implementing a strategy has been prohibitively time-consuming, focus on practicing a strategy instead.

If you try all those things and still aren't making progress, then accept your reality: you don't view doing strategy as particularly important. Spend some time thinking about why. If you're comfortable with your answer, then maybe this is a practice you should come back to later.

Final Words

At this point, you've read everything I have to offer on crafting engineering strategy. I hope this book has refined your view on what strategy can be in your organization, and has given you the tools to draft a more thoughtful future for your corner of the software engineering industry.

I'd never ask you to wholly agree with my ideas. They are my best thinking on this topic, but strategy is a topic where I'm certain Hegel's worldview is the correct one: even the best ideas here are wrong in interesting ways, and will be surpassed by better ones.

25

Strategy Resources

One of the hardest parts of learning about engineering strategy is finding useful resources on a topic where so much is kept private. This Appendix highlights some of the public resources that I've found valuable during my learning experience.

My Prior Writing

- "Writing an engineering strategy" (*https://lethain.com/eng-strategies*) is a chapter from *The Engineering Executive's Primer* (*https://lethain.com/eng-execs-primer*) on setting engineering strategy as an executive.
- "Write five, then synthesize" (*https://lethain.com/good-engineering-strategy-is-boring*) is a chapter from *Staff Engineer* (*https://staffeng.com*) on driving engineering strategy without executive authority (primarily through documentation).

Books

In addition to my own *Staff Engineer* (*https://staffeng.com*) and *The Engineering Executive's Primer* (*https://lethain.com/eng-execs-primer*), both of which have chapters on engineering strategy, I would encourage you to read:

- *Architecture Modernization* by Nick Tune with Jean-Georges Perrin (Manning, 2024) covers much of the same topics as *Technology Strategy Patterns* and *The Value Flywheel Effect*, but with more recent examples and references.
- *Enterprise Architecture as Strategy* (*https://lethain.com/notes-on-enterprise-architecture-as-strategy*) by Jeanne Ross, Peter Weill, and David Robertson (Harvard Business Review Press, 2006) is an interesting read on the

evolution of software (or "IT," in that era's vernacular), maturity within businesses, and deciding among strategies for coupling and integration across business units.

- *Technology Strategy Patterns* (*https://lethain.com/notes-on-the-technology-strategy-patterns*) by Eben Hewitt (O'Reilly, 2018) is a method-focused book on creating and communicating engineering strategy.
- *The Phoenix Project* by Gene Kim, Kevin Behr, and George Spafford (IT Revolution Press, 2013) is a modern retelling of Eliyahu Goldratt's 1984 *The Goal* (third edition available from North River Press, 2012), which shows how to model and resolve problems using constraint optimization. Previously, I would not have considered this a strategy book, but as my opinion on what strategy is evolves (mapping plus guiding policies), I think it demonstrates a useful mapping strategy.
- *The Value Flywheel Effect* (*https://lethain.com/notes-on-the-value-flywheel-effect*) by David Anderson, with Mark McCann and Michael O'Reilly (IT Revolution Press, 2022) introduces Wardley maps by exploring Liberty Mutual's rationale for serverless.
- *Wardley Maps* (*https://oreil.ly/MEXtt*) by Simon Wardley (2005) explains how to use Wardley maps to understand and improve strategy.

Additional books that don't focus on engineering strategy, but are quite useful:

- *Good Strategy, Bad Strategy* by Richard Rumelt (Crown Currency, 2011) is the most helpful strategy book that I have ever read, because it actually provides a usable definition of strategy.
- *How Big Things Get Done* by Bent Flyvbjerg and Dan Gardner (Crown Currency, 2023) is a fascinating look at why some megaprojects (*https://oreil.ly/CqfnH*) fail so resoundingly and why others succeed under budget and under schedule. It connects to many related topics, such as how benchmarking (*https://lethain.com/benchmarking*) can help evaluate guiding policies within a strategy.
- *The Crux* (*https://lethain.com/notes-on-the-crux*) by Richard Rumelt (PublicAffairs, 2022) is another good book by Rumelt, this one oriented on how to create strategies and why strategy creation often fails. (It's less

structurally focused on documenting strategies than *Good Strategy, Bad Strategy*.)

- *Thinking in Systems: A Primer* by Donella Meadows (Chelsea Green, 2008), a book on systems thinking and, for a long time, my sole tool for mapping things around me. This is not a software engineering book, but it provides a useful mapping mechanism that you can apply to software and software development. ("Why limiting work-in-progress works" (*https://lethain.com/limiting-wip*) is one example of me using systems thinking to model a software system.)

Case Studies

Every discussion of engineering strategy includes a weary remark about how few strategies are publicly documented. Acknowledging that concern, here are some case studies that I've found helpful:

- My "Magnitudes of Exploration" (*https://lethain.com/magnitudes-of-exploration*) (2019) documents a public version of Stripe's Engineering strategy.
- *The Value Flywheel Effect* (above) is a good case study of Liberty Mutual's engineering strategy, and additionally includes case studies for A Cloud Guru, Workgrid, and BBC.
- "Run Less Software" (*https://oreil.ly/X3693*) by Rich Archbold (2018) is a fantastic writeup of a cornerstone of Intercom's engineering strategy.
- "How Big Technical Changes Happen at Slack" (*https://oreil.ly/Hi8dO*) (2020) by Keith Adams and Johnny Rodgers is not quite Slack's engineering strategy, but includes many components of its engineering strategy.
- "The Difficult Teenage Years: Setting Tech Strategy After a Launch" (*https://oreil.ly/TftiO*) by Anna Shipman (2019) looks at the *Financial Times*' engineering strategy, particularly one that wasn't *really* defined until somewhat late in the lifecycle. (This is extremely common, even if we don't admit it.)

A few more resources that don't quite fit in the preceding list, but are nonetheless relevant reads:

- BoringTechnology.club (*https://oreil.ly/K11Lh*) by Dan McKinley offers a guiding principle that many engineering strategies include.
- GitLab Strategy (*https://oreil.ly/C1NCf*)—OK, it's actually the GitLab company strategy, but given that it's a technology company that builds technology for technologists, it's an interesting read at a slightly higher altitude than an engineering strategy.

The internet is an unruly place, and I'm sure that by the time you read this, many more excellent writeups will exist as well.

Index

A

D

E

F

G

H

O

P

R

S

About the Author

Will Larson is the chief technology officer at Imprint, and has held senior engineering leadership roles at Carta, Calm, Stripe, and Uber. He's the author of *An Elegant Puzzle*, *Staff Engineer*, and *The Engineering Executive's Primer*, and is a prolific writer on his blog, Irrational Exuberance.

Colophon

The cover illustration is by Susan Thompson. The cover fonts are Gilroy Semibold and Guardian Sans. The text fonts are Adobe Myriad Pro, Adobe Minion Pro, and Scala Pro, and the heading font is Benton Sans.

O'REILLY®

Learn from experts.
Become one yourself.

60,000+ titles | Live events with experts
Role-based courses | Interactive learning
Certification preparation

Try the O'Reilly learning platform free for 10 days.

©2025 O'Reilly Media, Inc. O'Reilly is a registered trademark of O'Reilly Media, Inc. 718900_6x9

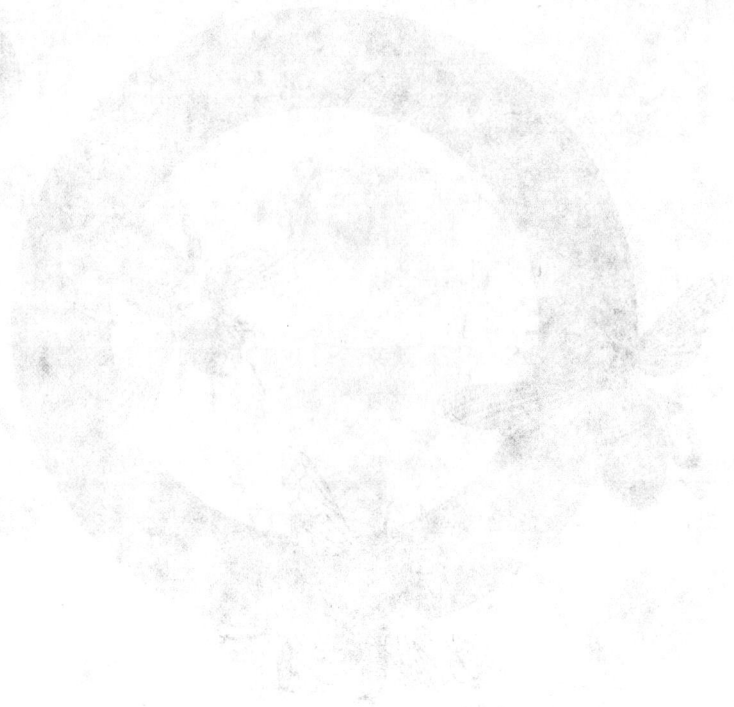

www.ingramcontent.com/pod-product-compliance
Lightning Source LLC
Chambersburg PA
CBHW061136220326
41599CB00025B/4262
* 9 7 9 8 3 4 1 6 4 5 5 2 3 *